THE LOEB CLASSICAL LIBRARY

FOUNDED BY JAMES LOEB 1911

EDITED BY

JEFFREY HENDERSON

EDITOR EMERITUS

G. P. GOOLD

CICERO

XXVII

LCL 230

CICERO

LETTERS TO FRIENDS

VOLUME III

EDITED AND TRANSLATED BY

D. R. SHACKLETON BAILEY

HARVARD UNIVERSITY PRESS
CAMBRIDGE, MASSACHUSETTS
LONDON, ENGLAND
2001

Copyright © 2001 by the President and Fellows
of Harvard College
All rights reserved

Library of Congress catalog card number 00-047259
CIP data available from the Library of Congress

ISBN 0-674-99588-0 (volume I)
ISBN 0-674-99589-9 (volume II)
ISBN 0-674-99590-2 (volume III)

21.50

CONTENTS

CICERO'S
LETTERS TO FRIENDS

281 (XIII.14)

Scr. Romae an. 46

CICERO BRUTO S.

1   L. Titio[1] Strabone, equite Romano in primis honesto et ornato, familiarissime utor. omnia mihi cum eo intercedunt iura summae necessitudinis. huic in tua provincia pecuniam debet P. Cornelius. ea res a Volcacio, qui Romae ius dicit, reiecta in Galliam est.

2   Peto a te, hoc diligentius quam si mea res esset quo est honestius de amicorum pecunia laborare quam de sua, ut negotium conficiendum cures, ipse suscipias transigas, operamque des, quoad tibi aequum et rectum videbitur, ut quam commodissima condicione libertus Strabonis, qui eius rei causa missus est, negotium conficiat ad nummosque perveniat. id et mihi gratissimum erit et tu ipse L. Titium cognosces amicitia tua dignissimum. quod ut tibi curae sit, ut omnia solent esse quae me velle scis, te vehementer etiam atque etiam rogo.

[1] Tidio *et* Tidium *infra coni. SB*

281 (XIII.14)
CICERO TO M. BRUTUS

Rome, 46

From Cicero to Brutus greetings.

L. Titius[1] Strabo, one of our most respected and distinguished Roman Knights, is on intimate terms with me, and we can claim from one another all that belongs to the closest of connections. He is owed money in your province by P. Cornelius. Volcacius, as City Praetor, has remitted the matter for adjudication in Gaul.

May I request you particularly (more so than if the case were mine, in so far as one is more respectably concerned about a friend's money than about one's own) to see that the affair is settled? Take it up personally and put it through. Try to arrange, so far as seems to you right and fair, that Strabo's freedman, who has been dispatched for the purpose, settles the business on the most favourable terms and collects the cash. I shall be deeply beholden, and you yourself will find L. Titius well worthy of your friendship. Let me once more earnestly beg of you to attend to this, as you habitually do to any wish of mine within your knowledge.

[1] Perhaps 'Tidius'; he may have been the father of the person mentioned in Letter 376.

282 (XIII.29)

Scr. Romae c. in. an. 46, ut vid.

M. CICERO L. PLANCO S.

1   Non dubito quin scias in iis necessariis qui tibi a patre relicti sint me tibi esse vel coniunctissimum, non iis modo causis quae speciem habeant magnae coniunctionis sed iis etiam quae familiaritate et consuetudine tenentur, quam scis mihi iucundissimam cum patre tuo et summam fuisse. ab his initiis noster in te amor profectus auxit paternam necessitudinem, et eo magis quod intellexi, ut primum per aetatem iudicium facere potueris quanti quisque tibi faciendus esset, me a te in primis coeptum esse observari, coli, diligi. accedebat non mediocre vinculum cum studiorum, quod ipsum est per se grave, tum eorum studiorum earumque artium quae per se ipsae eos qui voluntate eadem sunt etiam familiaritate devinciunt.

2   Exspectare te arbitror haec tam longe repetita principia quo spectent. id primum ergo habeto, non sine magna iustaque causa hanc a me commemorationem esse factam.

C. Ateio Capitone utor familiarissime. notae tibi sunt varietates meorum temporum. in omni genere et honorum et laborum meorum et animus et opera et auctoritas et gratia, etiam res familiaris C. Capitonis praesto fuit et patuit[1] et temporibus et fortunae meae.

3   Huius propinquus fuit T. Antistius. qui cum sorte quaestor Macedoniam obtineret neque ei successum es-

___
[1] paruit *(Man.)**

___
[1] In Africa with Caesar.

282 (XIII.29)
CICERO TO L. PLANCUS

Rome, ca. beginning of 46 (?)

From M. Cicero to L. Plancus[1] greetings.

I am sure you know that among the connections you inherited from your father I stand preeminently close to you, not only on such grounds as present the façade of an intimate association, but on those of familiar intercourse—for, as you are aware, I had such a relationship, most valid and most delightful, with your father. Such were the origins of my affection for yourself. It strengthened my association with your father, the more so because I observed that, from the time when you were old enough to discriminate in your regard for this person or that, I was the object of your special notice and fond attention. Add to this the strong attachment of common pursuits, important in itself, and of such pursuits and accomplishments as automatically link those who share the love of them in the bonds of familiar friendship.

I expect you are wondering where this long-drawn exordium may be tending. Well, let me begin by assuring you that I have not mentioned these points without good and ample reason.

I am on the closest terms with C. Ateius Capito. You know the vicissitudes of my career. In all the various advancements and tribulations which have come my way C. Capito has been mine to command. His spirit and his time, his public and personal influence, even his private fortune, have been at my service in good times and bad.

Capito had a relative, T. Antistius. As Quaestor he was appointed by lot to Macedonia, and was in charge of that

5

set, Pompeius in eam provinciam cum exercitu venit. facere Antistius nihil potuit; nam si potuisset, nihil ei fuisset
antiquius quam ad Capitonem, quem ut parentem dilige-
bat, reverti, praesertim <cum> sciret quanti is Caesarem
faceret semperque fecisset. sed oppressus tantum attigit
4 negoti quantum recusare non potuit. cum signaretur ar-
gentum Apolloniae, non possum dicere eum non prae-
fuisse neque possum negare adfuisse, sed non plus duobus
an tribus mensibus. deinde afuit a castris, fugit omne negotium. hoc mihi ut testi velim credas; meam enim ille
maestitiam in illo bello videbat, mecum omnia communi-
cabat. itaque abdidit se in intimam Macedoniam quo potuit longissime a castris, non modo ut non praeesset ulli negotio sed etiam ut ne interesset quidem. is post proelium
se ad hominem necessarium, A. Plautium, in Bithyniam
contulit. ibi eum Caesar cum vidisset, nihil aspere, nihil
acerbe dixit, Romam iussit venire. ille in morbum continuo
incidit, ex quo non convaluit; aeger Corcyram venit, ibi
est mortuus. testamento, quod Romae Paullo et Marcello
consulibus fecerat, heres ex parte dimidia et tertia est Capito; in sextante sunt ii quorum pars sine ulla cuiusquam
querela publica potest esse. ea est ad HS ⌜XXX⌝ . sed de hoc
Caesar viderit.
5   Te, mi Plance, pro paterna necessitudine, pro nostro
amore, pro studiis et omni cursu nostro totius vitae simil-
limo rogo et a te ita peto ut maiore cura, maiore studio

6

province, no one having come to replace him, when Pompey and his army arrived. There was nothing Antistius could do. Given the opportunity, he would have preferred above all things to rejoin Capito, whom he loved as a father, especially as he knew how strongly attached Capito was and has always been to Caesar. But taken as he was by surprise, he touched only such employment as he could not refuse. When money was minted at Apollonia, I cannot assert that he was not in charge, and I cannot deny that he was present, but for no more than two or perhaps three months. After that he kept away from the army and shunned all activity. I hope you will take my word for this as an eyewitness. He saw my despondency in that war, and shared all his thoughts with me. So he hid himself in a corner of Macedonia as far away as possible from the army, so as not to be present at any activity, let alone in command. After the battle he went to Bithynia, to a person with whom he had connections, A. Plautius. There Caesar saw him, and without a word of harshness or reproof told him to return to Rome. Directly afterwards he fell ill, and never recovered. He arrived in Corcyra a sick man, and there died. Under his will, made in Rome in the Consulship of Paullus and Marcellus, he left Capito five-sixths of his estate. The remaining sixth is left to persons whose portion may be confiscated to the state without exciting any complaint. It amounts to HS3,000,000. But this is Caesar's business.

Now, my dear Plancus, I appeal to you in the name of my friendship with your father and our mutual affection, of our studies and the whole tenor of our lives in which we are so much alike: I beg you with all possible earnestness and urgency to take this matter up and regard it as mine.

7

nullam possim, ut hanc rem suscipias, meam putes esse,
enitare, contendas, efficias ut mea commendatione, tuo
studio, Caesaris beneficio hereditatem propinqui sui C.
Capito obtineat. omnia quae potui in hac summa tua gratia
ac potentia a te impetrare, si petivissem,[2] ultro te ad me
detulisse putabo si hanc rem impetravero.

6   Illud fore tibi adiumento spero, cuius ipse Caesar opti-
mus esse iudex potest: semper Caesarem Capito coluit et
dilexit. sed ipse huius rei testis est; novi hominis memo-
riam. itaque nihil te doceo; tantum tibi sumito pro Capitone apud Caesarem quantum ipsum meminisse senties.

7 ego quod in me ipso experiri potui ad te deferam; in eo
quantum sit ponderis tu videbis. quam partem in re publica causamque defenderim, per quos homines ordinesque
steterim quibusque munitus[3] fuerim non ignoras. hoc mihi
velim credas, si quid fecerim hoc ipso in bello minus ex
Caesaris voluntate (quod intellexi[4] scire ipsum Caesarem
me invitissimum fecisse), id feci‹sse›[5] aliorum consilio,
hortatu, auctoritate; quo‹d› fuerim moderatior tempera-
tiorque quam in ea parte quisquam, id me fecisse maxime
auctoritate Capitonis. cuius similis si reliquos necessarios
habuissem, rei publicae fortasse non nihil, mihi certe
plurimum profuissem.

8   Hanc rem, mi Plance, si effeceris, meam de tua erga

[2] potuissem *(Man.)*
[3] inimicus *Man.**
[4] -llexerim *(Man.)*
[5] *(Lamb.)*

Press with all your strength. Bring it about that by dint of my recommendation, your active support, and Caesar's good favour C. Capito enjoys his relative's estate. If you grant me this, I shall feel that you have spontaneously laid in my lap all the advantages which, in your present plenitude of influence and power, I could have had of you for the asking.

There is a point which I hope will help you, one of which Caesar himself is in the best possible position to judge. Capito has always cultivated and regarded Caesar. But Caesar himself is witness to that. I know what an excellent memory he has, so I do not attempt to brief you. When you speak to Caesar, assume on Capito's behalf just so much as you find *his* recollection acknowledges. For my part, let me put before you what I have been able to test in personal experience—how much weight it should carry you must judge. You are not unaware what party and cause I championed in public life, and on what persons and classes I relied for support and protection. Please believe me when I say that in this very war any action of mine not in accordance with Caesar's wishes (and I know Caesar realizes that such action was very much contrary to my own inclination) was taken by the advice, instigation, and influence of others; whereas the fact that I was the most moderate and temperate member of that party was due above all to the influence of Capito. Had my other friends been similarly minded, I might have done something for the state and should certainly have greatly benefited myself.

If you put this matter through, my dear Plancus, you will confirm my hopes of your kindly disposition towards

9

me benevolentia spem confirmaveris, ipsum Capitonem, gratissimum, officiosissimum, optimum virum, ad tuam necessitudinem tuo summo beneficio adiunxeris.

283 (XIII.17)

Scr. Romae an. 46 vel 45

CICERO S. D. SER. SULPICIO

1   M'. Curius, qui Patris negotiatur, multis et magnis de causis a me diligitur. nam et amicitia pervetus mihi cum eo est, ut primum in forum veni[1] instituta, et Patris cum aliquotiens antea tum proxime hoc miserrimo bello domus eius tota mihi patuit; qua, si opus fuisset, tam essem usus quam mea. maximum autem mihi vinculum cum eo est quasi sanctioris cuiusdam necessitudinis quod est Attici nostri familiarissimus eumque unum praeter ceteros observat ac diligit.

2   Quem si tu iam forte cognosti, puto me hoc quod facio facere serius. ea est enim humanitate et observantia ut eum tibi iam ipsum per se commendatum putem. quod tamen si ita est, magno opere a te quaeso ut ad eam voluntatem, si quam in illum ante has meas litteras contulisti, quam maximus po‹te›st ‹m›ea[2] commendatione cumulus

3   accedat. sin autem propter verecundiam suam minus se tibi obtulit aut nondum eum satis habes cognitum aut quae causa est cur maioris commendationis indigeat, sic tibi eum commendo ut neque maiore studio quemquam

[1] venit χ *(cf. Beaujeu ad loc.)*
[2] *(Man.)*

me, and in Capito himself you will add to your connection a most appreciative, serviceable, and excellent person by conferring upon him so eminent a favour.

283 (XIII.17)
CICERO TO SERVIUS SULPICIUS RUFUS

Rome, 46 or 45

From Cicero to Servius Sulpicius greetings.

There are many good reasons for the regard I have for Manius Curius, who is in business in Patrae. My friendship with him is of very long standing, begun when I first entered public life; and at Patrae his whole house was open to me in this recent terrible war, as well as on several earlier occasions. Had I needed, I should have used it like my own. But my principal link with Curius has, if I may so put it, a more sacred character; for he is a great intimate of our friend Atticus, whom he cultivates and regards more than anybody in the world.

If you happen to have made Curius' acquaintance already, I imagine that this letter comes too late; for he is so agreeable and attentive that I expect he will have recommended himself to you by now. If that is so, I would none the less earnestly request of you that any measure of good will you have bestowed upon him prior to this letter of mine may be supplemented as largely as possible by my recommendation. If, on the other hand, his modesty has deterred him from putting himself in your way, or if you do not yet know him sufficiently, or if for some particular reason he requires a recommendation out of the common, then there is no man whom I could recommend to you

neque iustioribus de causis commendare possim, fa-
ciamque id quod debent facere ii qui religiose et sine am-
bitione commendant: spondebo enim tibi, vel potius spon-
deo in meque recipio, eos esse M'. Curi mores eamque
cum probitatem tum etiam humanitatem ut eum et amicitia tua et tam accurata commendatione, si tibi sit cognitus,
dignum sis existimaturus. mihi certe gratissimum feceris si
intellexero has litteras tantum quantum scribens confide-
bam apud te pondus habuisse.

284 (XIII.18)

Scr. Romae an. 46 vel 45

CICERO SERVIO S.

1   Non concedam ut Attico nostro, quem elatum laetitia
vidi, iucundiores tuae suavissime ad eum et humanissime
scriptae litterae fuerint, quam mihi. nam etsi utrique nostrum prope aeque gratae erant, tamen ego admirabar magis te, qui si rogatus aut certe admonitus liberaliter Attico
respondisses ⟨gratum mihi fecisses⟩,[1] quod tamen dubium
nobis quin ita futurum fuerit non erat, ultro ad eum scripsisse eique nec opinanti voluntatem tuam tantam per litteras detulisse. de quo non modo rogare te ut eo studiosius
mea quoque causa facias non debeo (nihil enim cumula-
tius fieri potest quam polliceris) sed ne gratias quidem
2   agere, quod tu et ipsius causa et tua sponte feceris. illud tamen dicam, mihi id quod fecisti esse gratissimum. tale
enim tuum iudicium de homine eo quem ego unice diligo

---

[1] *(SB, auct. Lehmann)*

more cordially or on better grounds. I will do what those who recommend a friend in conscience and simplicity ought to do—I will give you, or rather I do give you, my pledge and personal guarantee that Manius Curius' personality, character, and manners are such as will make you deem him, once you get to know him, worthy both of your friendship and of so studied a recommendation. Certainly I shall be deeply grateful if I find that my letter has carried as much weight with you as at the moment of writing I am confident it will.

284 (XIII.18)
CICERO TO SERVIUS SULPICIUS RUFUS

Rome, 46 or 45

From Cicero to Servius greetings.

I won't acknowledge that your kind and charming letter gave more pleasure to our friend Atticus, whose delight I witnessed, than to myself. Our gratification was about equal, but I was the more amazed. Had you *answered* Atticus handsomely, after a request or at any rate a hint (not that we had any doubt but that you would), I should have been beholden; but you have actually written to him of your own accord, and shown him by letter such a wealth of good will when he was not expecting it! I ought not to make a request of you in order to make you the more zealous on *my* account, for your promises go to the limit of liberality. I ought not even to thank you for what you have done for Atticus' sake and of your own volition. But this I will say, that I am deeply grateful for it. Such an expression of your esteem for my dearest friend cannot but give me

13

non potest mihi non summe esse iucundum; quod cum ita sit, esse gratum necesse est.

Sed tamen, quoniam mihi pro coniunctione nostra vel peccare apud te in scribendo licet, utrumque eorum quae negavi mihi facienda esse faciam. nam et ad id quod Attici causa te ostendisti esse facturum tantum velim addas quantum ex nostro amore accessionis fieri potest et, quod modo verebar tibi gratias agere, nunc plane ago teque ita existimare volo, quibuscumque officiis in Epiroticis reliquisque rebus Atticum obstrinxeris, iisdem me tibi obligatum fore.

285 (XIII.19)

Scr. Romae an. 46 vel 45

CICERO SERVIO S.

1   Cum Lysone Patrensi est mihi quidem hospitium vetus, quam ego necessitudinem sancte colendam puto; sed ea causa etiam cum aliis compluribus, familiaritas tanta nullo cum hospite, et ea cum officiis eius multis tum etiam consuetudine cottidiana sic est aucta ut nihil sit familiaritate nostra coniunctius. is cum Romae annum prope ita fuisset ut mecum viveret, etsi eramus in magna spe te meis litteris commendationeque diligentissime facturum, id quod fecisti, ut eius rem et fortunas absentis tuerere, tamen, quod in unius potestate erant omnia et quod Lyso

the liveliest satisfaction; and, that being so, I must needs
be grateful.

And yet we are so close that I may allow myself a slip
when I am writing to you. So I shall proceed to do both the
things I have said I must not do. I hope you *will* enhance
what you have told Atticus you are ready to do for his
sake by any additional favours your affection for me can
prompt. And whereas I did not venture a moment ago to
thank you, thank you now I do. I want you to feel that when
you oblige Atticus by your good offices in connection with
his affairs in Epirus or elsewhere you will by the same
token be obliging me.

285 (XIII.19)
CICERO TO SERVIUS SULPICIUS RUFUS

Rome, 46 or 45

From Cicero to Servius greetings.

With Lyso of Patrae I have an old tie of hospitality, a
connection which I believe should be religiously observed.
But that applies to a good many others, whereas the intimacy existing between myself and Lyso has no parallel
among my other relationships of this sort. It has been so
greatly furthered by his many services and by daily intercourse that our familiarity could not be closer. He has been
in Rome for almost a year, constantly in my company. We
were very hopeful that as a result of my letter of recommendation you would use your best endeavours to protect
his interests while he is away; and so you have. All the
same, remembering that all power resides in a single pair
of hands and that Lyso had been on our side, serving in our

fuerat in nostra causa nostrisque praesidiis, cottidie aliquid timebamus. effectum tamen est et ipsius splendore et nostro reliquorumque hospitum studio ut omnia quae vellemus a Caesare impetrarentur, quod intelleges ex iis litteris quas Caesar ad te dedit.

2   Nunc non modo non remittimus tibi aliquid ex nostra commendatione quasi adepti iam omnia sed eo vehementius a te contendimus ut Lysonem in fidem necessitudinemque tuam recipias. cuius dubia fortuna timidius tecum agebamus verentes ne quid accideret eius modi ut ne tu quidem mederi posses; explorata vero eius incolumitate omnia a te studio summo, ⟨summa⟩[1] cura peto. quae ne singula enumerem, totam tibi domum commendo, in his adulescentem filium eius, quem C. Maenius Gemellus, cliens meus, cum in calamitate exsili sui Patrensis civis factus esset, Patrensium legibus adoptavit, ut eius ipsius hereditatis ius causamque tueare.

3   Caput illud est ut Lysonem, quem ego virum optimum gratissimumque cognovi, recipias in necessitudinem tuam. quod si feceris, non dubito quin in eo diligendo ceterisque postea commendando idem quod ego sis iudici et voluntatis habiturus. quod cum fieri vehementer studeo tum etiam illud vereor, ne, si minus cumulate videbere fecisse aliquid eius causa, me ille neglegenter scripsisse putet, non te oblitum mei. quanti enim me faceres cum ex sermonibus cottidianis meis tum ex epistulis etiam tuis potuit cognoscere.

[1] *(Sjögren)*

ranks, we dreaded what each day might bring. However, his own distinction and the efforts of myself and his other erstwhile guests have carried the day. Caesar has acceded to our petitions in full, as you will gather from the letter which he has dispatched to you.

And now, far from at all abating my previous recommendation as though all our objectives were already achieved, I want to urge you all the more pressingly to take Lyso into your patronage and connection. When his fortunes hung in the balance, I was chary of saying too much to you in case of some mischance which even you would be powerless to remedy. But now that his status is secure, I most earnestly and particularly ask you for all possible assistance. Not to make a catalogue, I commend his whole household to your favour, including his young son, whom my client C. Maenius Gemellus adopted under the laws of Patrae, when he himself had become a citizen of that place during his unhappy exile. I trust that in this same matter of Maenius' inheritance you will defend his cause and rights.

The capital point is that you should admit Lyso, whom I know to be an excellent and appreciative fellow, into your connection. If you do, I have no doubt that you will form a regard for him, and in due course recommend him to others with sentiments and judgement corresponding to my own. This I ardently desire. And I also have some apprehension that, if in any particular you appear to have done less for him than you conceivably might, he will suspect that the perfunctory style of my letters has been to blame rather than your unmindfulness of myself. For how much you think of me he has been able to perceive from your own letters as well as my day-to-day conversation.

17

286 (XIII.20)

Scr. Romae an. 46 vel 45

CICERO SERVIO[1] S.

Asclapone Patrensi medico utor familiariter eiusque
cum consuetudo mihi iucunda fuit tum ars etiam, quam
sum expertus in valetudine meorum; in qua mihi cum ipsa
scientia tum etiam fidelitate benevolentiaque satis fecit.
hunc igitur tibi commendo et a te peto ut des operam ut
intellegat diligenter me scripsisse de sese meamque commendationem usui magno sibi fuisse. erit id mihi vehementer gratum.

287 (XIII.21)

Scr. Romae an. 46 vel 45

CICERO SERVIO S.

1   M. Aemilius Avia⟨nia⟩nus[1] ab ineunte adulescentia me
observavit semperque dilexit, vir cum bonus tum perhu-
manus et in omni genere offici diligen[du]s.[2] quem si arbitrarer esse Sicyone et nisi audirem ibi eum etiam nunc ubi
ego reliqui, Cibyrae, commorari, nihil esset necesse plura
me ad te de eo scribere. perficeret enim ipse profecto suis

[1] octavio
[1] *(Or.)*
[2] *(Man.)*

286 (XIII.20)
CICERO TO SERVIUS SULPICIUS RUFUS

Rome, 46 or 45

From Cicero to Servius greetings.

Asclapo, a physician of Patrae, is on familiar terms with me. I liked his company, and had favourable experience of his professional skill when members of my household[1] were taken sick. He gave me satisfaction in this connection as a knowledgeable doctor, and also a conscientious and kindly one. Accordingly I am recommending him to you, and would request you to let him understand that I have written about him with some particularity and that my recommendation has been to his no small advantage. I shall be truly obliged.

287 (XIII.21)
CICERO TO SERVIUS SULPICIUS RUFUS

Rome, 46 or 45

From Cicero to Servius greetings.

M. Aemilius Avianianus has cultivated my acquaintance from his early youth and always held me in regard. He is an honourable man and a very amiable one, most conscientious in serving his friends by every means in his power. If I thought he was now in Sicyon and had not heard that he is still staying where I left him, at Cibyra, there would be no need for me to write to you about him at any length. For I am sure that his own personality and manners

---

[1] Tiro 50–49, possibly others.

moribus suaque humanitate ut sine cuiusquam commendatione diligeretur abs te non minus quam et a me et a
2 ceteris suis familiaribus. sed cum illum abesse putem,
commendo tibi in maiorem modum domum eius, quae est
Sicyone, remque familiarem, maxime C. Avianium Ham-
monium, libertum eius, quem quidem tibi etiam suo nomine commendo. nam cum propterea mihi est probatus
quod est in patronum suum officio et fide singulari, tum
etiam in me ipsum magna officia contulit mihique mo-
lestissimis temporibus ita fideliter benevoleque praesto
fuit ut si a me manumissus esset. itaque peto a te ut eum
[Hammonium][3] et in patroni eius negotio sic tueare ut eius
procuratorem quem tibi commendo et ipsum suo nomine
diligas habeasque in numero tuorum. hominem pudentem
et officiosum cognosces et dignum qui a te diligatur.
  Vale.

288 (XIII.22)

Scr. Romae an. 46 vel 45
CICERO SERVIO S.
1   T. Manlium, qui negotiatur Thespiis, vehementer diligo. nam et semper me coluit diligentissimeque observavit
et a studiis nostris non abhorret. accedit eo quod Varro
Murena magno opere eius causa vult omnia; qui ita existi-
mavit, etsi suis litteris, quibus tibi Manlium commenda-
bat, valde confideret, tamen mea commendatione aliquid

___
    [3] *(Man.)**

without anybody's recommendation would have made you as fond of him as I and his other friends. But as I believe him to be away, let me warmly recommend to you his household in Sicyon and his interests—more especially his freedman C. Avianius Hammonius, whom I also recommend to you in his own right. I like him for his exceptional conscientiousness and fidelity towards his former master; moreover, he has rendered me personally important services, making himself available to me in the most difficult period of my life with as much loyalty and good will as if I had given him his freedom. So let me ask you to support him in his former master's affairs, as the agent of the person whom I am recommending to you, and also to hold him in regard for his own sake and admit him to your circle. You will find him a modest, serviceable person, worthy of your regard.

Good-bye.

288 (XIII.22)
CICERO TO SERVIUS SULPICIUS RUFUS

Rome, 46 or 45

From Cicero to Servius greetings.

I have a warm regard for T. Manlius, who carries on business at Thespiae. He has always made a point of cultivating my acquaintance and showing me courtesy, nor is he a stranger to our studies. Furthermore, Varro Murena takes the liveliest interest in his welfare. Although fully confident in the effect of his own letter of recommendation to you on Manlius' behalf, Varro was of the opinion that a letter of mine would contribute something addi-

accessionis fore. me quidem cum Manli familiaritas tum
Varronis studium commovit ut ad te quam accuratissime
scriberem.

2   Gratissimum igitur mihi feceris si huic commendationi
meae tantum tribueris quantum cui tribuisti plurimum, id
est, si T. Manlium quam maxime, quibuscumque rebus honeste ac pro tua dignitate poteris, iuveris atque ornaveris;
ex ipsiusque praeterea gratissimis et humanissimis moribus confirmo tibi te eum quem soles fructum a bonorum
virorum officiis exspectare esse capturum.

289 (XIII.23)

Scr. an. 46 vel 45

CICERO SERVIO S.

1   L. Cossinio, amico et tribuli meo,[1] valde familiariter
utor. nam et inter nosmet ipsos vetus usus intercedit et
Atticus noster maiorem etiam mihi cum Cossinio consuetudinem fecit. itaque tota Cossini domus me diligit in
primisque libertus eius, L. Cossinius Anchialus, homo et
patrono et patroni necessariis, quo in numero ego sum,
2   probatissimus. hunc tibi ita commendo ut, si meus libertus
esset eodemque apud me loco esset quo [et] est apud
suum patronum, maiore studio commendare non possem.
qua re pergratum mihi feceris si eum in amicitiam tuam
receperis atque eum, quod sine molestia tua fiat, si qua in
re opus ei fuerit, iuveris. id et mihi vehementer gratum erit

---

[1] tuo (*Man.*: amico ‹meo› et tribuli tuo *coni. SB*)

tional. As for me, my friendship with Manlius and Varro's urgency have induced me to write to you as pressingly as I can.

So then, I shall be deeply obliged if you will give as much attention to this recommendation of mine as you have ever given to such a document; that is to say, if you will assist and further T. Manlius as much as possible in any way consistent with your honour and dignity. And I assure you that you will reap from his own most appreciative and amiable character the reward you are accustomed to expect from the services of honourable men.

289 (XIII.23)
CICERO TO SERVIUS SULPICIUS RUFUS

Rome, 46 or 45

From Cicero to Servius greetings.

L. Cossinius, a friend of mine and a member of my Tribe, is on very friendly terms with me. We have an old-established acquaintance, and our friend Atticus has made me see even more of Cossinius than I otherwise should. His whole domestic circle has a regard for me, in particular his freedman L. Cossinius Anchialus, a person very highly thought of by his former master and his former master's connections, of whom I am one. I recommend him to you as warmly as I could if he was my own freedman and he stood in the same relation to me as to his former master. You will very much oblige me if you will admit him to your friendship and give him your assistance in any matter wherein he may require it, so far as you can do so without inconveniencing yourself. I shall be greatly obliged, and

et tibi postea iucundum; hominem enim summa probitate humanitate observantiaque cognosces.

290 (XIII.24)

Scr. Romae an. 46 vel 45

CICERO SERVIO S.

1   Cum antea capiebam ex officio meo voluptatem quod memineram quam tibi diligenter Lysonem, hospitem et familiarem meum, commendassem, tum vero, postea quam ex litteris eius cognovi tibi eum falso suspectum fuisse, vehementissime laetatus sum me tam diligentem in eo commendando fuisse. ita enim scripsit ad me, sibi meam commendationem maximo adiumento fuisse, quod ad te delatum diceret sese contra dignitatem tuam Romae de te
2 loqui solitum esse. de quo etsi pro tua facilitate et humanitate purgatum se tibi scribit esse, tamen primum, ut debeo, tibi maximas gratias ago, cum tantum litterae meae potuerunt ut iis lectis omnem offensionem suspicionis quam habueras de Lysone deponeres; deinde credas mihi adfirmanti velim me hoc non pro Lysone magis quam pro omnibus scribere, hominem esse neminem qui umquam mentionem tui sine tua summa laude fecerit. Lyso vero, cum mecum prope cottidie esset unaque viveret, non solum quia libenter me audire arbitrabatur sed quia libentius ipse loquebatur, omnia mihi tua et facta et dicta laudabat.
3   Quapropter, etsi a te ita tractatur ut iam non desideret

you will be glad of it later on, for you will find him a very
worthy, amiable, and attentive person.

290 (XIII.24)
CICERO TO SERVIUS SULPICIUS RUFUS

Rome, 46 or 45

From Cicero to Servius greetings.

In the consciousness of duty performed, I was already
happy to remember the pains with which I had recommended to you my host and friend Lyso; but after learning
in a letter from him that he had fallen under some un-
merited suspicion on your part, I was glad indeed to have
taken such trouble in recommending him. He tells me that
my recommendation has been of the greatest help to him,
because you had been informed that he was in the habit of
speaking disrespectfully about you in Rome. To be sure, he
writes that with your usual kindness and good nature you
accepted his exculpation. None the less I should, and do,
thank you most warmly for paying so much attention to my
letter as to put aside after reading it all offence arising from
the suspicion of Lyso which you had previously enter-
tained. I also hope that you will believe me when I assure
you that *nobody* (and in writing this I am not defending
Lyso any more than the community at large) has ever
spoken of you in other than the most complimentary
terms. As for Lyso, who has been with me almost daily, my
constant companion, he used to laud your every act and
word, not only because he thought I enjoyed listening to
such talk but because he enjoyed the talking even more.

Your treatment of him is such that he no longer re-

commendationem meam unisque se litteris meis omnia consecutum putet, tamen a te peto in maiorem modum ut eum etiam atque etiam tuis officiis liberalitate[1] complectare. scriberem ad te qualis vir esset, ut superioribus litteris feceram, nisi eum iam per se ipsum tibi satis esse notum arbitrarer.

291 (XIII.25)

Scr. Romae an. 46 vel 45

CICERO SERVIO S.

Hagesaretus Larisaeus magnis meis beneficiis ornatus in consulatu meo memor et gratus fuit meque postea diligentissime coluit. eum tibi magno opere commendo ut et hospitem meum et familiarem et gratum hominem et virum bonum et principem civitatis suae et tua necessitudine dignissimum. pergratum mihi feceris si dederis operam ut is intellegat hanc meam commendationem magnum apud te pondus habuisse.

292 (XIII.26)

Scr. Romae an. 46

CICERO SERVIO S.

1   L. Mescinius ea mecum necessitudine coniunctus est quod mihi quaestor fuit; sed hanc causam, quam ego, ut a

---

[1] ‹et› lib- *Benedict*: liberaliter ς

quires any recommendation from me and thinks that *one* letter of mine has accomplished all he needed. None the less I would particularly ask you to continue to favour him with your good offices and liberality. I should tell you what kind of a man he is, as I did in my previous letter, if I did not suppose that you know him well enough by now from personal acquaintance.

291 (XIII.25)
CICERO TO SERVIUS SULPICIUS RUFUS

Rome, 46 or 45

Cicero to Servius greetings.

Hagesaretus of Larisa received substantial favours at my hands when I was Consul and held them in grateful memory, paying me the most sedulous attention thereafter. I recommend him to you warmly as my host and friend, an honourable man who knows the meaning of gratitude, a leading member of his community, thoroughly worthy of your friendship. You will deeply oblige me if you make him sensible that my present recommendation has carried great weight with you.

292 (XIII.26)
CICERO TO SERVIUS SULPICIUS RUFUS

Rome, 46

From Cicero to Servius greetings.

I am bound to L. Mescinius by the fact that he was my Quaestor; but he has made that claim, to which I have

maioribus accepi, semper gravem duxi, fecit virtute et humanitate sua iustiorem. itaque eo sic utor ut nec familiarius ullo nec libentius.

Is, quamquam confidere videbatur te sua causa quae
honeste posses libenter esse facturum, magnum esse[1]
tamen speravit apud te meas quoque litteras ⟨pondus
habituras⟩. id cum ipse ita iudicabat tum pro familiari
consuetudine saepe ex me audierat quam suavis esset inter
nos et quanta coniunctio.

2   Peto igitur a te, tanto scilicet studio quanto intellegis
debere me petere pro homine tam mihi necessario et tam
familiari, ut eius negotia quae sunt in Achaia ex eo quod
heres est M. Mindio, fratri suo, qui Eli⟨de⟩[2] negotiatus
est, explices et expedias cum iure et potestate quam habes
tum etiam auctoritate et consilio tuo. sic enim praescripsi-
mus iis quibus ea negotia mandavimus, ut omnibus in
rebus quae in aliquam controversiam vocarentur te arbitro
et, quod commodo tuo fieri posset, te disceptatore uteren-
tur. id ut honoris mei causa suscipias vehementer te etiam
atque etiam rogo.

3   Illud praeterea, si non alienum tua dignitate putabis
esse, feceris mihi pergratum, si qui difficiliores erunt, ut
rem sine controversia confici nolint, si eos, quoniam cum
senatore res est, Romam reieceris. quod quo minore dubi-
tatione facere possis, litteras ad te a M. Lepido consule,
non quae te aliquid iuberent (neque enim id tuae dignitatis

1 *del. Beaujeu*
2 *(Man.)*

1 See Letter 128, n. 2.

always attached the importance prescribed by our traditions, all the more valid by his own merits of character and manners. I have no more familiar or pleasant acquaintance.

I think he is confident that you will be glad to do for his own sake all you properly can, but he hoped that a letter from me would carry much additional weight with you. That was his own impression, and in his familiar intercourse with me he had often heard me refer to the close and delightful connection between us.

Accordingly let me request you, with all the warmth which you will naturally understand to be appropriate in the case of so strong and familiar a connection, to smooth and straighten his affairs in Achaea, which arise from the fact that he is heir to the estate of his brother M. Mindius,[1] who was in business at Elis. This you can do by your influence and advice as well as by your official power and prerogative. We have instructed all our agents in these affairs to submit any disputed points to you as umpire and (so far as may be consistent with your convenience) as final arbiter. May I beg you most earnestly to take this responsibility upon yourself as a compliment to me?

One further point: should any parties show an unaccommodating disposition and prove unwilling to reach a settlement out of court, you will oblige me very greatly (provided you see nothing inconsistent therein with your own high standing) by referring them to Rome in view of the fact that a Senator is involved. In order that you may take this course with the less hesitation, we have obtained a letter from Consul M. Lepidus addressed to yourself—not directing you on any point (that we should consider less

29

esse arbitramur) sed quodam modo quasi commendati-
cias, sumpsimus.

4   Scriberem quam id beneficium bene apud Mescinium
positurus esses nisi et te scire confiderem et mihi peterem.
sic enim velim existimes, non minus me de illius re laborare quam ipsum de sua. sed cum illum studeo quam facill-
ime ad suum pervenire tum illud laboro, ut non minimum
hac mea commendatione se consecutum arbitretur.

293 (XIII.27)

Scr. Romae an. 46 vel 45

CICERO SERVIO S.

1   Licet eodem exemplo saepius tibi huius generis litteras
mittam, cum gratias agam quod meas commendationes
tam diligenter observes, quod feci in aliis et faciam, ut
video, saepius; sed tamen non parcam operae et, ut vo‹s
so›letis in formulis, sic ego in epistulis 'de eadem re alio
modo.'

2   C. Avianius igitur Hammonius incredibilis mihi gratias
per litteras egit et suo et Aemili Avianiani, patroni sui, nomine: nec liberalius nec honorificentius potuisse tractari
nec se praesentem nec rem familiarem absentis patroni
sui. id mihi cum iucundum est eorum causa quos tibi ego
summa necessitudine et summa coniunctione adductus
commendaveram, quod M. Aemilius unus est ex meis fa-

---

[1] Nothing is heard of this Aemilius except in letters of recommendation.

than respectful towards you), but a sort of letter of recommendation as it were.

I could say how wisely you will be placing such a favour with Mescinius. But I am sure you know that, and besides it is for myself that I am asking. For I hope you will take it that I am as much concerned for his interest as he is himself. But while I am anxious for him to come into his own with as little trouble as possible, I am also concerned to have him think that he owes this in no trifling degree to my present recommendation.

293 (XIII.27)
CICERO TO SERVIUS SULPICIUS RUFUS

Rome, 46 or 45

From Cicero to Servius greetings.

I might legitimately send you many letters of this kind in identical terms, thanking you for paying such careful attention to my recommendations, as I have done in other cases and shall clearly often be doing. None the less I shall not spare my pains. Like you jurists in your formulae I shall treat in my letters 'of the same matter in another way.'

C. Avianius Hammonius has written to me in transports of gratitude on his own behalf and that of his former master, Aemilius Avianianus. He writes that he himself on the spot and the interests of his absent ex-master could not have been dealt with more handsomely or with more flattering consideration. That makes me happy for their sakes. Close friendship and connection led me to recommend them to you, for of all my most intimate and familiar friends M. Aemilius is the nearest,[1] bound to me by sub-

31

miliarissimis atque intimis maxime necessarius, homo et
magnis meis beneficiis devinctus et prope omnium qui
mihi debere aliquid videntur gratissimus, tum multo iu-
cundius te esse in me tali voluntate ut plus prosis amicis
meis quam ego praesens fortasse prodessem, credo, quod
magis ego dubitarem quid illorum causa facerem quam tu
quid mea.

3   Sed hoc non dubito, quin existimes mihi esse gratum.
illud te rogo, ut illos quoque gratos esse homines putes;
quod ita esse tibi promitto atque confirmo. qua re velim
quicquid habent negoti des operam, quod commodo tuo
fiat, ut te obtinente Achaiam conficiant.

4   Ego cum tuo Servio iucundissime et coniunctissime
vivo magnamque cum ex ingenio eius singularique studio
tum ex virtute et probitate voluptatem capio.

294 (XIII.28)

Scr. Romae an. 46

CICERO SERVIO S.

1   Etsi libenter petere a te soleo si quid opus est meorum
cuipiam, tamen multo libentius gratias tibi ago, cum fecisti
aliquid commendatione mea, quod semper facis. incredi-
bile est enim quas mihi gratias omnes agant etiam medio-
criter a me tibi commendati. quae mihi omnia grata, sed de
L. Mescinio gratissimum. sic enim est mecum locutus, te,

stantial favours on my part, and the most grateful, I might almost say, of all those who may be thought to owe me anything. But it makes me far happier to find you so cordially disposed towards me that you do more for my friends than perhaps I should do myself, if I were on the spot. For I imagine that in serving them I should feel more hesitation as to how far I should go than you feel in serving me.

But of course you realize that I am grateful. What I ask you to believe is that they too are men of gratitude, which I hereby solemnly assure you is so. I hope you will try as far as you conveniently can to see that they settle whatever business they have on hand while you are governor of Achaea.

I have the closest and most agreeable association with your son Servius, and take great pleasure in observing his fine and upright character as well as his abilities and exceptional appetite for learning.

294 (XIII.28)
CICERO TO SERVIUS SULPICIUS RUFUS

Rome, 46

From Cicero to Servius greetings.

I am generally ready enough to ask your assistance when any of my friends stands in need, but it is with far greater readiness that I write to thank you when you have acted on my recommendation, as you always do. The gratitude expressed to me by everyone I recommend to you, even without special emphasis, passes belief. All this makes me beholden, but most of all in the case of Mescinius. He tells me that as soon as you read my letter

ut meas litteras legeris, statim procuratoribus suis pollici-
tum esse omnia, multo vero plura et maiora fecisse. id
igitur (puto enim etiam atque etiam mihi dicendum esse)
2 velim existimes mihi te fecisse gratissimum. quod quidem
hoc vehementius laetor quod ex ipso Mescinio te video
magnam capturum voluptatem; est enim in eo cum virtus
et probitas et summum officium summaque observantia
tum studia illa nostra quibus antea delectabamur, nunc
etiam vivimus. quod reliquum est, velim augeas tua in eum
beneficia omnibus rebus quae te erunt dignae; sed ‹sunt›[1]
duo quae te nominatim rogo: primum ut, si quid satis dan-
dum erit amplius eo nomine non peti, cures ut satis detur
fide mea; deinde, cum fere consistat hereditas in its rebus
quas avertit Oppia, quae uxor Mindi fuit, adiuves ineasque
rationem quem ad modum ea mulier Romam perducatur.
quod si putarit illa fore, ut opinio nostra est, negotium
conficiemus. hoc ut adsequamur te vehementer etiam
atque etiam rogo.
3   Illud quod supra scripsi, id tibi confirmo in meque recipio, te ea quae fecisti Mescini causa quaeque feceris ita
bene collocaturum ut ipse iudices homini te gratissimo
iucundissimo benigne fecisse. volo enim ad id quod mea
causa fecisti hoc etiam accedere.

[1] *(Purser)*

you immediately promised his agents all they asked, and
that you actually did far more and better than your word. I
hope you realize (I feel I cannot say it too often) that I am
most deeply beholden on this score. It makes me all the
happier because I am clear that Mescinius himself will
prove a source of great satisfaction to you. He is a man of
fine, upright character, in the highest degree obliging and
attentive, and he shares those literary interests which used
to be our diversion and are now our very life. As for the
future, I hope you will increase your benefactions to him
by all means befitting yourself. But I have two specific re-
quests. Firstly, if security has to be given in respect of final
settlement of any claim, please see that security is given on
my guarantee. Secondly, the estate consists, as near as
makes no matter, of those items which Mindius' widow,
Oppia, has made away with; please assist and find some
means whereby the woman may be brought to Rome. It is
our opinion that, if she thinks this is going to happen, we
shall settle the business. Let me beg you most particularly
to gain us this point.

In confirmation of what I have written above, let me
personally guarantee that your past and future good offices
to Mescinius will be well placed, and that you will find for
yourself that you have obliged a most grateful and agreeable individual. I want this to add something to what you
have done on my account.

295 (XIII.28a)

Scr. Romae an. 46 vel 45

‹ CICERO SERVIO S. ›

1   Nec Lacedaemonios dubitare arbitror quin ipsi sua maiorumque suorum auctoritate satis commendati sint fidei et iustitiae tuae et ego, qui te optime novissem, non dubitavi quin tibi notissima et iura et merita populorum essent. itaque cum a me peteret Philippus Lacedaemonius ut tibi civitatem commendarem, etsi memineram me ei civitati omnia debere, tamen respondi commendatione Lacedaemonios apud te non egere.

2   Itaque sic velim existimes, me omnis Achaiae civitates arbitrari pro horum temporum perturbatione felicis quod iis tu praesis, eundemque me ita iudicare, te, quod unus optime nosses non nostra solum sed etiam Graeciae monumenta omnia, tua sponte amicum Lacedaemoniis et esse et fore. qua re tantum a te peto ut, cum ea facies Lacedaemoniorum causa quae tua fides, amplitudo, iustitia postulat, ut iis, si tibi videbitur, significes te non moleste ferre quod intellegas ea quae facias mihi quoque grata esse. pertinet enim ad officium meum eos existimare curae mihi suas res esse. hoc te vehementer etiam atque etiam rogo.

295 (XIII.28a)
CICERO TO SERVIUS SULPICIUS RUFUS

Rome, 46 or 45

From Cicero to Servius greetings.

The Lacedaemonians are confident, I imagine, that their own prestige and that of their forefathers is all the recommendation they need to your sense of duty and justice, nor was I in any doubt, knowing you so well, that you are fully conversant with the rights and deserts of peoples. Accordingly, when Philippus of Lacedaemon asked me to recommend his community to you, I replied, though conscious of my great obligations to them, that the Lacedaemonians require no recommendation where you are concerned.

So please take it that I regard all the communities of Achaea as fortunate, considering the disorders of the present time, in having you as their governor; and, further, that I judge you to be of your own accord a good friend, now and in the future, to the people of Lacedaemon, better versed as you are in the whole history of Greece as well as Rome than any man alive. Let me then request only this: when you do for the Lacedaemonians what your conscience, your dignity, and your sense of justice will demand, indicate to them, if you please, that you are not sorry to understand that I too shall take it kindly. I have an obligation to let them feel that their interests concern me. Allow me to ask this as a particular favour.

296 (XIII.67)

Scr. Romae an. 46–44

M. CICERO P. SERVILIO PRO COS.[1] S.

1   Ex provincia mea Ciliciensi, cui scis τρεῖς[2] διοικήσεις
Asiaticas attributas fuisse, nullo sum familiarius usus quam
Androne, Artemonis filio, Laodicensi, eumque habui in ea
civitate cum hospitem tum vehementer ad meae vitae rationem et consuetudinem accommodatum; quem quidem
multo etiam pluris postea quam decessi facere coepi, quod
multis rebus expertus sum gratum hominem meique memorem. itaque eum Romae libentissime vidi. non te enim
fugit, qui plurimis in ista provincia benigne fecisti, quam
multi grati reperiantur.

2   Haec propterea scripsi ut et me non sine causa laborare
intellegeres et tu ipse eum dignum hospitio tuo iudicares.
feceris igitur mihi gratissimum si ei declararis quanti me
facias, id est si receperis eum in fidem tuam et, quibuscumque rebus honeste ac sine molestia tua poteris, adiu-
veris. hoc mihi erit vehementer gratum, idque ut facias te
etiam atque etiam rogo.

[1] propr(aetore) *(SB)*
[2] tris *coni. SB*

296 (XIII.67)
CICERO TO SERVILIUS ISAURICUS

Rome, 46–44

From M. Cicero to P. Servilius, Proconsul, greetings.

In all my province of Cilicia (to which, as you know, three districts of Asia were assigned) there was nobody with whom I was on a more friendly footing than with Andro, son of Artemo, of Laodicea. He was my host in that town and one that eminently suited my way of life and daily habit. Since leaving the province, I have come to value him far more even than at the time, having experienced in many contexts his grateful disposition and mindfulness of me. I was therefore very glad to see him in Rome. You, who have done good turns to so many people in your province, are well aware that the proportion of the grateful is less than overwhelming.

I have written the above to let you realize that my concern is not idle, and so that you yourself may account him worthy to be your host. You will oblige me very much indeed if you make it plain to him how much you think of me; that is to say, if you take him under your wing, and help him in every way you can with propriety and without inconvenience to yourself. That will oblige me indeed, and I would earnestly beg you so to do.

297 (XIII.69)

Scr. Romae an. 46–44

CICERO P. SERVILIO COLLEGAE S. P.

1   C. Curtius Mithres est ille quidem, ut scis, libertus Postumi, familiarissimi mei, sed me colit et observat aeque atque illum ipsum patronum suum. apud eum ego sic Ephesi fui, quotienscumque fui, tamquam domi meae, multaque acciderunt in quibus et benevolentiam eius erga me experirer et fidem. itaque si quid aut mihi aut meorum cuipiam in Asia opus est, ad hunc scribere consuevi, huius cum opera et fide tum domo et re uti tamquam mea.

Haec ad te eo pluribus scripsi ut intellegeres me non vulga⟨ri mo⟩re[1] nec ambitiose sed ut pro homine intimo ac 2 mihi pernecessario scribere. peto igitur a te ut in ea controversia quam habet de fundo cum quodam Colophonio et in ceteris rebus quantum fides tua patietur quantumque tuo commodo poteris tantum ei honoris mei causa commodes; etsi, ut eius modestiam cognovi, gravis tibi nulla in re erit. si et mea commendatione et sua probitate adsecutus erit ut de se bene existimes, omnia se adeptum arbitrabitur. ut igitur eum recipias in fidem habeasque in numero tuorum te vehementer etiam atque etiam rogo.

Ego quae te velle quaeque ad te pertinere arbitrabor omnia studiose diligenterque curabo.

[1] *(R. Klotz)*

---

[1] As Augur.

HORACE

ODES AND EPODES

WITH AN ENGLISH TRANSLATION BY

C. E. BENNETT

HARVARD UNIVERSITY PRESS

CAMBRIDGE, MASSACHUSETTS

LONDON, ENGLAND

First published 1914
Reprinted 1918, 1919, 1921, 1924, 1925
Revised and reprinted 1927
Reprinted 1929, 1930, 1934, 1939, 1946, 1947, 1960, 1964
Revised and reprinted 1968
Reprinted 1978, 1988, 1995

ISBN 0-674-99037-4

Printed in Great Britain by St Edmundsbury Press Ltd,
Bury St Edmunds, Suffolk, on acid-free paper.
Bound by Hunter & Foulis Ltd, Edinburgh, Scotland.

CONTENTS

LIFE AND WORKS OF HORACE

QUINTUS HORATIUS FLACCUS was born at the little town of Venusia, on the borders of Apulia and Lucania, December 8, 65 B.C. His father was a freedman, who seems to have been a collector of taxes. In this business he saved some money, and, dissatisfied with the advantages offered by the school at Venusia, took the young Horace to Rome for his education. This plan evidently involved no little personal and financial sacrifice on the father's part—a sacrifice appreciated to the full by Horace, if not at this time, at least in his later life. In a touching passage almost unique in ancient literature (*Sat.* i. 6, 72*ff.*) the poet tells us of the father's devotion at this period. Ambitious only for his son's mental and moral improvement, without a thought of the larger material prizes of life, he not only provided Horace with the best instruction the capital afforded, but watched with anxious care over the boy's moral training as well, even accompanying him to school and back again to his lodgings.

In his nineteenth year or thereabouts (*i.e.* about 46 B.C.) Horace went to Athens to add the finishing touches to his education by the study of philosophy. The Greek poets also largely occupied his attention at this time. Among his friends during this Athenian

period may be mentioned the young Cicero, son of the orator, and M. Valerius Messalla, who, with many other young Romans, were residing at Athens for the purpose of study.

After some two years Horace's studies were interrupted by political events. Caesar had been assassinated in March of 44 B.C., and in September of that year Brutus arrived in Athens, burning with the spirit of republicanism. Horace was easily induced to join his standard, and, though lacking previous military training or experience, received the important appointment of *tribunus militum* in Brutus' army. The battle of Philippi (November, 42 B.C.) sounded the death-knell of republican hopes and left Horace in bad case. His excellent father had died, and the scant patrimony which would have descended to the poet had been confiscated by Octavian in consequence of the son's support of Brutus and Cassius.

Taking advantage of the general amnesty granted by Octavian, Horace returned to Rome in 41 B.C., and there secured a position as quaestor's clerk (*scriba*), devoting his intervals of leisure to composition in verse. He soon formed a warm friendship with Virgil, then just beginning his career as a poet, and with Varius; through their influence he was admitted (39 B.C.) to the friendship and intimacy of Maecenas, the confidential adviser of Octavian, and a generous patron of literature. About six years later (probably 33 B.C.) he received from Maecenas the Sabine Farm, situated some twenty-five miles to the northeast of Rome, in the valley of the Digentia, a small stream flowing into the Anio. This estate was not merely adequate for his support, enabling him to devote his entire energy to study and poetry, but

viii

was an unfailing source of happiness as well ; Horace
never wearies of singing its praises.

Horace's friendship with Maecenas, together with
his own admirable social qualities and poetic gifts,
won him an easy entrance into the best Roman
society. His *Odes* bear eloquent testimony to his
friendship with nearly all the eminent Romans of
his time. Among these were : Agrippa, Octavian's
trusted general and later his son-in-law ; Messalla,
the friend of Horace's Athenian student days, and
later one of the foremost orators of the age ; Pollio,
distinguished alike in the fields of letters, oratory,
and arms. The poets Virgil and Varius have already
been mentioned. Other literary friends were : Quintilius Varus, Valgius, Plotius, Aristius Fuscus, and
the poet Tibullus.

With the Emperor, Horace's relations were intimate and cordial. Though the poet had fought
with conviction under Brutus and Cassius at Philippi,
yet he possessed too much sense and patriotism
to be capable of ignoring the splendid promise of
stability and good government held out by the new
régime inaugurated by Augustus. In sincere and
loyal devotion to his sovereign, he not merely
accepted the new order, but lent the best efforts
of his verse to glorifying and strengthening it.

He died November 27, 8 B.C., shortly before the
completion of his fifty-seventh year, and but a few
weeks after the death of his patron and friend
Maecenas.

Horace's first published work was Book I of the
Satires, which appeared in 35 B.C. Five years later
Book II was published. Though conventionally called
" Satires," and alluded to by Horace himself as
satirae, these were entitled by him *Sermones,* as being

talks, so to speak, couched in the familiar language of everyday life. In Horace's hands satire consists in the main of urbane comment upon the vices and foibles of the day, coupled with amusing incidents of personal experience and good-natured raillery at the defects of the prevailing philosophical systems, of which he was always an earnest and intelligent student.

The *Epodes*, published about 29 B.C., mark the transition from the *Satires* to the *Odes*. They resemble the *Satires* in their frequent polemical character, the *Odes* in the lyric form in which they are cast.

Books I–III of the *Odes* were published in 23 B.C., when Horace was forty-two years old. Many of them had unquestionably been written several years before—some apparently as early as 32 B.C. These *Odes* at once raised Horace to the front rank of Roman poets, and assured his permanent fame. Six years later he was the natural choice of Augustus for the composition of the *Carmen Saeculare* to be sung at the celebration of the Saecular Games in that year. A fourth book of *Odes* was published about 13 B.C.

Horace also issued two books of *Epistles*, the first about 20 B.C., the second about 14 B.C. Besides these we have the *Epistula ad Pisones*, often called *Ars Poetica*, a letter dealing with the principles of poetic composition, especially with the drama. This work belongs to the last years of the poet's life.

As a master of lyric form Horace is unexcelled among Roman poets. In content also many of his odes represent the highest order of poetry. His patriotism was genuine, his devotion to Augustus was profound, his faith in the moral law was deep

x

and clear. Wherever he touches on these themes he speaks with conviction and sincerity, and often rises to a lofty level. But the very qualities of reason and reflection that made him successful here, naturally limited his success in treating of love and sentiment—the topics most frequently chosen for lyric treatment by other poets. On this account he has not infrequently been challenged as without title to high poetic rank. But fortunately the question is not an academic one. Generation after generation continues to own the spell of Horace's verse. So long as this is true, we may properly ignore theoretical discussions concerning the character of his lyric work.

BIBLIOGRAPHY

THE *editio princeps* of Horace was published at Venice, probably in the year 1470. The name of the printer, as well as the date, is uncertain. Of especial present value are the following:

Text; translation:

    Bentley, Richard. Opera, Cambridge, 1711. Most accessible now in the reprint of Weidmann, Berlin, 1869. With Zangemeister's Index Verborum.

    Hofman-Peerlkamp. Carmina II, Amsterdam, 1862.

    Page, T. E. Opera, London, 1895.

    Müller, Lucian. Carmina III, Leipzig, 1879, and often reprinted. Teubner text.

    Keller, Otto. Carmina, Epodi, Carmen Saeculare, Leipzig, 1899. With Index Verborum.

    Vollmer, Friedrich. Opera II, Leipzig, 1912. Teubner.

    Kiessling A. and Heinze R. i Odes and Epodes (ed. 8); ii Satires (ed. 6); iii Epistles (ed. 5). Berlin, 1955–1957.

    Klinger F. ed. 2. Leipzig, 1950

    Villeneuve F. ed. and French translation. Odes and Epodes, 1954. Epistles, 1934. Satires, 1951, Paris, Budé.

BIBLIOGRAPHY

Michie J. Odes. Translation. Penguin Classics, 1967.

Wallace F. W. Odes. Translation. Hove, 1964.

Hermann L. Epodes. ed. and French translation Coll. Latomus. Brussels, 1953.

Campbell A. Y. The Odes. Liverpool, 1945.

Commentaries :

Kiessling, A. Oden und Epoden, Fünfte Auflage, besorgt von Richard Heinze. Berlin, 1908.

Orelli, Io. Gaspar. Odae, Carmen Saeculare, Epodi IV, curavit Guilelmus Hirschfelder. Berlin. 1886.

Page, T. E. Odes and Epodes. London, 1909.

Müller, Lucian. Oden und Epoden. St. Petersburg, 1900.

Wickham, E. C. Odes, Epodes, and Carmen Saeculare III. Oxford, 1904.

Nauck, C. W. Oden und Epoden XVII, von P. Hoppe. Leipzig, 1910.

Miscellaneous :

Pomponi Porfyrionis commentum in Horatium Flaccum, ed. A. Holder. Innsbruck, 1894.

Pseudoacronis Scholia in Horatium Vetustiora, ed. Otto Keller. Leipzig, 1901.

Keller, Otto. Epilegomena zu Horaz. Leipzig, 1879. An exhaustive presentation and discussion of variant readings.

Sellar, W. Y. Horace and the Elegiac Poets II. Oxford, 1899.

Ribbeck, Otto. Geschichte der römischen Dichtung. Stuttgart, 1900. II, chap. ii.

Tyrrell, Robert Y. Lectures on Latin Poetry. Boston, 1895. Chap. ii.

BIBLIOGRAPHY

Miscellaneous (cont.):

Fraenkel, E. Horace. Oxford, 1957. A study of many of the poems.

Perret, J. Horace. Paris, 1959. A general study.

La Penna, A. Orazio lirico. Studi. Florence, 1966.

Rudd, N. The Satires of Horace. Cambridge, 1966. A study.

Dilke, O. A. W. Epistles I, London, ed. 1, 1954, ed. 2, 1961, 1966.

Rostagni, A. Arte Poetica (edition). Turin, 1930.

Hermann, L. Ars Poetica ed. with French translation. Coll. Latomus, Brussels, 1951.

METRES USED BY HORACE

1. *Alcaic Strophe.*

⏓ | ‿ ◡ | ‿ ‿‖‿ ◡ ◡ | ‿ ◡ | ⏓ (twice)

◡ | ‿ ◡ | ‿ ‿ | ‿ ◡ | ‿ ⏓

‿ ◡ ◡ | ‿ ◡ ◡ | ‿ ◡ | ‿ ⏓

In the first two lines a diaeresis regularly occurs after the second complete foot, but this is sometimes neglected, *e.g. Odes,* I, 37, 14 ; IV, 14, 17.

The extra syllable at the beginning of the first three lines of each stanza is called an anacrusis.

This metre occurs in *Odes,* I, 9, 16, 17, 26, 27, 29, 31, 34, 35, 37 ; II, 1, 3, 5, 7, 9, 11, 13, 14, 15, 17, 19, 20 ; III, 1-6, 17, 21, 23, 26, 29 ; IV, 4, 9, 14, 15.

2. *Sapphic and Adonic.*

‿ ◡ | ‿ ‿ | ‿‖◡ ◡ | ‿ ◡ | ‿ ⏓ (three times)

‿ ◡ ◡ | ‿ ⏓

The regular caesura of the first three lines falls after the long syllable of the dactyl ; but a feminine caesura, after the first short of the dactyl, sometimes

occurs. This is especially frequent in Book IV of the *Odes*, and in the *Carmen Saeculare*.

Now and then we find a hypermetric verse, *e.g. Odes*, II, 16, 34.

This metre occurs in *Odes*, I, 2, 10, 12, 20, 22, 25, 30, 32, 38 ; II, 2, 4, 6, 8, 10, 16 ; III, 8, 11, 14, 18, 20, 22, 27 ; IV, 2, 6, 11 ; *Carmen Saeculare*.

3. *First Asclepiadean.*

$$\_\_|\_\cup\cup|\_\||\_\cup\cup|\_\cup|\smile$$

A diaeresis regularly occurs after the sixth syllable of the verse, but exceptions occur in *Odes*, II, 12, 25, and IV, 8, 17.

This metre occurs in *Odes*, I, 1 ; III, 30 ; IV, 8.

4. *Second Asclepiadean.*

$$\_\_|\_\cup\cup|\_\cup|\smile$$
$$\_\_|\_\cup\cup|\_\||\_\cup\cup|\_\cup|\smile$$

The second line of the couplet is the First Asclepiadean. The special name Glyconic is given to the metre of the first line.

This metre occurs in *Odes*, I, 3, 13, 19, 36 ; III, 9, 15, 19, 24, 25, 28 ; IV, 1, 3.

5. *Third Asclepiadean.*

$$\_\_|\_\cup\cup|\_\||\_\cup\cup|\_\cup|\smile \quad \text{(three times)}$$
$$\_\_|\_\cup\cup|\_\cup|\smile$$

This consists of the First Asclepiadean and the Glyconic.

This metre occurs in *Odes*, I, 6, 15, 24, 33 ; II, 12 ; III, 10, 16 ; IV, 5, 12.

6. *Fourth Asclepiadean.*

$$\_ \_ | \_ \smile \smile | \_ \| \_ \smile \smile | \_ \smile | \smile \text{ (twice)}$$
$$\_ \_ | \_ \smile \smile | \_ \smile$$
$$\_ \_ | \_ \smile \smile | \_ \smile | \smile$$

The first two lines are the First Asclepiadean. The third is called Pherecratean. The fourth is the Glyconic.

This metre occurs in *Odes*, I, 5, 14, 21, 23 ; III, 7, 13 ; IV, 13.

7. *Fifth Asclepiadean.*

$$\_ \_ | \_ \smile \smile | \_ \| \_ \smile \smile | \_ \| \_ \smile \smile | \_ \smile | \smile$$

This metre occurs in *Odes*, I, 11, 18 ; IV, 10.

8. *Iambic Trimeter.*

The strict scheme is:

$$\smile \_ | \smile \_ | \smile \| \_ | \smile \_ | \smile \_ | \smile \_ ;$$

but the spondee is occasionally substituted for the iambus in the odd feet of the verse, and at times even other substitutes occur, *e.g.* the tribrach ($\smile \smile \smile$), dactyl, and rarely the anapaest ($\smile \smile \_$). A caesura regularly occurs after the short syllable of the third foot (penthemimeral caesura), less

frequently after the short syllable of the fourth foot (hepthemimeral caesura).

This metre occurs in *Epode* 17.

9. *Iambic Strophe.*

This consists of the iambic trimeter (see § 8) followed by the iambic dimeter, which admits the same substitutes as the trimeter.

This metre occurs in *Epodes* 1-10.

10. *Alcmanic Strophe.*

This consists of the dactylic hexameter followed by a dactylic tetrameter. The spondee is freely substituted for the dactyl, as in Virgil.

This metre occurs in *Odes*, I, 7, 28; *Epode* 12.

11. *First Pythiambic.*

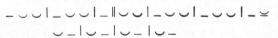

A dactylic hexameter followed by an iambic dimeter (§ 9).

This metre occurs in *Epodes* 14, 15.

12. *Second Pythiambic.*

_‿‿|_‿‿|_‖‿‿|_‿‿|_‿‿|_‿

‿_|‿_|‿‖‖_|‿_|‿_|‿_

A dactylic hexameter followed by an iambic trimeter (§ 8). In this metre no substitutes for the
iambus are permitted.

This metre occurs in *Epode* 16.

13. *First Archilochian.*

_‿‿|_‿‿|_‖‿‿|_‿‿|_‿‿|_‿

_‿‿|_‿‿|_

A dactylic hexameter followed by a dactylic trimeter catalectic ("stopping short").
This metre occurs in *Odes,* IV, 7.

14. *Second Archilochian.*

_‿‿|_‿‿|_‖‿‿|_‿‿|_‿‿|_‿

‿_|‿_|‿_|‿_‖_‿‿|_‿‿|_

A dactylic hexameter followed by a line consisting
of an iambic dimeter combined with a dactylic trimeter catalectic (§ 13). In the first and third feet
of the dimeter, the spondee may take the place of
the iambus.

This metre occurs in *Epode* 13.

15. *Third Archilochian.*

⏑ _ | ⏑ _ | ⏑ ‖ _ | ⏑ _ | ⏑ _ | ⏑ _ | ⏑ _

⏑ ⏑ | _ ⏑ ⏑ | _ ‖ ⏑ _ | ⏑ _ | ⏑ _ | ⏑ _ | ⏑ _

The first line is an iambic trimeter (§ 8).   The second is the same as the second line of the Second Archilochian (§ 14), with the two parts reversed.

This metre occurs in *Epode* 11.

16. *Fourth Archilochian Strophe.*

_ ⏑ ⏑ | _ ⏑ ⏑ | _ ‖ ⏑ ⏑ | _ ⏑ ⏑ | _ ⏑ | _ ⏑ | _ ⏑

⏑ _ | ⏑ _ | ⏑ ‖ _ | ⏑ _ | ⏑ _ | ⏑

The first line is called a greater Archilochian, and admits the substitution of the spondee for the dactyl in the first three feet.   The second line is an iambic trimeter catalectic ("stopping short") ; *cf.* § 8.

This metre occurs in *Odes*, I, 4.

17. *Second Sapphic Strophe.*

_ ⏑ ⏑ | _ ⏑ | _ ⏓

_ ⏑ | _ _ | _ | _ ‖ ⏑ ⏑ | _ | _ ⏑ ⏑ | _ ⏑ | _ ⏓

A so-called Aristophanic verse, followed by a greater Sapphic.

This metre occurs in *Odes*, I, 8.

18. *Trochaic Strophe.*

‒ ∪ | ‒ ‒ ∪ | ‒ ∪ | ‒
∪ ‒ | ∪ ‒ | ∪ ‒ | ∪ ‒ | ∪ ‒ | ‒

A so-called Euripidean verse, followed by an iambic trimeter catalectic ("stopping short"); *cf.* § 8.
This metre occurs in *Odes*, II, 18.

19 *Ionic a Minore.*

∪ ∪ ‒ ‒ | ∪ ∪ ‒ ‒ | ∪ ∪ ‒ ‒ | ∪ ∪ ‒ ‒ (twice)
∪ ∪ ‒ ‒ | ∪ ∪ ‒ ‒

This metre occurs in *Odes*, III, 12.

THE ODES OF HORACE

LIBER I

I

MAECENAS atavis edite regibus,
o et praesidium et dulce decus meum,
sunt quos curriculo pulverem Olympicum
collegisse iuvat metaque fervidis
evitata rotis palmaque nobilis
terrarum dominos evehit ad deos;
hunc, si mobilium turba Quiritium
certat tergeminis tollere honoribus;
illum, si proprio condidit horreo,
quicquid de Libycis verritur areis.   10
gaudentem patrios findere sarculo
agros Attalicis condicionibus
numquam demoveas, ut trabe Cypria
Myrtoum pavidus nauta secet mare.
luctantem Icariis fluctibus Africum
mercator metuens otium et oppidi
laudat rura sui; mox reficit rates
quassas, indocilis pauperiem pati.
est qui nec veteris pocula Massici

BOOK I

ODE I

Dedication to Maecenas

MAECENAS, sprung from royal stock, my bulwark and
my glory dearly cherished, some there are whose one
delight it is to gather Olympic dust upon the racing
car, and whom the turning-post cleared with glowing
wheel and the glorious palm exalt as masters of the
earth to the very gods.   One man is glad if the mob
of fickle Romans strive to raise him to triple honours ;
another, if he has stored away in his own granary
everything swept up from Libyan threshing-floors.
The peasant who loves to break the clods of his
ancestral acres with the hoe, you could never induce
by the terms of an Attalus to become a trembling sailor
and to plough the Myrtoan Sea in Cyprian bark.   The
trader, fearing the southwester as it wrestles with the
Icarian waves, praises the quiet of the fields about
his native town, yet presently refits his shattered
barks, untaught to brook privation.   Many a one
there is who scorns not bowls of ancient Massic
nor to steal a portion of the day's busy hours,

3

nec partem solido demere de die   20
spernit, nunc viridi membra sub arbuto
stratus, nunc ad aquae lene caput sacrae.
multos castra iuvant et lituo tubae
permixtus sonitus bellaque matribus
detestata.   manet sub Iove frigido
venator tenerae coniugis immemor,
seu visa est catulis cerva fidelibus,
seu rupit teretes Marsus aper plagas.
me doctarum hederae praemia frontium
dis miscent superis, me gelidum nemus   30
nympharumque leves cum Satyris chori
secernunt populo, si neque tibias
Euterpe cohibet nec Polyhymnia
Lesboum refugit tendere barbiton.
quodsi me lyricis vatibus inseris,
sublimi feriam sidera vertice.

stretching his limbs now 'neath the verdant arbute-tree, now by the sacred source of some gently murmuring rill.

Many delight in the camp, in the sound of the trumpet mingled with the clarion, and in the wars that mothers hate. Out beneath the cold sky, forgetful of his tender wife, stays the hunter, whether a deer has been sighted by the trusty hounds, or a Marsian boar has broken the finely twisted nets.

Me the ivy, the reward of poets' brows, links with the gods above; me the cool grove and the lightly tripping bands of the nymphs and satyrs withdraw from the vulgar throng, if only Euterpe withhold not the flute, nor Polyhymnia refuse to tune the Lesbian lyre. But if you rank me among lyric bards, I shall touch the stars with my exalted head.

II

Iam satis terris nivis atque dirae
grandinis misit Pater et rubente
dextera sacras iaculatus arces
    terruit urbem,

terruit gentis, grave ne rediret
saeculum Pyrrhae nova monstra questae,
omne cum Proteus pecus egit altos
    visere montes,

piscium et summa genus haesit ulmo,
nota quae sedes fuerat columbis,   10
et superiecto pavidae natarunt
    aequore dammae.

vidimus flavum Tiberim, retortis
litore Etrusco violenter undis,
ire deiectum monumenta regis
    templaque Vestae,

Iliae dum se nimium querenti
iactat ultorem, vagus et sinistra
labitur ripa, Iove non probante, ux-
    orius amnis.   20

ODE II

To Augustus, the Deliverer and Hope of the State

ENOUGH already of dire snow and hail has the Father sent upon the earth, and smiting with his red right hand the sacred hill-tops has filled with fear the City and the people, lest there should come again the gruesome age of Pyrrha, who complained of marvels strange, when Proteus drove all his herd to visit the lofty mountains, and the tribe of fishes lodged in elm-tops, that till then had been the wonted haunt of doves, and the terror-stricken does swam in the overwhelming flood.

We saw the yellow Tiber, its waves hurled back in fury from the Tuscan shore, advance to overthrow the King's Memorial [1] and Vesta's shrines, showing himself too ardent an avenger of complaining Ilia, and spreading far and wide o'er the left bank without Jove's sanction,—fond river-god.

[1] The Regia, the official residence of the Pontifex Maximus, said to have been built by King Numa.

7

audiet civis acuisse ferrum,
quo graves Persae melius perirent,
audiet pugnas vitio parentum
    rara iuventus.

quem vocet divom populus ruentis
imperi rebus ?   Prece qua fatigent
virgines sanctae minus audientem
    carmina Vestam ?

cui dabit partes scelus expiandi
Iuppiter ?   Tandem venias, precamur,   30
nube candentes umeros amictus,
    augur Apollo ;

sive tu mavis, Erycina ridens,
quam Iocus circum volat et Cupido ;
sive neglectum genus et nepotes
    respicis, auctor,

heu nimis longo satiate ludo,
quem iuvat clamor galeaeque leves
acer et Mauri[1] peditis cruentum
    vultus in hostem.   40

sive mutata iuvenem figura
ales in terris imitaris almae
filius Maiae, patiens vocari
    Caesaris ultor :

[1] Marsi *Faber, Bentley.*

8

Our children, made fewer by their sires' sins, shall hear that citizen whetted against citizen the sword whereby the Parthian foe had better perished,— shall hear of battles too.

Whom of the gods shall the folk call to the needs of the falling empire? With what entreaty shall the holy Maidens importune Vesta, who heedeth not their litanies? To whom shall Jupiter assign the task of atoning for our guilt? Come thou at length, we pray thee, prophetic Apollo, veiling thy radiant shoulders in a cloud; or thou, if thou wilt rather, blithe goddess of Eryx, about whom hover Mirth and Desire; or thou, our author, if thou regardest the neglected race of thy descendants, thou glutted with the game of war, alas! too long continued, thou whose delight is in the battle-shout and glancing helms and the grim visage of the Moorish foot-soldier facing his blood-stained foe. Or thou, wingèd son of benign Maia, if changing thy form, thou assumest on earth the guise of man, right ready to be called the avenger of Caesar: late mayest thou return to

9

serus in caelum redeas, diuque
laetus intersis populo Quirini,
neve te nostris vitiis iniquum
    ocior aura

tollat ; hic magnos potius triumphos,
hic ames dici pater atque princeps,   50
neu sinas Medos equitare inultos,
    te duce, Caesar.

the skies and long mayest thou be pleased to dwell amid Quirinus' folk ; and may no untimely gale waft thee from us angered at our sins !   Here rather mayest thou love glorious triumphs, the name of " Father " and of " Chief " ; nor suffer the Medes to ride on their raids unpunished, whilst thou art our leader, O Caesar !

III

Sɪc te diva potens Cypri,
  sic fratres Helenae, lucida sidera,
ventorumque regat pater
  obstrictis aliis praeter Iapyga,

navis, quae tibi creditum
  debes Vergilium; finibus Atticis
reddas incolumem, precor,
  et serves animae dimidium meae.

illi robur et aes triplex
  circa pectus erat, qui fragilem truci   10
commisit pelago ratem
  primus, nec timuit praecipitem Africum

decertantem Aquilonibus
  nec tristes Hyadas nec rabiem Noti,
quo non arbiter Hadriae
  maior, tollere seu ponere volt freta.

quem mortis timuit gradum,
  qui siccis oculis monstra natantia,
qui vidit mare turbidum et
  infames scopulos, Acroceraunia?   20

ODES BOOK I

ODE III

To Virgil setting out for Greece

MAY the goddess who rules over Cyprus, may Helen's brothers, gleaming fires, and the father of the winds, confining all but Iapyx, guide thee so, O ship, which owest to us Virgil entrusted to thee,—guide thee so that thou shalt bring him safe to Attic shores, I pray thee, and preserve the half of my own soul!

Oak and triple bronze must have girt the breast of him who first committed his frail bark to the angry sea, and who feared not the furious south-west wind battling with the blasts of the north, nor the gloomy Hyades, nor the rage of Notus, than whom there is no mightier master of the Adriatic, whether he choose to raise or calm the waves. What form of Death's approach feared he who with dry eyes gazed on the swimming monsters, on the stormy sea, and the ill-famed cliffs of Acroceraunia? Vain was the

nequiquam deus abscidit
   prudens Oceano dissociabili
terras, si tamen impiae
   non tangenda rates transiliunt vada.

audax omnia perpeti
   gens humana ruit per vetitum nefas.
audax Iapeti genus
   ignem fraude mala gentibus intulit.

post ignem aetheria domo
   subductum macies et nova febrium   30
terris incubuit cohors,
   semotique prius tarda necessitas

leti corripuit gradum.
   expertus vacuum Daedalus aëra
pinnis non homini datis;
   perrupit Acheronta Herculeus labor.

nil mortalibus ardui est;
   caelum ipsum petimus stultitia, neque
per nostrum patimur scelus
   iracunda Iovem ponere fulmina.   40

purpose of the god in severing the lands by the estranging main, if in spite of him our impious ships dash across the depths he meant should not be touched.   Bold to endure all things, mankind rushes even through forbidden wrong. Iapetus' daring son by impious craft brought fire to the tribes of men. After fire was stolen from its home in heaven, wasting disease and a new throng of fevers fell upon the earth, and the doom of death, that before had been slow and distant, quickened its pace.   Daedalus essayed the empty air on wings denied to man ; the toiling Hercules burst through Acheron.   No ascent is too steep for mortals.   Heaven itself we seek in our folly, and through our sin we let not Jove lay down his bolts of wrath.

IV

Solvitvr acris hiems grata vice veris et Favoni,
  trahuntque siccas machinae carinas,
ac neque iam stabulis gaudet pecus aut arator igni,
  nec prata canis albicant pruinis.

iam Cytherea choros ducit Venus imminente luna,
  iunctaeque Nymphis Gratiae decentes
alterno terram quatiunt pede, dum graves Cyclopum
  Volcanus ardens visit[1] officinas.

nunc decet aut viridi nitidum caput impedire myrto
  aut flore, terrae quem ferunt solutae ;   10
nunc et in umbrosis Fauno decet immolare lucis,
  seu poscat agna sive malit haedo.

pallida Mors aequo pulsat pede pauperum tabernas
  regumque turres.   o beate Sesti,
vitae summa brevis spem nos vetat incohare longam.
  iam te premet nox fabulaeque Manes

et domus exilis Plutonia ; quo simul mearis,
  nec regna vini sortiere talis,
nec tenerum Lycidan mirabere, quo calet iuventus
  nunc omnis et mox virgines tepebunt.   20

[1] visit *most MSS.*: urit *a few poorer MSS.*

ODES BOOK I

ODE IV

Spring's Lesson

KEEN winter is breaking up at the welcome change to spring and the Zephyr, and the tackles are hauling dry hulls toward the beach. No longer now does the flock delight in the fold, or the ploughman in his fireside, nor are the meadows longer white with hoary frost. Already Cytherean Venus leads her dancing bands beneath the o'erhanging moon, and the comely Graces linked with Nymphs tread the earth with tripping feet, while blazing Vulcan visits the mighty forges of the Cyclopes. Now is the fitting time to garland our glistening locks with myrtle green or with the blossoms that the unfettered earth brings forth. Now also is it meet in shady groves to bring sacrifice to Faunus, whether he demand a lamb or prefer a kid.

Pale Death with foot impartial knocks at the poor man's cottage and at princes' palaces. Despite thy fortune, Sestius, life's brief span forbids thy entering on far-reaching hopes. Soon shall the night of Death enshroud thee, and the phantom shades and Pluto's cheerless hall. As soon as thou com'st thither, no longer shalt thou by the dice obtain the lord-ship of the feast, nor gaze with wonder on the tender Lycidas, of whom all youths are now enamoured and for whom the maidens soon shall glow with love.

V

Qvis multa gracilis te puer in rosa
perfusus liquidis urget odoribus
   grato, Pyrrha, sub antro?
     cui flavam religas comam,

simplex munditiis? heu quotiens fidem
mutatosque deos flebit et aspera
   nigris aequora ventis
     emirabitur insolens,

qui nunc te fruitur credulus aurea,
qui semper vacuam, semper amabilem   10
   sperat, nescius aurae
     fallacis. miseri, quibus

intemptata nites. me tabula sacer
votiva paries indicat uvida
   suspendisse potenti
     vestimenta maris deo.

ODE V

To a Flirt

WHAT slender youth, bedewed with perfumes, embraces thee amid many a rose, O Pyrrha, in the pleasant grotto? For whom dost thou tie up thy golden hair in simple elegance? Alas! How often shall he lament changed faith and gods, and marvel in surprise at waters rough with darkening gales, who now enjoys thee, fondly thinking thee all golden, who hopes that thou wilt ever be free of passion for another, ever lovely,—ignorant he of the treacherous breeze. Ah, wretched they to whom thou, untried, dost now appear so dazzling! As for me, the temple wall with its votive tablet shows I have hung up my dripping garments to the god who is master of the sea.

VI

SCRIBERIS Vario fortis et hostium
victor Maeonii carminis alite,
quam rem cumque ferox navibus aut equis
   miles te duce gesserit.

nos, Agrippa, neque haec dicere nec gravem
Pelidae stomachum cedere nescii
nec cursus duplicis per mare Vlixei
   nec saevam Pelopis domum

conamur, tenues grandia, dum pudor
imbellisque lyrae Musa potens vetat   10
laudes egregii Caesaris et tuas
   culpa deterere ingeni.

quis Martem tunica tectum adamantina
digne scripserit aut pulvere Troico
nigrum Merionen aut ope Palladis
   Tydiden superis parem?

nos convivia, nos proelia virginum
sectis in iuvenes unguibus acrium
cantamus, vacui, sive quid urimur,
   non praeter solitum leves.   20

ODES BOOK I

ODE VI

Horace is unable worthily to sing the Praises of Agrippa

THOU shalt be heralded by Varius, a poet of Homeric flight, as valiant and victorious o'er the foe, whatever exploit with ships or horse the daring soldier has achieved under thy leadership. No such deeds, Agrippa, do I essay to sing nor the fell anger of Peleus' son, who knew not how to yield, nor the wanderings o'er the sea of the crafty Ulysses, nor the cruel house of Pelops,—too feeble I for such lofty themes, since modesty and the Muse that presides over the lyre of peace forbid me lessen by defect of skill noble Caesar's glory and thine own. Who could fittingly tell of Mars clad in his adamantine tunic? Of Meriones begrimed with Trojan dust, or Tydides, a match, with Pallas's help, for the immortals? I sing but of banquets, I sing but of combats of maidens fiercely attacking the young men with trimmed nails, easy as is my wont, whether fancy free or fired by a spark of love.

VII

Lavdabvnt alii claram Rhodon aut Mytilenen
  aut Ephesum bimarisve Corinthi
moenia vel Baccho Thebas vel Apolline Delphos
  insignes aut Thessala Tempe.

sunt quibus unum opus est, intactae Palladis urbem
  carmine perpetuo celebrare et
undique decerptam fronti praeponere olivam.
  plurimus in Iunonis honorem

aptum dicet equis Argos ditesque Mycenas.
  me nec tam patiens Lacedaemon   10
nec tam Larisae percussit campus opimae,
  quam domus Albuneae resonantis

et praeceps Anio ac Tiburni lucus et uda
  mobilibus pomaria rivis.
albus ut obscuro deterget nubila caelo
  saepe Notus neque parturit imbres

perpetuos, sic tu sapiens finire memento
  tristitiam vitaeque labores
molli, Plance, mero, seu te fulgentia signis
  castra tenent seu densa tenebit   20

22

ODES BOOK I

ODE VII

In Praise of Tibur

LET others praise famed Rhodes, or Mitylene, or Ephesus, or the walls of Corinth, that overlooks two seas, or Thebes renowned for Bacchus, Delphi for Apollo, or Thessalian Tempe. Some there are whose only task it is to hymn in unbroken song the town of virgin Pallas and to place upon their brows a wreath of olive gathered from every quarter. Many a one in Juno's honour shall sing of horse-breeding Argos and of rich Mycenae. As for me, not hardy Lacedaemon, or the plain of bounteous Larisa has so struck my fancy as Albunea's echoing grotto and the tumbling Anio, Tiburnus' grove and the orchards watered by the coursing rills.

As Notus is oft a clearing wind and dispels the clouds from darkened skies nor breeds perpetual showers, so do thou, O Plancus, remember wisely to end life's gloom and troubles with mellow wine, whether the camp gleaming with standards holds thee

Tiburis umbra tui.   Teucer Salamina patremque
  cum fugeret, tamen uda Lyaeo
tempora populea fertur vinxisse corona,
  sic tristes adfatus amicos :

" quo nos cumque feret melior fortuna parente,
  ibimus, o socii comitesque !
nil desperandum Teucro duce et auspice Teucro !
  certus enim promisit Apollo

" ambiguam tellure nova Salamina futuram.
  o fortes peioraque passi   30
mecum saepe viri, nunc vino pellite curas ;
  cras ingens iterabimus aequor."

or the dense shade of thine own Tibur shall encompass thee   Teucer, as he fled from Salamis and his father, is yet said to have bound garlands of poplar about his temples flushed with wine, addressing thus his sorrowing friends: " Whithersoever Fortune, kinder than my sire, shall bear us, thither let us go, O friends and comrades! Never despair under Teucer's lead and Teucer's auspices! For the unerring Apollo pledged us that there should be a second Salamis in a new land.   O ye brave heroes, who with me have often suffered worse misfortunes, now banish care with wine! To-morrow we will take again our course over the mighty main."

VIII

LYDIA, dic, per omnes
  te deos oro, Sybarin cur properes amando
perdere; cur apricum
  oderit campum, patiens pulveris atque solis;

cur neque militaris
  inter aequales equitet, Gallica nec lupatis
temperet ora frenis.
  cur timet flavum Tiberim tangere? cur olivum

sanguine viperino
  cautius vitat, neque iam livida gestat armis   10
bracchia, saepe disco,
  saepe trans finem iaculo nobilis expedito?

quid latet, ut marinae
  filium dicunt Thetidis sub lacrimosa Troiae
funera, ne virilis
  cultus in caedem et Lycias proriperet catervas?

ODE VIII

Sybaris' Infatuation for Lydia

In the name of all the gods, tell me, Lydia, why thou art bent on ruining Sybaris with love; why he hates the sunny Campus, he who once was patient of the dust and sun; why he rides no more among his soldier mates, nor restrains the mouth of his Gallic steed with jagged bit! Why does he fear to touch the yellow Tiber? Why does he shun the wrestling-oil more warily than viper's blood, nor longer show his arms bruised with weapon practice, he who once was famed for hurling, oft the discus, oft the javelin, beyond the farthest mark? Why does he skulk, as they say the son of sea-born Thetis did, when the time of Troy's tearful destruction drew near, for fear that the garb of men should hurry him to slaughter and the Lycian bands?

IX

Vides ut alta stet nive candidum
Soracte, nec iam sustineant onus
   silvae laborantes, geluque
    flumina constiterint acuto?

dissolve frigus ligna super foco
large reponens atque benignius
   deprome quadrimum Sabina,
    o Thaliarche, merum diota.

permitte divis cetera, qui simul
stravere ventos aequore fervido   10
   deproeliantes, nec cupressi
    nec veteres agitantur orni.

quid sit futurum cras, fuge quaerere et
quem Fors dierum cumque dabit, lucro
   appone nec dulces amores
    sperne puer neque tu choreas,

donec virenti canities abest
morosa. nunc et campus et areae
   lenesque sub noctem susurri
    composita repetantur hora,   20

nunc et latentis proditor intumo
gratus puellae risus ab angulo
   pignusque dereptum lacertis
    aut digito male pertinaci.

ODE IX

Winter without Bids Us Make merry within

SEEST thou how Soracte stands glistening in its mantle of snow, and how the straining woods no longer uphold their burden, and the streams are frozen with the biting cold? Dispel the chill by piling high the wood upon the hearth, and right generously bring forth in Sabine jar the wine four winters old, O Thaliarchus! Leave to the gods all else; for so soon as they have stilled the winds battling on the seething deep, the cypresses and ancient ash-trees are no longer shaken. Cease to ask what the morrow will bring forth, and set down as gain each day that Fortune grants! Nor in thy youth neglect sweet love nor dances, whilst life is still in its bloom and crabbed age is far away! Now let the Campus be sought and the squares, with low whispers at the trysting-hour as night draws on, and the merry tell-tale laugh of maiden hiding in farthest corner, and the forfeit snatched from her arm or finger that but feigns resistance.

X

MERCVRI, facunde nepos Atlantis,
qui feros cultus hominum recentum
voce formasti catus et decorae
    more palaestrae,

te canam, magni Iovis et deorum
nuntium curvaeque lyrae parentem,
callidum, quicquid placuit, iocoso
    condere furto.

te, boves olim nisi reddidisses
per dolum amotas, puerum minaci   10
voce dum terret, viduos pharetra
    risit Apollo.

quin et Atridas duce te superbos
Ilio dives Priamus relicto
Thessalosque ignes et iniqua Troiae
    castra fefellit.

tu pias laetis animas reponis
sedibus virgaque levem coerces
aurea turbam, superis deorum
    gratus et imis.   20

ODES BOOK I

ODE X

Hymn to Mercury

O MERCURY, grandson eloquent of Atlas, thou that
with wise insight didst mould the savage ways of
men just made, by giving speech and setting up the
grace-bestowing wrestling-ground, thee will I sing,
messenger of mighty Jove and of the gods, and father
of the curving lyre; clever, too, to hide in sportive
stealth whate'er thy fancy chose. Once in thy boyhood, as Apollo strove with threatening words to fright
thee, should'st thou not return the kine thy craft had
stolen, he laughed to find himself bereft of quiver too.
'Twas by *thy* guidance also that Priam, laden with
rich gifts, when leaving Ilium, escaped the proud
Atridae, the Thessalian watch-fires, and the camp that
menaced Troy. 'Tis thou dost bring the pious souls
to their abodes of bliss, marshalling the shadowy
throng with golden wand, welcome alike to gods
above and those below.

XI

Tv ne quaesieris—scire nefas—quem mihi, quem tibi
finem di dederint, Leuconoë, nec Babylonios
temptaris numeros.   ut melius, quicquid erit, pati!
seu plures hiemes, seu tribuit Iuppiter ultimam,
quae nunc oppositis debilitat pumicibus mare
Tyrrhenum.   sapias, vina liques, et spatio brevi
spem longam reseces.   dum loquimur, fugerit invida
aetas : carpe diem, quam minimum credula postero.

ODE XI

Enjoy the Passing Hour!

Ask not, Leuconoë (we cannot know), what end the gods have set for me, for thee, nor make trial of the Babylonian tables[1]! How much better to endure whatever comes, whether Jupiter allots us added winters or whether this is last, which now wears out the Tuscan Sea upon the barrier of the cliffs! Show wisdom! Busy thyself with household tasks; and since life is brief, cut short far-reaching hopes! Even while we speak, envious Time has sped. Reap the harvest of to-day, putting as little trust as may be in the morrow!

[1] Referring to the calculations of the Chaldaean astrologers.

XII

Qvem virum aut heroa lyra vel acri
tibia sumis celebrare, Clio?
quem deum?   cuius recinet iocosa
    nomen imago

aut in umbrosis Heliconis oris
aut super Pindo gelidove in Haemo,
unde vocalem temere insecutae
    Orphea silvae,

arte materna rapidos morantem
fluminum lapsus celeresque ventos,   10
blandum et auritas fidibus canoris
    ducere quercus?

quid prius dicam solitis parentis
laudibus, qui res hominum ac deorum,
qui mare et terras variisque mundum
    temperat horis?

unde nil maius generatur ipso,
nec viget quicquam simile aut secundum
proximos illi tamen occupavit
    Pallas honores,   20

ODE XII

The Praises of Augustus

WHAT man, what hero dost thou take to herald on the lyre or clear-toned flute, O Clio ? What god ? Whose name shall the playful echo make resound on the shady slopes of Helicon or on Pindus' top or on cool Haemus, whence in confusion the trees followed after tuneful Orpheus, who by the skill his mother had imparted stayed the swift courses of the streams and rushing winds ; persuasive, too, with his melodious lyre to draw the listening oaks in his train.

What shall I sing before the wonted praises of the Father, who directs the destinies of men and gods, who rules the sea and lands and the sky with its shifting seasons ? From whom is begotten nothing greater than himself, nor doth aught flourish like or even next to him. Yet the glory nearest his, Pallas, bold in battle, hath secured. Nor will I fail to mention

proeliis audax ; neque te *uilebo*,
Liber, et saevis inimica virgo
beluis, nec te, metuende certa
    Phoebe sagitta.

dicam et Alciden puerosque Ledae,
hunc equis, illum superare pugnis
nobilem ; quorum simul alba nautis
    stella refulsit,

defluit saxis agitatus umor,
concidunt venti fugiuntque nubes,   30
et minax, quod sic voluere, ponto
    unda recumbit.

Romulum post hos prius an quietum
Pompili regnum memorem an superbos
Tarquini fasces, dubito, an Catonis
    nobile letum.

Regulum et Scauros animaeque magnae
prodigum Paulum, superante Poeno,
gratus insigni referam camena
    Fabriciumque.   40

hunc et intonsis Curium capillis
utilem bello tulit et Camillum
saeva paupertas et avitus apto
    cum lare fundus.

thee, O Bacchus, nor thee, O virgin goddess, a foe to savage creatures, nor thee, O Phoebus, to be dreaded for thine unerring arrow. I will sing Alcides, too, and Leda's sons, famed, the one for victories with horses, the other for his skill in boxing; as soon as their clear star shines out for sailors, down from the cliffs flows the storm-tossed water, the winds subside, the clouds flee, and the threatening billow, because they so have willed, falls to rest upon the deep.

After these I know not whether to tell first of Romulus, of Pompilius' peaceful reign, or the proud fasces of Tarquinius, or of Cato's noble death. Regulus and the Scauri and Paulus, generous of his noble life, what time the Carthaginian prevailed, will I gratefully celebrate in glorious song,—Fabricius, too. Him and Curius with his unshorn locks and Camillus, stern poverty bred fit for war and a farm handed down from father to son with homestead to

crescit occulto velut arbor aevo
fama Marcelli[1]; micat inter omnes
Iulium sidus, velut inter ignes
    luna minores.

gentis humanae pater atque custos,
orte Saturno, tibi cura magni   50
Caesaris fatis data : tu secundo
    Caesare regnes.

ille seu Parthos Latio imminentes
egerit iusto domitos triumpho,
sive subiectos Orientis orae
    Seras et Indos,

te minor latum reget aequus orbem :
tu gravi curru quaties Olympum,
tu parum castis inimica mittes
    fulmina lucis.   60

[1] Marcelli *MSS.* : Marcellis, *Peerlkamp's conjecture, is adopted by many editors.*

match. The glory of Marcellus, like a tree, grows by the silent lapse of time. As the moon among the lesser lights, so shines the Julian constellation amid all others.

O Father and Guardian of the human race, thou son of Saturn, to thee by fate has been entrusted the charge of mighty Caesar; mayst thou be lord of all, with Caesar next in power! Whether he lead in well-earned triumph the humbled Parthians, that now threaten Latium, or the Seres and Indians lying along the borders of the East, second to thee alone shall he with justice rule the broad earth; be it thine to shake Olympus with thy ponderous chariot, thine to hurl thy angry bolts upon polluted groves!

XIII

Cvm tu, Lydia, Telephi
  cervicem roseam, cerea Telephi
laudas bracchia, vae, meum
  fervens difficili bile tumet iecur.

tunc nec mens mihi nec color
  certa sede manet, umor et in genas
furtim labitur, arguens
  quam lentis penitus macerer ignibus.

uror, seu tibi candidos
  turparunt umeros immodicae mero   10
rixae, sive puer furens
  impressit memorem dente labris notam.

non, si me satis audias,
  speres perpetuum dulcia barbare
laedentem oscula, quae Venus
  quinta parte sui nectaris imbuit.

felices ter et amplius,
  quos inrupta tenet copula nec malis
divulsus querimoniis
  suprema citius solvet amor die.   20

ODE XIII

Jealousy

WHEN thou, O Lydia, praisest Telephus' rosy neck, Telephus' waxen arms, alas! my burning heart swells with angry passion. Then my senses abide no more in their firm seat, nor does my colour remain unchanged, and the moist tear glides stealthily down my cheek, proving with what lingering fires I am inwardly devoured. I kindle with anger whether a quarrel waxing hot with wine has harmed thy gleaming shoulders, or the frenzied lad has with his teeth imprinted a lasting mark upon thy lips. Didst thou but give heed to me, thou wouldst not hope for constancy in him who savagely profanes the sweet lips that Venus has imbued with the quintessence of her own nectar. Thrice happy and more are they whom an unbroken bond unites and whom no sundering of love by wretched quarrels shall separate before life's final day.

XIV

O NAVIS, referent in mare te novi
fluctus.   o quid agis!   fortiter occupa
   portum.   nonne vides, ut
     nudum remigio latus

et malus celeri saucius Africo
antemnaeque gemant, ac sine funibus
   vix durare carinae
     possint imperiosius

aequor?   non tibi sunt integra lintea,
non di, quos iterum pressa voces malo.   10
   quamvis Pontica pinus,
     silvae filia nobilis,

iactes et genus et nomen inutile:
nil pictis timidus navita puppibus
   fidit.   tu, nisi ventis
     debes ludibrium, cave.

nuper sollicitum quae mihi taedium,
nunc desiderium curaque non levis,
   interfusa nitentes
     vites aequora Cycladas.   20

ODE XIV

To the Ship of State

O sHIP, new billows threaten to bear thee out to sea
again. Beware! Haste valiantly to reach the haven!
Seest thou not how thy bulwarks are bereft of oars,
how thy shattered mast and yards are creaking in the
driving gale, and how thy hull without a girding-
rope can scarce withstand the overmastering sea?
Thy canvas is no longer whole, nor hast thou gods
to call upon when again beset by trouble. Though
thou be built of Pontic pine, a child of far-famed
forests, and though thou boast thy stock and useless
name, yet the timid sailor puts no faith in gaudy
sterns. Beware lest thou become the wild gale's sport!
Do thou, who wert not long ago to me a source of
worry and of weariness, but art now my love and
anxious care, avoid the seas that course between the
glistening Cyclades!

XV

Pastor cum traheret per freta navibus
Idaeis Helenen perfidus hospitam,
ingrato celeres obruit otio
    ventos, ut caneret fera

Nereus fata: " mala ducis avi domum,
quam multo repetet Graecia milite,
coniurata tuas rumpere nuptias
    et regnum Priami vetus.

eheu, quantus equis, quantus adest viris
sudor! quanta moves funera Dardanae   10
genti! iam galeam Pallas et aegida
    currusque et rabiem parat.

nequicquam Veneris praesidio ferox
pectes caesariem grataque feminis
imbelli cithara carmina divides;
    nequicquam thalamo graves

hastas et calami spicula Cnosii
vitabis strepitumque et celerem sequi
Aiacem: tamen, heu serus! adulteros
    crines pulvere collines.   20

44

ODE XV

The Prophecy of Nereus

As the treacherous shepherd youth was hurrying his
whilom hostess Helen o'er the waves in Trojan bark,
Nereus checked the swift gales with an unwelcome
calm, that he might foretell the cruel fates: " 'Tis
under evil auspices that thou art leading home a
bride whom Greece with many a champion shall
seek again, sworn to break thy wedlock and destroy
the ancient realm of Priam. Alas! What toil for
steeds, what toil for men is looming near! What
disaster art thou bringing on the Trojan folk!
Already Pallas makes ready her helmet, her aegis,
her car, and is whetting her fury. In vain, em-
boldened by Venus' help, shalt thou comb thy
tresses and sing to the music of the unwarlike lyre
the songs that women love; vainly in thy chamber's
retreat shalt thou shun the heavy spears and darts
of Cretan reed, the battle's din, and Ajax fleet to
follow. In spite of all, thou shalt yet (alas! too
late) defile in the dust thy adulterous locks. Heedest

non Laërtiaden, exitium tuae
gentis, non Pylium Nestora respicis ?
urgent impavidi te Salaminius
    Teucer, te Sthenelus, sciens

pugnae, sive opus est imperitare equis,
non auriga piger.   Merionen quoque
nosces. ecce furit te reperire atrox
    Tydides melior patre,

quem tu, cervos uti vallis in altera
visum parte lupum graminis immemor,   30
sublimi fugies mollis anhelitu,
    non hoc pollicitus tuae.

iracunda diem proferet Ilio
matronisque Phrygum classis Achillei ;
post certas hiemes uret Achaicus
    ignis Pergameas [1] domos.''

[1] Pergameas *Petrus van Os*, 1500 : Iliacas *MSS.*

thou not Laertes' son, the scourge of thy race?
No? Nor Pylian Nestor? Dauntlessly upon thee
press Teucer of Salamis and Sthenelus skilled in
battle, or, if occasion call to guide the car, no
sluggish charioteer. Meriones, too, shalt thou come
to know. Lo! Fierce Tydides, brave father's braver
son, is furious to hunt thee out. Him shalt thou flee
faint-hearted, panting with head thrown high, as the
deer forgets its pasturage and flees the wolf seen
across the valley, though to thy mistress thou didst
promise a far different prowess.

The wrath of Achilles' followers may put off the
day of doom for Ilium and the Trojan matrons; yet
after the allotted years the fires of Greece shall burn
the homes of Pergamus."

47

XVI

O matre pulchra filia pulchrior,
quem criminosis cumque voles modum
    pones iambis, sive flamma
      sive mari libet Hadriano.

non Dindymene, non adytis quatit
mentem sacerdotum incola Pythius,
    non Liber aeque, non acuta
      sic [1] geminant Corybantes aera,

tristes ut irae, quas neque Noricus
deterret ensis nec mare naufragum   10
    nec saevus ignis nec tremendo
      Iuppiter ipse ruens tumultu.

fertur Prometheus addere principi
limo coactus particulam undique
    desectam et insani leonis
      vim stomacho apposuisse nostro.

irae Thyesten exitio gravi
stravere et altis urbibus ultimae
    stetere causae, cur perirent
      funditus imprimeretque muris   20

[1] sic *MSS.:* si *Bentley, followed by many editors*

ODE XVI

The Poet's Recantation

O MAIDEN, fairer than thy mother fair, make any end thou wilt of my abusive lines, be it with fire or in the waters of the Adriatic !

Not Dindymene, not the god who dwells in Pytho's shrine, when he thrills the priestess' soul, not Bacchus, not the Corybants, when they clash their shrill-sounding cymbals, so agitate the breast as doth grim anger, which neither the Noric sword represses, nor the sea that wrecketh ships, nor fierce fire, nor Jupiter himself, when he dashes down in awful fury.

Prometheus, as goes the tale, when forced to add to our primeval clay a portion drawn from every creature, put also in our breasts the fury of the ravening lion. 'Twas anger that laid Thyestes low in dire destruction, and that has ever been the primal cause why lofty cities perished utterly, and

49

hostile aratrum exercitus insolens.
compesce mentem : me quoque pectoris
    temptavit in dulci iuventa
        fervor et in celeres iambos

misit furentem ; nunc ego mitibus
mutare quaero tristia, dum mihi
    fias recantatis amica
        opprobriis animumque reddas.

the hostile hosts in exultation ran the plough over
their fallen walls. Restrain thy spirit! Me too in
youth's sweet day eager passion tempted and drove
in madness to impetuous verse. Now I would change
those bitter lines for sweet, wouldst thou only become
my friend and give me again thy heart, since I have
recanted my harsh words.

XVII

VELOX amoenum saepe Lucretilem
mutat Lycaeo Faunus et igneam
    defendit aestatem capellis
        usque meis pluviosque ventos.

impune tutum per nemus arbutos
quaerunt latentes et thyma deviae
    olentis uxores mariti,
        nec virides metuunt colubras

nec Martialis haediliae [1] lupos,
utcumque dulci, Tyndari, fistula   10
    valles et Vsticae cubantis
        levia personuere saxa.

di me tuentur, dis pietas mea
et Musa cordi est.   hic tibi copia
    manabit ad plenum benigno
        ruris honorum opulenta cornu.

hic in reducta valle Caniculae
vitabis aestus, et fide Teia
    dices laborantis in uno
        Penelopen vitreamque Circen ;   20

[1] haediliae *MSS., supported by ancient glosses: formerly taken
as a proper name (Haediliae).*

ODE XVII

An Invitation to Country Joys

In swift passage Faunus often changes Lycaeus for fair Lucretilis, and wards off from my goats the fiery heat and rainy winds during all his stay. Harmlessly through safe thickets do the roaming consorts of the rank he-goat hunt the hiding arbutus and thyme. Nor do the kids have fear of poisonous snakes or of the wolf, the war god's favourite, when once, O Tyndaris, sloping Ustica's vales and smooth-worn rocks have echoed with the sweet pipe (of Pan). The gods are my protection; to the gods both my devotion and my muse are dear. In this spot shall rich abundance of the glories of the field flow to the full for thee from bounteous horn. Here in retired valley shalt thou escape the dog-star's heat, and sing on Teian lyre Penelope and Circe of the glassy sea,

CARMINVM LIBER I

hic innocentis pocula Lesbii
duces sub umbra, nec Semeleius
    cum Marte confundet Thyoneus
        proelia, nec metues protervum

suspecta Cyrum, ne male dispari
incontinentes iniciat manus
    et scindat haerentem coronam
        crinibus immeritamque vestem.

enamoured of the self-same hero. Here shalt thou quaff bowls of harmless Lesbian wine beneath the shade, nor shall Thyoneus, child of Semele, engage in broils with Mars. Nor shalt thou, watched with jealous eye, fear the wanton Cyrus, lest he lay rude hands on thee, a partner ill-suited to his cruel ways, or lest he rend the garland clinging to thy locks, or thy unoffending robe.

XVIII

Nvllam, Vare, sacra vite prius severis arborem
circa mite solum Tiburis et moenia Catili ;
siccis omnia nam dura deus proposuit neque
mordaces aliter diffugiunt sollicitudines.
quis post vina gravem militiam aut pauperiem crepat ?
quis non te potius, Bacche pater, teque, decens Venus ?
ac ne quis modici transiliat munera Liberi,
Centaurea monet cum Lapithis rixa super mero
debellata, monet Sithoniis non levis Euhius,
cum fas atque nefas exiguo fine libidinum   10
discernunt avidi.   non ego te, candide Bassareu,
invitum quatiam nec variis obsita frondibus
sub divum rapiam.   saeva tene cum Berecyntio
cornu tympana, quae subsequitur caecus Amor sui
et tollens vacuum plus nimio Gloria verticem
arcanique Fides prodiga, perlucidior vitro.

ODE XVIII

The Praises of Wine

O VARUS, plant no tree in preference to the sacred vine about the mellow soil of Tibur and by the walls of Catilus! For to the abstemious has the god ordained that everything be hard, nor are cankering cares dispelled except by Bacchus' gift. Who, after his wine, harps on the hardships of campaigns or poverty? Who does not rather glorify thee, O Father Bacchus, and thee, O comely Venus? And yet, that no one pass the bounds of moderation in enjoying Liber's gifts, we have a lesson in the Centaurs' contest with the Lapithae, fought out to the bitter end over the festal board; we have a lesson, too, in the Sithonians, hated by Bacchus when, furious with desire, they distinguish right and wrong only by the narrow line their passions draw. I'll not be the one, fair Bassareus, to rouse thee against thy will, nor to expose to the light of day thy mystic emblems covered with leaves of many kinds. Repress the wild cymbal along with Berecyntian horn, orgies followed by blind self-love, by vainglory that lifts its empty head too high aloft, and by a faith that betrays its trust, transparent more than glass!

XIX

MATER saeva Cupidinum
  Thebanaeque iubet me Semelae puer
et lasciva Licentia
  finitis animum reddere amoribus.

urit me Glycerae nitor,
  splendentis Pario marmore purius ;
urit grata protervitas
  et vultus nimium lubricus aspici.

in me tota ruens Venus
  Cyprum deseruit, nec patitur Scythas   10
et versis animosum equis
  Parthum dicere, nec quae nihil attinent.

hic vivum mihi caespitem, hic
  verbenas, pueri, ponite turaque
bimi cum patera meri :
  mactata veniet lenior hostia.

ODE XIX

The Charms of Glycera

THE Cupids' cruel mother with the son of Theban Semele and sportive Wantonness bid me give heed again to loves I dreamed were ended. I am enamoured of Glycera's beauty, more dazzling than Parian marble; I am enamoured of her sweet forwardness and her face seductive to behold. Upon me Venus, leaving her Cyprus, has fallen with all her power, and permits me not to sing of the Scythians, of the Parthians bold in flight, or of aught irrelevant. Here set me up, O slaves, an altar of verdant turf! Here put sprays of leaves, and incense, with a bowl of last year's unmixed wine! The goddess will be less cruel at her coming, if I sacrifice a victim.

XX

Vɪʟᴇ potabis modicis Sabinum
cantharis, Graeca quod ego ipse testa
conditum levi, datus in theatro
    cum tibi plausus,

care [1] Maecenas eques, ut paterni
fluminis ripae simul et iocosa
redderet laudes tibi Vaticani
    montis imago.

Caecubum et prelo domitam Caleno
tum [2] bibes [3] uvam; mea nec Falernae   10
temperant vites neque Formiani
    pocula colles.

[1] care : clare *interpolated MSS.*
[2] tum *Porphyrion :* tu *MSS.*
[3] bibas *Keller.*

ODE XX

An Invitation to Maecenas

COME, drink with me—cheap Sabine, to be sure, and out of common tankards, yet wine that I with my own hand put up and sealed in a Grecian jar, on the day, dear Knight Maecenas, when such applause was paid thee in the Theatre that with one accord the banks of thy native stream and the sportive echo of Mount Vatican returned thy praises. Then thou shalt drink Caecuban and the juice of grapes crushed by Cales' presses; my cups are flavoured neither with the product of Falernum's vines nor of the Formian hills.

XXI

DIANAM tenerae dicite virgines,
intonsum, pueri, dicite Cynthium
    Latonamque supremo
      dilectam penitus Iovi.

vos laetam fluviis et nemorum coma,
quaecumque aut gelido prominet Algido,
    nigris aut Erymanthi
      silvis aut viridis Cragi ;

vos Tempe totidem tollite laudibus
natalemque, mares, Delon Apollinis,   10
    insignemque pharetra
      fraternaque umerum lyra.

hic bellum lacrimosum, hic miseram famem
pestemque a populo et principe Caesare in
    Persas atque Britannos
      vestra motus aget prece.

ODE XXI

In Praise of Latona and Her Children

PRAISE Diana, O ye maidens tender! Praise, O ye lads, unshorn Apollo, and Latona, fondly loved by Jove supreme! Praise ye, O maidens, her who delights in streams and in the foliage of the groves that stand out on cool Algidus or amid the black woods of Erymanthus and verdant Cragus! Do ye, O lads, with praises just as many, glorify Tempe and Delos, Apollo's natal isle, and the god's shoulder, adorned with quiver and with the lyre invented by his brother's cunning! Moved by your prayer he shall ward off tearful war, wretched plague and famine from the folk and from our sovereign Caesar, and send these woes against the Parthian and the Briton.

XXII

INTEGER vitae scelerisque purus
non eget Mauris iaculis neque arcu
nec venenatis gravida sagittis,
    Fusce, pharetra,

sive per Syrtes iter aestuosas
sive facturus per inhospitalem
Caucasum vel quae loca fabulosus
    lambit Hydaspes.

namque me silva lupus in Sabina,
dum meam canto Lalagen et ultra   10
terminum curis vagor expeditis,
    fugit inermem ;

quale portentum neque militaris
Daunias latis alit aesculetis
nec Iubae tellus generat, leonum
    arida nutrix.

pone me pigris ubi nulla campis
arbor aestiva recreatur aura,
quod latus mundi nebulae malusque
    Iuppiter urget ;   20

pone sub curru nimium propinqui
solis in terra domibus negata :
dulce ridentem Lalagen amabo,
    dulce loquentem.

ODE XXII

*From the Righteous Man even the Wild Beasts Run
away*

HE who is upright in his way of life and unstained by
guilt, needs not Moorish darts nor bow nor quiver
loaded with poisoned arrows, Fuscus, whether his way
shall be through the sweltering Syrtes or the cheerless
Caucasus or the regions that storied Hydaspes waters.
For as I was singing of my Lalage and wandering far
beyond the boundaries of my farm in Sabine woods,
unarmed and free from care, there fled from me a
wolf, a monster such as not martial Daunia nurtures
in her broad oak forests, nor the parched land of
Juba, nurse of lions, breeds.

Place me on the lifeless plains where no tree
revives under the summer breeze, a region of the
world o'er which brood mists and a gloomy sky; set
me beneath the chariot of the sun where it draws too
near the earth, in a land denied for dwellings! I will
love my sweetly laughing, sweetly prattling Lalage.

XXIII

Vitas hinnuleo me similis, Chloë,
quaerenti pavidam montibus aviis
   matrem non sine vano
     aurarum et siluae metu.

nam seu mobilibus veris[1] inhorruit
adventus foliis, seu virides rubum
   dimovere lacertae,
     et corde et genibus tremit.

atqui non ego te tigris ut aspera
Gaetulusve leo frangere persequor: 10
   tandem desine matrem
     tempestiva sequi viro.

[1] vepris inhorruit ad ventos *Bentley, Keller.*

ODE XXIII

Fear me not, Chloë!

Thou shunnest me, Chloë, like a fawn that seeks its
timid mother o'er trackless hills, filled with needless
terror of the breezes and the woods.   For it quivers
in heart and limb, if through the light hung leaves
hath run the shiver of spring's approach, or the
green lizards have pushed aside the bramble.   Yet
my purpose is not to crush thee like a savage tiger
or Gaetulian lion.   Cease at length to follow thy
mother, since now thou art ripe for a mate !

XXIV

Qvis desiderio sit pudor aut modus
tam cari capitis ?   praecipe lugubres
cantus, Melpomene, cui liquidam pater
    vocem cum cithara dedit.

ergo Quintilium perpetuus sopor
urget ?   cui Pudor et Iustitiae soror,
incorrupta Fides, nudaque Veritas,
    quando ullum inveniet parem ?

multis ille bonis flebilis occidit,
nulli flebilior quam tibi, Vergili.   10
tu frustra pius heu non ita creditum
    poscis Quintilium deos.

quid, si Threicio blandius Orpheo
auditam moderere arboribus fidem ?
num vanae redeat sanguis imagini,
    quam virga semel horrida,

non lenis precibus fata recludere,
nigro compulerit Mercurius gregi ?
durum : sed levius fit patientia,
    quicquid corrigere est nefas.   20

ODE XXIV

A Dirge for Quintilius

WHAT restraint or limit should there be to grief for one so dear? Teach me a song of mourning, O Melpomene, thou to whom the Father gave a liquid voice and music of the lyre!

Does, then, the sleep that knows no waking lie heavy on Quintilius! When shall Honour, and Justice' sister, Loyalty unshaken, and candid Truth e'er find a peer to him? Many are the good who mourn his death; but no one more than thou, O Virgil. In vain, despite thy fond devotion, dost thou ask the gods to give Quintilius back, entrusted to this mortal life, alas! on no such terms. Even wert thou to strike more tunefully than Thracian Orpheus the lyre once heeded by the trees, would then the life return to the unsubstantial ghost, which with his gruesome wand Mercury, not kind to ope the portals of the Fates to our entreaty, has gathered once to the shadowy throng? 'Tis hard; but by endurance that grows lighter which Heaven forbids to change for good.

69

XXV

Parcivs iunctas quatiunt fenestras
ictibus [1] crebris iuvenes protervi,
nec tibi somnos adimunt, amatque
　　ianua limen,

quae prius multum facilis movebat
cardines.　audis minus et minus iam :
" me tuo longas pereunte noctes,
　　Lydia, dormis?"

invicem moechos anus arrogantes
flebis in solo levis angiportu,　　　　　　　　　　　10
Thracio bacchante magis sub inter-
　　lunia vento,

cum tibi flagrans amor et libido,
quae solet matres furiare equorum,
saeviet circa iecur ulcerosum,
　　non sine questu,

laeta quod pubes hedera virenti
gaudeat pulla magis atque myrto,
aridas frondes hiemis sodali
　　dedicet Euro.[2]　　　　　　　　　　　20

[1] ictibus: iactibus *most MSS.*
[2] Euro *Strassburg ed.* 1516 : Hebro *MSS.*

ODE XXV

Lydia's Charms are Past

LESS often now do riotous youths shake thy shutters with repeated blows; no longer do they steal thy slumbers from thee; and the door that once right willingly did move its hinges now hugs its threshold. Less and less often hearest thou such plaints as this: "Sleepest thou, Lydia, while I, thy lover true, die throughout the livelong night?" Thy turn shall come, and thou, a hag forlorn in deserted alley, shalt weep o'er thy lovers' disdain, when on moon-less nights the Thracian north-wind rises in its fury, while burning love and passion, such as are wont to goad the stallions' dams, shall rage about thy wounded heart. Then shalt thou make moan that merry youths take more delight in ivy green and myrtle dark, consigning withered leaves to the east-wind, winter's mate.

XXVI

Mvsis amicus tristitiam et metus
tradam protervis in mare Creticum
portare ventis, quis sub Arcto
    rex gelidae metuatur orae,

quid Tiridaten terreat, unice
securus.   o quae fontibus integris
gaudes, apricos necte flores,
    necte meo Lamiae coronam,

Pimplei dulcis.   nil sine te mei
prosunt honores: hunc fidibus novis,   10
    hunc Lesbio sacrare plectro
    teque tuasque decet sorores.

ODE XXVI

Immortalise Lamia, Ye Muses!

DEAR to the Muses, I will banish gloom and fear to the wild winds to carry o'er the Cretan Sea, all unconcerned what ruler of the frozen borders of the North is object of our fear, or what dangers frighten Tiridates.

Do thou, sweet Muse, that takest joy in fountains fresh, weave gay blossoms, yea, weave them as a garland for my Lamia! Naught without thee avail my tributes. Him in new measures, him with Lesbian plectrum,[1] 'tis meet that thou and thy sisters should make immortal.

[1] An instrument of metal or ivory with which the strings of the lyre were struck or picked.

XXVII

Natis in usum laetitiae scyphis
pugnare Thracum est: tollite barbarum
   morem, verecundumque Bacchum
     sanguineis prohibete rixis.

vino et lucernis Medus acinaces
immane quantum discrepat: impium
   lenite clamorem, sodales,
     et cubito remanete presso.

vultis severi me quoque sumere
partem Falerni? dicat Opuntiae   10
   frater Megyllae, quo beatus
     vulnere, qua pereat sagitta.

cessat voluntas? non alia bibam
mercede. quae te cumque domat Venus,
   non erubescendis adurit
     ignibus ingenuoque semper

amore peccas. quicquid habes, age,
depone tutis auribus.—a miser,
   quanta laboras in Charybdi,
     digne puer meliore flamma!   20

quae saga, quis te solvere Thessalis
magus venenis, quis poterit deus?
   vix inligatum te triformi
     Pegasus expediet Chimaera.

74

ODE XXVII

Let Moderation Reign!

To fight with goblets meant for pleasure's service is
fit for none but Thracians. Banish such barbarous
ways! Protect from bloody brawls our Bacchus, who
loves what's seemly. With wine and lamps the Persian sword is sadly out of keeping. Repress your
impious uproar, mates, and lie with elbow resting on
the couch! You wish that I too drink my portion
of stout Falernian? Then let Opuntian Megylla's
brother tell with what wound, what shaft, he lan-
guishes in bliss. Thy inclination falters? On no
other terms will I consent to touch the draught.
Whatever passion masters thee, it burns thee with a
flame for which thou needst not blush, and free-born
always is the object of thy weakness. Whatever 'tis,
come, confide it to my trusty ear!—Ah! Wretched
youth! In what a fatal whirlpool art thou caught,
lad worthy of a better flame! What witch, what
wizard with Thessalian charms,—nay, what god, can
rescue thee! Entangled, as thou art, in the triple-
formed Chimaera's toils, scarce Pegasus shall set
thee free.

XXVIII—1

TE maris et terrae numeroque carentis harenae
    mensorem cohibent, Archyta,
pulveris exigui prope litus parva Matinum
    munera, nec quicquam tibi prodest

aërias temptasse domos animoque rotundum
    percurrisse polum morituro.
occidit et Pelopis genitor, conviva deorum,
    Tithonusque remotus in auras

et Iovis arcanis Minos admissus, habentque
    Tartara Panthoiden iterum Orco   10
demissum, quamvis clipeo Troiana refixo
    tempora testatus nihil ultra

nervos atque cutem morti concesserat atrae,
    iudice te non sordidus auctor
naturae verique.   sed omnes una manet nox,
    et calcanda semel via leti.

dant alios Furiae torvo spectacula Marti,
    exitio est avidum mare nautis;
mixta senum ac iuvenum densentur funera, nullum
    saeva caput Proserpina fugit.   20

ODE XXVIII—1 [1]

Death the Doom of All

THOU, Archytas, measurer of the sea and land and countless sands, art confined in a small mound of paltry earth near the Matinian shore; nor doth it aught avail thee that thou didst once explore the gods' ethereal homes and didst traverse in thought the circling vault of heaven. For thou wast born to die! Death befell also Pelops' sire, though once he sat at the table of the gods; Tithonus, too, translated to the skies, and Minos, partner of Jove's own secrets; and Tartarus holds the son of Panthous, sent down a second time to Orcus, though by taking down the shield he bore witness to Trojan times, and yielded to black Death naught but his sinews and his frame,—to thy mind no common judge of Nature and of truth.

But a common night awaiteth every man, and Death's path must be trodden once for all. Some, the Furies offer as a sight for cruel Mars; the hungry sea is the sailor's ruin. Without distinction the deaths of old and young follow close on each other's heels; cruel Proserpine spares no head.

[1] In our *MSS.* and in most editions, this Ode forms a part of the one that here follows.

XXVIII—2

Me quoque devexi rapidus comes Orionis
 Illyricis Notus obruit undis.
at tu, nauta, vagae ne parce malignus harenae
 ossibus et capiti inhumato

particulam dare : sic, quodcumque minabitur Eurus
 fluctibus Hesperiis, Venusinae
plectantur silvae te sospite, multaque merces,
 unde potest, tibi defluat aequo

ab Iove Neptunoque sacri custode Tarenti.
 neglegis immeritis nocituram   10
postmodo te natis fraudem committere ? fors et
 debita iura vicesque superbae

te maneant ipsum : precibus non linquar inultis,
 teque piacula nulla resolvent.
quamquam festinas, non est mora longa ; licebit
 iniecto ter pulvere curras.

ODE XXVIII—2 [1]

A Petition for Sepulture

ME, too, Notus, whirling mate of setting Orion, overwhelmed in the Illyrian waves. But do thou, O mariner, begrudge me not the shifting sand, nor refuse to bestow a little of it on my unburied head and bones! Then, whatever threats Eurus shall vent against the Hesperian waves, when the Venusian woods are beaten by the gale, mayst thou be safe, and may rich reward redound to thee from the sources whence it can,—from kindly Jove and Neptune, sacred Tarentum's guardian god!

Thou thinkest it a light matter to do a wrong that after this will harm thine unoffending children? Perchance the need of sepulture and a retribution of like disdain may await thyself sometime. I shall not be left with my petition unavenged, and for thee no offerings shall make atonement. Though thou art eager to be going, 'tis a brief delay I ask. Only three handfuls of earth! Then thou mayst speed upon thy course.

---

[1] In our *MSS.* and in most editions, this Ode forms a part of the one that here precedes.

XXIX

Icci, beatis nunc Arabum invides
gazis et acrem militiam paras
   non ante devictis Sabaeae
     regibus, horribilique Medo

nectis catenas?   quae tibi virginum
sponso necato barbara serviet?
   puer quis ex aula capillis
     ad cyathum statuetur unctis,

doctus sagittas tendere Sericas
arcu paterno?   quis neget arduis   10
   pronos relabi posse rivos
     montibus et Tiberim reverti,

cum tu coëmptos undique nobilis
libros Panaeti, Socraticam et domum
   mutare loricis Hiberis,
     pollicitus meliora, tendis?

ODE XXIX

The Scholar Turned Adventurer

Iccius, art thou looking now with envious eye at the rich treasures of the Arabians, and making ready for dire warfare on Sabaean kings as yet unconquered, and art thou forging fetters for the dreadful Mede? What barbarian maiden, her lover slain by thee, shall become thy slave? What page from royal halls, with perfumed locks, shall be thy cup-bearer, taught with his father's bow to speed the arrows of the East? Who'll deny that the descending streams can glide backwards to the lofty hills and the Tiber reverse its course, when thou, that gavest promise of better things, art bent on changing Panaetius' famous books, purchased from every quarter, and the Socratic school for Spanish corselets?

XXX

O Venvs, regina Cnidi Paphique,
sperne dilectam Cypron et vocantis
ture te multo Glycerae decoram
    transfer in aedem.

fervidus tecum puer et solutis
Gratiae zonis properentque Nymphae
et parum comis sine te Iuventas
    Mercuriusque.

ODE XXX

Invocation to Venus

O VENUS, queen of Cnidos and of Paphos, forsake thy
beloved Cyprus and betake thyself to the fair shrine
of Glycera, who summons thee with bounteous
incense! And with thee let hasten thy ardent
child; the Graces, too, with girdles all unloosed,
the Nymphs, and Youth, unlovely without thee,
and Mercury!

XXXI

Qvid dedicatum poscit Apollinem
vates ?   quid orat, de patera novum
    fundens liquorem ?   non opimae
        Sardiniae segetes feraces,

non aestuosae grata Calabriae
armenta, non aurum aut ebur Indicum,
    non rura, quae Liris quieta
        mordet aqua taciturnus amnis.

prcmant Calena falce quibus dedit
Fortuna vitem, dives ut aureis   10
    mercator exsiccet culillis
        vina Syra reparata merce,

dis carus ipsis, quippe ter et quater
anno revisens aequor Atlanticum
    impune.   me pascunt olivae,
        me cichorea levesque malvae.

frui paratis et valido mihi,
Latoe, dones et, precor, integra
    cum mente, nec turpem senectam
        degere nec cithara carentem.   20

ODE XXXI
The Poet's Prayer

WHAT is the poet's prayer to the newly enshrined
Apollo? For what is his petition as he pours new wine
from the bowl? Not for the rich harvests of fertile
Sardinia, not for the pleasant herds of hot Calabria,
not for Indian gold or ivory, nor for the fields that
the Liris' silent stream frets with its placid flow. Let
those to whom Fortune has vouchsafed it, trim
the vine with Calenian pruning-knife, that the rich
trader may drain from golden chalice the wine for
which he barters Syrian wares, dear to the very
gods, since thrice and four times yearly he revisits
all unscathed the Atlantic main. My fare is the
olive, the endive, and the wholesome mallow. Grant
me, O Latona's son, to be content with what I
have, and, sound of body and of mind, to pass an
old age lacking neither honour nor the lyre!

XXXII

Poscimvr.   siquid vacui sub umbra
lusimus tecum, quod et hunc in annum
vivat et plures, age dic Latinum,
    barbite, carmen,

Lesbio primum modulate civi,
qui ferox bello tamen inter arma,
sive iactatam religarat udo
    litore navim,

Liberum et Musas Veneremque et illi
semper haerentem puerum canebat,   10
et Lycum nigris oculis nigroque
    crine decorum.

o decus Phoebi et dapibus supremi
grata testudo Iovis, o laborum
dulce lenimen medicumque,[1] salve
    rite vocanti !

[1] medicumque *Lachmann :* mihicumque *MSS.*

ODE XXXII

Invocation to the Lyre

I AM asked for a song. If ever in idle hour beneath the shade I have sung with thee any trivial lay that shall live not merely for this year, but for many, come, give forth now a Roman song, thou lyre first tuned by the Lesbian patriot who, though bold in war, yet, whether amid arms or having moored his storm-tossed bark on the watery strand, was wont to sing of Bacchus, the Muses, Venus, and the boy that ever clings to her, and Lycus beautiful for black eyes and raven locks.

O shell, thou glory of Phoebus and welcome at the feasts of Jove Supreme, O sweet and healing balm of troubles, be propitious to me, whenever I invoke thee duly!

XXXIII

Albɪ, ne doleas plus nimio memor
immitis Glycerae neu miserabiles
decantes elegos, cur tibi iunior
    laesa praeniteat fide.

insignem tenui fronte Lycorida
Cyri torret amor, Cyrus in asperam
declinat Pholoën : sed prius Apulis
    iungentur capreae lupis,

quam turpi Pholoë peccet adultero.
sic visum Veneri, cui placet impares   10
formas atque animos sub iuga aënea
    saevo mittere cum ioco.

ipsum me melior cum peteret Venus,
grata detinuit compede Myrtale
libertina, fretis acrior Hadriae
    curvantis Calabros sinus.

ODE XXXIII

The Faithless Fair

GRIEVE not o'ermuch, O Albius, for thought of cruel Glycera, nor sing unceasing plaintive elegies, asking why a younger rival outshines thee in her eyes, and why her plighted troth is broken! Fair Lycoris with forehead low is consumed with love for Cyrus; Cyrus in turn inclines to unresponsive Pholoë; but sooner shall does mate with Apulian wolves than Pholoë shall go astray with so mean a paramour. Such the decree of Venus, whose delight it is in cruel sport to force beneath her brazen yoke bodies and hearts ill-mated. I myself, when a worthier passion called, was held fast in pleasing bonds by slave-born Myrtale, more tempestuous than the waves of Hadria, where it rounds into Calabria's gulf.

XXXIV

Parcvs deorum cultor et infrequens,
insanientis dum sapientiae
   consultus erro, nunc retrorsum
     vela dare atque iterare cursus

cogor relictos : namque Diespiter,
igni corusco nubila dividens
   plerumque, per purum tonantes
     egit equos volucremque currum ;

quo bruta tellus et vaga flumina
quo Styx et invisi horrida Taenari   10
   sedes Atlanteusque finis
     concutitur.   valet ima summis

mutare et insignem attenuat deus,
obscura promens ; hinc apicem rapax
   Fortuna cum stridore acuto
     sustulit, hic posuisse gaudet.

ODE XXXIV

The Poet's Conversion

I, A CHARY and infrequent worshipper of the gods, what time I wandered, the votary of a foolish wisdom, am now compelled to spread my sails for the voyage back, and to retrace the course I had abandoned. For though it is the clouds that Jove is wont to cleave with his flashing bolts, this time he drove his thundering steeds and flying car through a sky serene— his steeds and car, whereby the lifeless earth and wandering streams were shaken, Styx, and hated Taenarus' dread seat, and the bourne where Atlas has his stand. Power the god does have. He can interchange the lowest and the highest; the mighty he abases and exalts the lowly. From one man Fortune with shrill whirring of her wings swiftly snatches away the crown; on another she delights to place it.

XXXV

O DIVA, gratum quae regis Antium,
praesens vel imo tollere de gradu
    mortale corpus vel superbos
        vertere funeribus triumphos,

te pauper ambit sollicita prece
ruris colonus, te dominam aequoris,
    quicumque Bithyna lacessit
        Carpathium pelagus carina,

te Dacus asper, te profugi Scythae
urbesque gentesque et Latium ferox   10
    regumque matres barbarorum et
        purpurei metuunt tyranni,

iniurioso ne pede proruas
stantem columnam, neu populus frequens
    " ad arma " cessantes, " ad arma "
        concitet imperiumque frangat.

te semper anteit saeva [1] Necessitas,
clavos trabales et cuneos manu
    gestans aëna, nec severus
        uncus abest liquidumque plumbum.   20

[1] *Excellent MSS. also have* serva.

92

ODE XXXV

To Fortuna

O GODDESS that rulest pleasant Antium, mighty to raise our mortal clay from low estate or change proud triumphs into funeral trains, thee the poor peasant entreats with anxious prayer; thee, as sovereign of the deep, whoever braves the Carpathian Sea in Bithynian bark; thee the wild Dacian, the roving Scythian, cities, tribes, and martial Latium, and mothers of barbarian kings, and tyrants clad in purple, fearing lest with wanton foot thou overturn the standing pillar of the State, and lest the thronging mob arouse the peaceable "to arms, to arms!" and thus wreck the ruling power.

Before thee ever stalks Necessity, grim goddess, with spikes and wedges in her brazen hand; the stout clamp and molten lead are also there. Thee,

te Spes et albo rara Fides colit
velata panno, nec comitem abnegat,
　　utcumque mutata potentis
　　　　veste domos inimica linquis.

at vulgus infidum et meretrix retro
periura cedit, diffugiunt cadis
　　cum faece siccatis amici,
　　　　ferre iugum pariter dolosi.

serves iturum Caesarem in ultimos
orbis Britannos et iuvenum recens　　　　　　　30
　　examen, Eois timendum
　　　　partibus Oceanoque rubro.

eheu, cicatricum et sceleris pudet
fratrumque.　quid nos dura refugimus
　　aetas?　quid intactum nefasti
　　　　liquimus?　unde manum iuventus

metu deorum continuit?　quibus
pepercit aris?　o utinam nova
　　incude diffingas retusum in
　　　　Massagetas Arabasque ferrum!　　　　　40

Hope cherishes and rare Fidelity, her hand bound[1] with cloth of white, nor refuses her companionship, whenever thou in hostile mood forsakest the houses of the great in mourning plunged. But the faithless rabble and the perjured harlot turn away; friends scatter so soon as they have drained our winejars to the dregs, too treacherous to help us bear the yoke of trouble.

Do thou preserve our Caesar, soon to set forth against the Britons, farthest of the world! Preserve the freshly levied band of youthful soldiers who shall raise fear in Eastern parts beside the Red Sea's coast.

Alas, the shame of our scars, and crimes, and brothers slain! What have we shrunk from, hardened generation that we are? What iniquity have we left untouched? From what have our youth kept back their hands through fear of the gods? What altars have they spared? O mayst thou on fresh anvils reforge our blunted swords, and turn them against the Arabs and Massagetae!

---

[1] The priests of Fides performed sacrifice with a band of white cloth wrapped around the hand.

XXXVI

Et ture et fidibus iuvat
  placare et vituli sanguine debito
custodes Numidae deos,
  qui nunc Hesperia sospes ab ultima

caris multa sodalibus,
  nulli plura tamen dividit oscula
quam dulci Lamiae, memor
  actae non alio rege puertiae

mutataeque simul togae.
  Cressa ne careat pulchra dies nota,   10
neu promptae modus amphorae,
  neu morem in Salium sit requies pedum,

neu multi Damalis meri
  Bassum Threicia vincat amystide.
neu desint epulis rosae
  neu vivax apium neu breve lilium;

omnes in Damalin putres
  deponent oculos, nec Damalis novo
divelletur adultero,
  lascivis hederis ambitiosior.   20

ODE XXXVI

A Joyful Return

WITH incense and with music and due offering of a bullock's blood, let us appease the gods that have guarded Numida, who, now returned in safety from the farthest West, bestows kisses in abundance on each fond mate, yet on no one more than well-loved Lamia, recalling their boyhood passed under the self-same teacher and their togas changed together.

Let this fair day not lack a mark of white, nor be there limit of devotion to the wine-jar that has been brought out, nor pause of dancing after the Salian fashion! Nor let Bassus be outdone by strong-headed Damalis in drinking the long, deep Thracian draught. Nor let roses, lasting parsley, or the quickly fading lily be wanting to our feast! All shall cast their languishing eyes on Damalis; yet shall Damalis not be torn from her new lover, holding closer to him than the fond ivy (to the oak).

XXXVII

Nvnc est bibendum, nunc pede libero
pulsanda tellus, nunc Saliaribus
   ornare pulvinar deorum
      tempus erat dapibus, sodales.

antehac nefas depromere Caecubum
cellis avitis, dum Capitolio
   regina dementes ruinas,
      funus et imperio parabat

contaminato cum grege turpium
morbo virorum, quidlibet impotens   10
   sperare fortunaque dulci
      ebria.   sed minuit furorem

vix una sospes navis ab ignibus,
mentemque lymphatam Mareotico
   redegit in veros timores
      Caesar, ab Italia volantem

remis adurgens, accipiter velut
molles columbas aut leporem citus
   venator in campis nivalis
      Haemoniae, daret ut catenis   20

ODE XXXVII

The Fall of Cleopatra

Now is the time to drain the flowing bowl, now with unfettered foot to beat the ground with dancing, now with Salian feast to deck the couches of the gods, my comrades! Before this day it had been wrong to bring our Caecuban forth from ancient bins, while yet a frenzied queen was plotting ruin 'gainst the Capitol and destruction to the empire, with her polluted crew of creatures foul with lust—a woman mad enough to nurse the wildest hopes, and drunk with Fortune's favours. But the escape of scarce a single galley from the flames sobered her fury, and Caesar changed the wild delusions bred by Mareotic wine to the stern reality of terror, chasing her with his galleys, as she sped away from Italy, even as the hawk pursues the gentle dove, or the swift hunter follows the hare over the plains of snow-clad Thessaly, with

fatale monstrum.   quae generosius
perire quaerens nec muliebriter
    expavit ensem nec latentes
        classe cita reparavit oras.

ausa et iacentem visere regiam
vultu sereno, fortis et asperas
    tractare serpentes, ut atrum
        corpore combiberet venenum,

deliberata morte ferocior;
saevis Liburnis scilicet invidens   30
    privata deduci superbo
        non humilis mulier triumpho.

purpose fixed to put in chains the accursed monster.
Yet she, seeking to die a nobler death, showed for
the dagger's point no woman's fear, nor sought to
win with her swift fleet some secret shore; she even
dared to gaze with face serene upon her fallen palace;
courageous, too, to handle poisonous asps, that she
might draw black venom to her heart, waxing bolder
as she resolved to die; scorning, in sooth, the thought
of being borne, a queen no longer, on hostile galleys
to grace a glorious triumph—no craven woman she!

XXXVIII

PERSICOS odi, puer, apparatus,
displicent nexae philyra coronae ;
mitte sectari, rosa quo locorum
    sera moretur.

simplici myrto nihil adlabores
sedulus, cura : neque te ministrum
dedecet myrtus neque me sub arta
    vite bibentem.

ODE XXXVIII

Away with Oriental Luxury!

PERSIAN elegance, my lad, I hate, and take no pleasure in garlands woven on linden bast.   A truce to searching out the haunts where lingers late the rose ! Strive not to add aught else to the plain myrtle ! The myrtle befits both thee, the servant, and me, the master, as I drink beneath the thick-leaved vine,

BOOK II

LIBER II

I

Motvm ex Metello consule civicum
bellique causas et vitia et modos
　　ludumque Fortunae gravesque
　　　principum amicitias et arma

nondum expiatis uncta cruoribus,
periculosae plenum opus aleae,
　　tractas et incedis per ignes
　　　suppositos cineri doloso.

paulum severae Musa tragoediae
desit theatris : mox, ubi publicas　　　　　10
　　res ordinaris, grande munus
　　　Cecropio repetes cothurno,

insigne maestis praesidium reis
et consulenti, Pollio, curiae,
　　cui laurus aeternos honores
　　　Delmatico peperit triumpho.

BOOK II

ODE I

To Pollio Writing a History of the Civil Wars

THOU art treating of the civil strife that with
Metellus' consulship began, the causes of the war,
its blunders, and its phases, and Fortune's game,
friendships of leaders that boded ill, and weapons
stained with blood as yet unexpiated—a task full
of dangerous hazard—and art walking, as it were, over
fires hidden beneath treacherous ashes.

For a brief time only let it be that thy stern tragic
muse is missing from the stage; but soon, when thou
hast chronicled events of state, renew thy lofty calling
in the Attic buskin, Pollio, famed support of anxious
clients and bulwark of the Senate in its councils,
thou for whom, too, the laurel won lasting glory in
thy Dalmatian triumph. Even now with threaten-

iam nunc minaci murmure cornuum
perstringis auris, iam litui strepunt,
    iam fulgor armorum fugaces
        terret equos equitumque vultus.   20

audire magnos iam videor duces,
non indecoro pulvere sordidos,
    et cuncta terrarum subacta
        praeter atrocem animum Catonis.

Iuno et deorum quisquis amicior
Afris inulta cesserat impotens
    tellure, victorum nepotes
        rettulit inferias Iugurthae.

quis non Latino sanguine pinguior
campus sepulcris impia proelia   30
    testatur auditumque Medis
        Hesperiae sonitum ruinae ?

qui gurges aut quae flumina lugubris
ignara belli ? quod mare Dauniae
    non decoloravere caedes ?
        quae caret ora cruore nostro ?

sed ne relictis, Musa procax, iocis
Ceae retractes munera neniae,
    mecum Dionaeo sub antro
        quaere modos leviore plectro.   40

ing blare of horns thou strik'st our ears; even now the clarions sound; even now the gleam of weapons strikes terror into timid horses and into the horsemen's faces. Already I seem to hear the shouts of mighty captains begrimed with no inglorious dust, and to see all the world subdued, except stern Cato's soul. Juno and all the gods who, friendlier to Africa, had helplessly withdrawn, powerless to avenge the land, have offered on Jugurtha's grave the grandsons of his conquerors.

What plain is not enriched with Latin blood, to bear witness with its graves to our unholy strife and to the sound of Hesperia's fall, heard even by the Medes! What pool or stream has failed to taste the dismal war! What sea has Italian slaughter not discoloured! What coast knows not our blood!

But, lest, O heedless Muse, thou leave sportive themes and essay again the Cean dirge, seek with me in the shadow of some Dionean grotto measures of lighter mood!

II

Nvllvs argento color est avaris
abdito terris, inimice lamnae
Crispe Sallusti, nisi temperato
　　splendeat usu.

vivet extento Proculeius aevo,
notus in fratres animi paterni:
illum aget pinna metuente solvi
　　Fama superstes.

latius regnes avidum domando
spiritum, quam si Libyam remotis　　10
Gadibus iungas et uterque Poenus
　　serviat uni.

crescit indulgens sibi dirus hydrops,
nec sitim pellit, nisi causa morbi
fugerit venis et aquosus albo
　　corpore languor.

redditum Cyri solio Phraaten
dissidens plebi numero beatorum
eximit Virtus populumque falsis
　　dedocet uti　　20

vocibus, regnum et diadema tutum
deferens uni propriamque laurum,
quisquis ingentes oculo inretorto
　　spectat acervos.

ODE II

Money—Its Use and Abuse

No lustre is there to silver hidden away in the greedy earth, O Sallustius Crispus, thou foe to metal unless it shine by well-ordered use. Proculeius shall live through distant ages, known for his fatherly spirit towards his brothers; him shall enduring fame bear on pinions that refuse to droop.

Thou shalt rule a broader realm by subduing a greedy heart than shouldst thou join Libya to distant Gades, and should Punic settlers on both sides the Strait become subjects of a single lord. By indulgence the dreadful dropsy grows apace, nor can the sufferer banish thirst, unless the cause of the malady has first departed from the veins and the watery languor from the pale body.

Though Phraates has been restored to the throne of Cyrus, yet Virtue, dissenting from the rabble, will not admit him to the number of the happy, and teaches the folk to discard wrong names, conferring power, the secure diadem, and lasting laurels on him alone who can gaze upon huge piles of treasure without casting an envious glance behind.

III

Aeqvam memento rebus in arduis
servare mentem, non secus in bonis
    ab insolenti temperatam
      laetitia, moriture Delli,

seu maestus omni tempore vixeris,
seu te in remoto gramine per dies
    festos reclinatum bearis
      interiore nota Falerni.

quo pinus ingens albaque populus
umbram hospitalem consociare amant   10
    ramis?   quid obliquo laborat
      lympha fugax trepidare rivo?

huc vina et unguenta et nimium breves
flores amoenae ferre iube rosae,
    dum res et aetas et sororum
      fila trium patiuntur atra.

cedes coëmptis saltibus et domo
villaque, flavus quam Tiberis lavit,
    cedes, et exstructis in altum
      divitiis potietur heres.   20

ODE III

Enjoy the Fleeting Hour!

REMEMBER, when life's path is steep, to keep an even mind, and likewise, in prosperity, a spirit restrained from over-weening joy, Dellius, seeing thou art doomed to die, whether thou live always sad, or reclining in grassy nook take delight on holidays in some choice vintage of Falernian wine. Why do the tall pine and poplar white love to interlace their branches in inviting shade? Why does the hurrying water strive to press onward in the winding stream? Hither bid slaves bring wines and perfumes and the too brief blossoms of the lovely rose, while Fortune and youth allow, and the dark threads of the Sisters three. Thou shalt leave thy purchased pastures, thy house, and thy estate that yellow Tiber washes; yea, thou shalt leave them, and an heir shall become master of the wealth thou hast heaped up high.

divesne, prisco natus ab Inacho,
nil interest an pauper et infima
    de gente sub divo moreris;
        victima nil miserantis Orci.

omnes eodem cogimur, omnium
versatur urna serius ocius
    sors exitura et nos in aeternum
        exsilium impositura cumbae.

Whether thou be rich and sprung from ancient Inachus, or dwell beneath the canopy of heaven poor and of lowly birth, it makes no difference : thou art pitiless Orcus' victim. We are all being gathered to one and the same fold. The lot of every one of us is tossing about in the urn, destined sooner, later, to come forth and place us in Charon's skiff for everlasting exile.

IV

Ne sit ancillae tibi amor pudori,
Xanthia Phoceu.   prius insolentem
serva Briseis niveo colore
    movit Achillem ;

movit Aiacem Telamone natum
forma captivae dominum Tecmessae ;
arsit Atrides medio in triumpho
    virgine rapta,

barbarae postquam cecidere turmae
Thessalo victore et ademptus Hector   10
tradidit fessis leviora tolli
    Pergama Grais.

nescias an te generum beati
Phyllidis flavae decorent parentes :
regium certe genus, et penates
    maeret iniquos.

crede non illam tibi de scelesta
plebe dilectam neque sic fidelem,
sic lucro aversam potuisse nasci
    matre pudenda.   20

bracchia et voltum teretesque suras
integer laudo ; fuge suspicari,
cuius octavum trepidavit aetas
    claudere lustrum.

ODES BOOK II

ODE IV

Love for a Slave-Girl

LET not affection for thy handmaiden put thee to the blush, O Phocian Xanthias! Before thy day the slave Briseis with her snow-white skin stirred the heart of proud Achilles; yea, and captive Tecmessa's beauty stirred the heart of her master, Ajax, son of Telamon; and Atrides in the midst of triumph was inflamed with love for a captured maid, what time the barbarian hosts were overcome by the Thessalian's victory, and Hector's loss gave Pergamos over to the toil-worn Greeks, an easier prey.

Thou can'st not tell but that the parents of thy blond Phyllis are rich and will lend glory to their new-found son; surely her lineage must be of royal origin, and she mourns the cruelty of her household gods. Rest assured that the maid thou lovest belongs not to the wretched rabble, and that one so loyal, so aloof from greed could be the child of no mean mother. 'Tis with no touch of passion that I praise her arms, her face, and her shapely ankles. Suspect not one whose life in rapid course has already brought its eighth lustrum to a close!

V

Nondvm subacta ferre iugum valet
cervice, nondum munia comparis
　　aequare nec tauri ruentis
　　　　in venerem tolerare pondus.

circa virentes est animus tuae
campos iuvencae, nunc fluviis gravem
　　solantis aestum, nunc in udo
　　　　ludere cum vitulis salicto

praegestientis.　tolle cupidinem
immitis uvae : iam tibi lividos　　　　　　　　　　10
　　distinguet autumnus racemos
　　　　purpureo varius colore.

iam te sequetur (currit enim ferox
aetas, et illi, quos tibi dempserit,
　　apponet annos), iam proterva
　　　　fronte petet Lalage maritum,

dilecta, quantum non Pholoë fugax,
non Chloris, albo sic umero nitens,
　　ut pura nocturno renidet
　　　　luna mari Cnidiusve Gyges,　　　　　　　　20

quem si puellarum insereres choro,
mire sagaces falleret hospites
　　discrimen obscurum solutis
　　　　crinibus ambiguoque vultu.

ODE V

Not Yet!

NOT yet can she bear the yoke on submissive neck, not yet fulfil the duties of a mate, or endure the vehemence of a lover. Upon the verdant meads dwell the thoughts of thy love, who now allays the oppressive heat amid the streams, and now is eager to sport with her comrades in the moist willow-grove. Away with desire for the unripe grape! Soon for thee shall many-coloured Autumn paint the darkening clusters purple. Soon shall she follow thee. For Time courses madly on, and shall add to her the years it takes from thee. Soon with eager forwardness shall Lalage herself make quest of thee to be her mate, beloved as was not shy Pholoë, nor Chloris, gleaming with shoulder white, even as the unclouded moon beams on midnight sea, nor Cnidian Gyges, so fair that should you put him in a band of maids, those who knew him not would, for all their insight, fail to note his difference from the rest, disguised by his flowing locks and his girl-boy face.

VI

Sᴇᴘᴛɪᴍɪ, Gadis aditure mecum et
Cantabrum indoctum iuga ferre nostra et
barbaras Syrtes, ubi Maura semper
    aestuat unda,

Tibur Argeo positum colono
sit meae sedes utinam senectae,
sit modus lasso maris et viarum
    militiaeque.

unde si Parcae prohibent iniquae
dulce pellitis ovibus Galaesi   10
flumen et regnata petam Laconi
    rura Phalantho.

ille terrarum mihi praeter omnes
angulus ridet, ubi non Hymetto
mella decedunt viridique certat
    baca Venafro ;

ver ubi longum tepidasque praebet
Iuppiter brumas, et amicus Aulon
fertili Baccho minimum Falernis
    invidet uvis.   20

ille te mecum locus et beatae
postulant arces ; ibi tu calentem
debita sparges lacrima favillam
    vatis amici.

ODES BOOK II

ODE VI

Praise of Tibur and Tarentum

O SEPTIMIUS, ready to go with me to Gades and to the
Cantabrians not yet schooled to bear our yoke, and
to the wild Syrtes, where the Moorish wave is ever
tossing, may Tibur, founded by Argive settlers, be the
home of my old age!   May it be my final goal when
I am weary with sea, with roaming, and with war!
But if the cruel Fates bar me from that spot, I
will seek the river of Galaesus, loved by its skin-clad [1]
sheep, and the fields once ruled by Spartan Phalanthus.
That corner of the world smiles for me beyond all
others, where the honey yields not to Hymettus, and
the olive vies with green Venafrum, where Jupiter
vouchsafes long springs and winters mild, and where
Aulon, dear to fertile Bacchus, envies not the clusters
of Falernum.   That place and its blessed heights
summon thee and me; there shalt thou bedew with
affection's tear the warm ashes of thy poet friend!

[1] The fine fleeces of certain sheep were protected from injury
by means of skins fastened about their bodies.

VII

O SAEPE mecum tempus in ultimum
deducte Bruto militiae duce,
   quis te redonavit Quiritem
     dis patriis Italoque caelo,

Pompei, meorum prime sodalium,
cum quo morantem saepe diem mero
   fregi, coronatus nitentes
     malobathro Syrio capillos?

tecum Philippos et celerem fugam
sensi relicta non bene parmula,   10
   cum fracta Virtus et minaces
     turpe solum tetigere mento.

sed me per hostes Mercurius celer
denso paventem sustulit aëre;
   te rursus in bellum resorbens
     unda fretis tulit aestuosis.

ergo obligatam redde Iovi dapem,
longaque fessum militia latus
   depone sub lauru mea nec
     parce cadis tibi destinatis.   20

ODE VII

A Joyful Return

O FRIEND oft led with me into extremest peril, when Brutus was leader of our hosts, who hath restored thee as a citizen to thy country's gods and to the sky of Italy, O Pompey, first of my comrades, with whom I many a time have beguiled the lagging day with wine, first garlanding my locks glistening with Syrian nard? With thee I knew Philippi's day and its headlong rout, leaving my shield ingloriously behind, when Valour's self was beaten down and threatening hosts ignobly bit the dust. But me in my terror Mercury bore swiftly through the foe in a dense cloud; thee the wave drew back again into the abyss of war and bore once more on troubled waters. So render unto Jove the banquet pledged, and lay thy limbs, with long campaigning wearied, beneath my laurel-tree, nor spare the jars set apart for thee!

CARMINVM LIBER II

oblivioso levia Massico
ciboria exple, funde capacibus
   unguenta de conchis.   quis udo
     deproperare apio coronas

curatve myrto ?   quem Venus arbitrum
dicet bibendi ?   non ego sanius
   bacchabor Edonis : recepto
     dulce mihi furere est amico.

Fill to the brim with care-dispelling Massic the polished goblets! Pour out perfumes from generous phials! Who will make haste to weave garlands of pliant parsley or of myrtle? Whom shall the Venus-throw [1] make the master of our drinking? I'll revel as wildly as the Edonians. 'Tis sweet to make mad holiday when a friend has been regained.

[1] The name given to the highest throw of the dice.

VIII

Vlla si iuris tibi peierati
poena, Barine, nocuisset umquam,
dente si nigro fieres vel uno
    turpior ungui,

crederem.   sed tu simul obligasti
perfidum votis caput, enitescis
pulchrior multo iuvenumque prodis
    publica cura.

expedit matris cineres opertos
fallere et toto taciturna noctis   10
signa cum caelo gelidaque divos
    morte carentes.

ridet hoc, inquam, Venus ipsa ; rident
simplices Nymphae ferus et Cupido,
semper ardentis acuens sagittas
    cote cruenta.

adde quod pubes tibi crescit omnis,
servitus crescit nova, nec priores
impiae tectum dominae relinquunt,
    saepe minati.   20

te suis matres metuunt iuvencis,
te senes parci miseraeque, nuper
virgines, nuptae, tua ne retardet
    aura maritos.

ODE VIII

Barine's Baleful Charms

HAD ever any penalty for violated vows visited thee, Barine; didst thou ever grow uglier by a single blackened tooth or spotted nail, I'd trust thee now. But with thee, no sooner hast thou bound thy perfidious head by promises than thou shinest forth much fairer and art the cynosure of all eyes when thou appearest. 'Tis actually of help to thee to swear falsely by the buried ashes of thy mother, by the silent sentinels of night, with the whole heaven, and by the gods, who are free from chilly death. All this but makes sport for Venus (upon my word, it does!) and for the artless Nymphs, and cruel Cupid, ever whetting his fiery darts on blood-stained stone. Not only this! All our youth are growing up for thee alone, to be a fresh band of slaves, while thy old admirers leave not the roof of their heartless mistress, oft as they have threatened this. Thee mothers fear for their sons, thee frugal sires, thee wretched brides, who but yesterday were maidens, lest thy radiance make their husbands linger.

IX

Non semper imbres nubibus hispidos
manant in agros aut mare Caspium
    vexant inaequales procellae
      usque nec Armeniis in oris,

amice Valgi, stat glacies iners
menses per omnes, aut Aquilonibus
    querqueta Gargani laborant
      et foliis viduantur orni:

tu semper urges flebilibus modis
Mysten ademptum, nec tibi Vespero   10
    surgente decedunt amores
      nec rapidum fugiente solem.

at non ter aevo functus amabilem
ploravit omnes Antilochum senex
    annos, nec impubem parentes
      Troilon aut Phrygiae sorores

flevere semper.   desine mollium
tandem querellarum, et potius nova
    cantemus Augusti tropaea
      Caesaris, et rigidum Niphaten   20

Medumque flumen gentibus additum
victis minores volvere vertices,
    intraque praescriptum Gelonos
      exiguis equitare campis.

ODE IX

A Truce to Sorrow, Valgius!

NOT for ever do the showers fall from the clouds on
the sodden fields, nor the rough blasts always fret
the Caspian waves, nor on Armenian borders, friend
Valgius, does the lifeless ice linger through every
month, nor are Garganus' oak-groves always lashed
by the blasts of the North and the ash-trees reft
of their leaves.   But thou in tearful strains dwellest
ever on the loss of thy Mystes, nor do thy words
of love cease either when Vesper comes out at
evening, or when he flies before the swiftly coursing
sun.   Yet the aged hero who had lived three gene-
rations did not for ever mourn his loved Antilochus,
nor did his Phrygian parents and sisters weep without end for youthful Troilus. Cease at length thy weak
laments, and let us rather sing of the new trophies
of Augustus Caesar, ice-bound Niphates and the
river of the Medes rolling in smaller eddies, now 'tis
added to the list of vanquished nations, and the
Geloni riding now within bounds prescribed over
their narrowed plains.

X

Rectivs vives, Licini, neque altum
semper urgendo neque, dum procellas
cautus horrescis, nimium premendo
　　litus iniquum.

auream quisquis mediocritatem
diligit, tutus caret obsoleti
sordibus tecti, caret invidenda
　　sobrius aula.

saepius ventis agitatur ingens
pinus et celsae graviore casu　　　　　　　　10
decidunt turres feriuntque summos
　　fulgura montis.

sperat infestis, metuit secundis
alteram sortem bene praeparatum
pectus. informes hiemes reducit
　　Iuppiter; idem

summovet. non, si male nunc, et olim
sic erit: quondam cithara tacentem
suscitat Musam neque semper arcum
　　tendit Apollo.　　　　　　　　　　　　20

rebus angustis animosus atque
fortis appare: sapienter idem
contrahes vento nimium secundo
　　turgida vela.

ODE X

" The Golden Mean "

BETTER wilt thou live, Licinius, by neither always pressing out to sea nor too closely hugging the dangerous shore in cautious fear of storms. Whoso cherishes the golden mean, safely avoids the foulness of an ill-kept house and discreetly, too, avoids a hall exciting envy. 'Tis oftener the tall pine that is shaken by the wind; 'tis the lofty towers that fall with the heavier crash, and 'tis the tops of the mountains that the lightning strikes. Hopeful in adversity, anxious in prosperity, is the heart that is well prepared for weal or woe. Though Jupiter brings back the unlovely winters, he, also, takes them away. If we fare ill to-day, 'twill not be ever so. At times Apollo wakes with the lyre his slumbering song, and does not always stretch the bow. In time of stress shew thyself bold and valiant! Yet wisely reef thy sails when they are swollen by too fair a breeze!

XI

Qvid bellicosus Cantaber et Scythes,
Hirpine Quincti, cogitet Hadria
   divisus obiecto, remittas
     quaerere, nec trepides in usum

poscentis aevi pauca : fugit retro
levis iuventas et decor, arida
   pellente lascivos amores
     canitie facilemque somnum.

non semper idem floribus est honor
vernis, neque uno luna rubens nitet   10
   voltu : quid aeternis minorem
     consiliis animum fatigas ?

cur non sub alta vel platano vel hac
pinu iacentes sic temere et rosa
   canos odorati capillos,
     dum licet, Assyriaque nardo

potamus uncti ?   dissipat Euhius
curas edaces.   quis puer ocius
   restinguet ardentis Falerni
     pocula praetereunte lympha ?   20

quis devium scortum eliciet domo
Lyden ? eburna, dic age, cum lyra
   maturet, in comptum Lacaenae
     more comas religata nodum ! [1]

    [1] incomptam comam nodo *Bentley.*

ODE XI

Enjoy the Passing Hour !

WHAT the warlike Cantabrian is plotting, Quinctius Hirpinus, and the Scythian, divided from us by the intervening Adriatic, cease to inquire, and be not anxious for the needs of life, since 'tis little that it asks. Fresh youth and beauty are speeding fast away behind us, while wizened age is banishing sportive love and slumbers soft. Not for ever do the flowers of spring retain their glory, nor does blushing Luna shine always with the selfsame face. Why, with planning for the future, weary thy soul unequal to the task ? Why not rather quaff the wine, while yet we may, reclining under this lofty plane or pine, in careless ease, our grey locks garlanded with fragrant roses and perfumed with Syrian nard ? Bacchus dispels carking cares. What slave will swiftly temper the bowls of fiery Falernian with water from the passing stream ? Who will lure from her home Lyde, coy wench ? With ivory lyre, come bid her haste, her hair neatly fastened in a knot, like some Laconian maid.

XII

Nolis longa ferae bella Numantiae
nec durum Hannibalem nec Siculum mare
Poeno purpureum sanguine mollibus
    aptari citharae modis,

nec saevos Lapithas et nimium mero
Hylaeum domitosque Herculea manu
telluris iuvenes, unde periculum
    fulgens contremuit domus

Saturni veteris : tuque pedestribus
dices historiis proelia Caesaris,   10
Maecenas, melius ductaque per vias
    regum colla minacium.

me dulces dominae Musa Licymniae
cantus, me voluit dicere lucidum
fulgentes oculos et bene mutuis
    fidum pectus amoribus ;

quam nec ferre pedem dedecuit choris
nec certare ioco nec dare bracchia
ludentem nitidis virginibus sacro
    Dianae celebris die.   20

ODE XII

The Charms of Terentia

You would not wish to have the themes of fierce Numantia's tedious wars wedded to soft measures of the lyre, or doughty Hannibal, or the Sicilian Sea crimson with Punic blood, or the savage Lapithae and Hylaeus mad with wine, or the triumph of Hercules' hand over the sons of earth, at the danger of whose assault the shining house of ancient Saturn shook with terror. So you yourself, Maecenas, would better treat, and treat in storied prose, of Caesar's battles and of kings, once threatening, led by the neck along the streets.

Me the Muse has bidden to celebrate the sweet singing of Mistress Licymnia, her brightly flashing eyes, and her heart right faithful in mutual love— her whom it graced so well to trip amid the dancers' bands, to parry jest with jest, and to offer her arms to festal maids on the sacred day that fills Diana's shrine.

135

num tu quae tenuit dives Achaemenes
aut pinguis Phrygiae Mygdonias opes
permutare velis crine Licymniae,
    plenas aut Arabum domos,

cum flagrantia detorquet ad oscula
cervicem, aut facili saevitia negat,
quae poscente magis gaudeat eripi,
    interdum rapere occupat? [1]

[1] *Most MSS. and editors read* occupet.

Would you exchange a lock of Licymnia's tresses for all that rich Achaemenes once owned, or for the Mygdonian wealth of fertile Phrygia, or the well-stocked homes of the Arabians, as she bends her neck toward your eager kisses, or in teasing playfulness refuses to give them (yea, refuses, since, more than he who asks them, she delights to have them snatched), or at times is first herself to snatch them?

XIII

ILLE et nefasto te posuit die,
quicumque primum, et sacrilega manu
    produxit, arbos, in nepotum
        perniciem opprobriumque pagi.

illum et parentis crediderim sui
fregisse cervicem et penetralia
    sparsisse nocturno cruore
        hospitis ; ille venena Colcha

et quicquid usquam concipitur nefas
tractavit, agro qui statuit meo   10
    te, triste lignum, te caducum
        in domini caput immerentis.

quid quisque vitet, numquam homini satis
cautum est in horas : navita Bosphorum
    Poenus perhorrescit neque ultra
        caeca timet aliunde fata ;

miles sagittas et celerem fugam
Parthi, catenas Parthus et Italum
    robur ; sed improvisa leti
        vis rapuit rapietque gentes.   20

ODES BOOK II

ODE XIII

A Narrow Escape

THE man who first planted thee did it upon an evil day and reared thee with a sacrilegious hand, O tree, for the destruction of posterity and the countryside's disgrace. I could believe that he actually strangled his own father and spattered his hearthstone with a guest's blood at dead of night; he too has dabbled in Colchic poisons and whatever crime is anywhere conceived—the man that set thee out on my estate, thou miserable stump, to fall upon the head of thy unoffending master.

Man never heeds enough from hour to hour what he should shun. The Punic sailor dreads the Bosphorus, but fears not the unseen fates beyond that threaten from other quarters. The soldier dreads the arrows of the Parthians and their swift retreat; the Parthian fears the chains and rugged strength of Italy; but the fatal violence that has snatched away, and again will snatch away, the tribes of men, is something unforeseen.

quam paene furvae regna Proserpinae
et iudicantem vidimus Aeacum
  sedesque discriptas piorum et
    Aeoliis fidibus querentem

Sappho puellis de popularibus
et te sonantem plenius aureo,
  Alcaee, plectro dura navis,
    dura fugae mala, dura belli.

utrumque sacro digna silentio
mirantur umbrae dicere ; sed magis   30
  pugnas et exactos tyrannos
    densum umeris bibit aure volgus.

quid mirum, ubi illis carminibus stupens
demittit atras belua centiceps
  auris, et intorti capillis
    Eumenidum recreantur angues ?

quin et Prometheus et Pelopis parens
dulci laborum [1] decipitur sono,
  nec curat Orion leones
    aut timidos agitare lyncas.   40

[1] laborum : *good MSS. read also* laborem.

How narrowly did I escape beholding the realms of dusky Proserpine and Aeacus on his judgment-seat, and the abodes set apart for the righteous, and Sappho complaining on Aeolian lyre of her countrywomen, and thee, Alcaeus, rehearsing in fuller strain with golden plectrum [1] the woes of seaman's life, the cruel woes of exile, and the woes of war. The shades marvel at both as they utter words worthy of reverent silence; but the dense throng, shoulder to shoulder packed, drinks in more eagerly with listening ear stories of battles and of tyrants banished. What wonder, when lulled by such strains, the hundred-headed monster lowers his black ears, and the serpents writhing in the locks of the Furies stop for rest! Yea, even Prometheus and Pelops' sire are beguiled of their sufferings by the soothing sound, nor does Orion care to chase the lions or the wary lynxes.

[1] See note on p. 73.

XIV

Eheu fugaces, Postume, Postume,
labuntur anni, nec pietas moram
    rugis et instanti senectae
      adferet indomitaeque morti;

non, si trecenis, quotquot eunt dies,
amice, places inlacrimabilem
    Plutona tauris, qui ter amplum
      Geryonen Tityonque tristi

compescit unda, scilicet omnibus,
quicumque terrae munere vescimur,   10
    enaviganda, sive reges
      sive inopes erimus coloni.

frustra cruento Marte carebimus
fractisque rauci fluctibus Hadriae,
    frustra per autumnos nocentem
      corporibus metuemus Austrum :

visendus ater flumine languido
Cocytos errans et Danai genus
    infame damnatusque longi
      Sisyphus Aeolides laboris.   20

ODES BOOK II

ODE XIV

Death is Inevitable

ALAS, O Postumus, Postumus, the years glide swiftly by, nor will righteousness give pause to wrinkles, to advancing age, or Death invincible—no, not if with three hecatombs of bulls a day, my friend, thou strivest to appease relentless Pluto, who imprisons Geryon of triple frame and Tityos, by the gloomy stream that surely must be crossed by all of us who feed upon Earth's bounty, be we princes or needy husbandmen. In vain shall we escape from bloody Mars and from the breakers of the roaring Adriatic; in vain through autumn tide shall we fear the south-wind that brings our bodies harm. At last we needs must gaze on black Cocytos winding with its sluggish flow, and Danaus' daughters infamous, and Sisyphus, the son of Aeolus, condemned to ceaseless toil. Earth we must

linquenda tellus et domus et placens
uxor, neque harum, quas colis, arborum
   te praeter invisas cupressos
     ulla brevem dominum sequetur.

absumet heres Caecuba dignior
servata centum clavibus et mero
   tinguet pavimentum superbo
     pontificum potiore cenis.

leave, and home and darling wife; nor of the trees thou tendest now, will any follow thee, its short-lived master, except the hated cypress. A worthier heir shall drink thy Caecuban now guarded by a hundred keys, and drench the pavement with glorious wine choicer than that drunk at the pontiffs' feasts.

XV

I‍AM pauca aratro iugera regiae
moles relinquent, undique latius
    extenta visentur Lucrino
        stagna lacu, platanusque caelebs

evincet ulmos; tum violaria et
myrtus et omnis copia narium
    spargent olivetis odorem
        fertilibus domino priori.

tum spissa ramis laurea fervidos
excludet ictus.   non ita Romuli   10
    praescriptum et intonsi Catonis
        auspiciis veterumque norma.

privatus illis census erat brevis,
commune magnum : nulla decempedis
    metata privatis opacam
        porticus excipiebat Arcton,

nec fortuitum spernere caespitem
leges sinebant, oppida publico
    sumptu iubentes et deorum
        templa novo decorare saxo.   20

ODE XV

The Invasion of Luxury

A SHORT time and our princely piles will leave but few acres to the plough ; on all sides will be seen our fish-ponds spreading wider than the Lucrine Lake, and the lonely plane-tree will drive out the elm ; then will beds of violets and copses of myrtle and the whole company of sweet perfumes scatter their fragrance amid olive groves that once bore increase to their former owner ; then will laurel thickets shut out the sun's hot rays. Not so was it prescribed under the rule of Romulus and unshorn Cato or by the standard of our sires. With them private estates were small, and great was the common weal. No private citizen had a portico measuring its tens of feet, lying open to the shady north ; nor did the laws permit our fathers to scorn the chance turf,[1] but bade them at common cost adorn their towns and the temples of the gods with marbles rare.

---

[1] For building a simple altar.

XVI

Otivm divos rogat in patenti
prensus Aegaeo, simul atra nubes
condidit lunam neque certa fulgent
    sidera nautis;

otium bello furiosa Thrace,
otium Medi pharetra decori,
Grosphe, non gemmis neque purpura ve-
    nale neque auro.

non enim gazae neque consularis
summovet lictor miseros tumultus   10
mentis et curas laqueata circum
    tecta volantes.

vivitur parvo bene, cui paternum
splendet in mensa tenui salinum
nec leves somnos timor aut cupido
    sordidus aufert.

quid brevi fortes iaculamur aevo
multa?   quid terras alio calentes
sole mutamus?   patriae quis exsul
    se quoque fugit?   20

ODES BOOK II

ODE XVI

Contentment the Only True Happiness

FOR peace the mariner prays, storm-caught on the open Aegean, when dark clouds have hid the moon and the stars shine no longer sure for sailors; for peace prays Thrace furious in war; for peace the Parthian with quiver richly dight—peace, Grosphus, that cannot be bought with gems, with purple, or with gold.   For 'tis not treasure nor even the consul's lictor that can banish the wretched tumults of the soul and the cares that flit about the panelled ceilings.   He lives happily upon a little on whose frugal board gleams the ancestral salt-dish, and whose soft slumbers are not banished by fear or sordid greed. Why do we strive so hard in our brief lives for great possessions?   Why do we change our own land for climes warmed by a foreign sun?   What exile from his country ever escaped himself as well?   Morbid care

scandit aeratas vitiosa naves
cura nec turmas equitum relinquit,
ocior cervis et agente nimbos
    ocior Euro.

laetus in praesens animus quod ultra est
oderit curare et amara lento
temperet risu.   nihil est ab omni
    parte beatum.

abstulit clarum cita mors Achillem,
longa Tithonum minuit senectus ;   30
et mihi forsan, tibi quod negarit,
    porriget hora.

te greges centum Siculaeque circum
mugiunt vaccae, tibi tollit hinnitum
apta quadrigis equa, te bis Afro
    murice tinctae

vestiunt lanae ; mihi parva rura et
spiritum Graiae tenuem Camenae
Parca non mendax dedit et malignum
    spernere vulgus.   40

boards even the brass-bound galley, nor fails to over-
take the troops of horse, swifter than stags, swifter
than Eurus when he drives the storm before him.
Let the soul be joyful in the present, let it disdain
to be anxious for what the future has in store, and
temper bitterness with smile serene! Nothing is happy
altogether. Achilles for all his glory was snatched
away by an early death; Tithonus, though granted a
long old age, wasted to a shadow; and to me mayhap
the passing hour will grant what it denies to thee.
Around thee low a hundred herds of Sicilian kine;
in thy stables whinnies the racing-mare; thou art
clothed in wool twice dipped in Afric purple. To
me Fate that does not belie her name [1] has given a
small domain, but she has vouchsafed the fine breath
of Grecian song and a scorn for the envious crowd.

[1] *i.e.* because she is *parca :* " sparing in her gifts."

XVII

CVR me querellis exanimas tuis?
nec dis amicum est nec mihi te prius
    obire, Maecenas, mearum
        grande decus columenque rerum.

a, te meae si partem animae rapit
maturior vis, quid moror altera,
    nec carus aeque nec superstes
        integer? ille dies utramque

ducet ruinam. non ego perfidum
dixi sacramentum: ibimus, ibimus,   10
    utcumque praecedes, supremum
        carpere iter comites parati.

me nec Chimaerae spiritus igneae
nec, si resurgat, centimanus Gyas [1]
    divellet umquam: sic potenti
        Iustitiae placitumque Parcis.

seu Libra seu me Scorpios adspicit
formidolosus pars violentior
    natalis horae seu tyrannus
        Hesperiae Capricornus undae,   20

[1] Gyas *Lambinus:* gigas *MSS*

ODES BOOK II

ODE XVII

Despair not, Maecenas! One Star Links our Destinies

WHY dost thou crush out my life by thy complaints?
'Tis the will neither of the gods nor of myself that I
should pass away before thee, Maecenas, the great
glory and prop of my own existence. Alas, if some
untimely blow snatches thee, the half of my own life,
away, why do I, the other half, still linger on, neither
so dear as before nor surviving whole? That fatal day
shall bring the doom of both of us. No false oath have
I taken; both, both together, will we go, whene'er
thou leadest the way, prepared as comrades to travel
the final journey. Me no fiery breath of Chimaera, nor
hundred-handed Gyas, should he rise against me, shall
ever tear from thee. Such is the will of mighty Justice and the Fates. Whether Libra or dread Scorpio
or Capricornus, lord of the Hesperian wave, dominates
my horoscope as the more potent influence of my

utrumque nostrum incredibili modo
consentit astrum.   te Iovis impio
   tutela Saturno refulgens
      eripuit volucrisque Fati

tardavit alas, cum populus frequens
laetum theatris ter crepuit sonum ;
   me truncus inlapsus cerebro
      sustulerat, nisi Faunus ictum

dextra levasset, Mercurialium
custos virorum.   reddere victimas   30
   aedemque votivam memento ;
      nos humilem feriemus agnam.

natal hour, the stars of us twain are wondrously linked together. To thee the protecting power of Jove, outshining that of baleful Saturn, brought rescue, and stayed the wings of swift Fate what time the thronging people thrice broke into glad applause in the theatre. Me the trunk of a tree, descending on my head, had snatched away, had not Faunus, protector of poets, with his right hand warded off the stroke. Remember then to offer the victims due and to build a votive shrine! I will sacrifice a humble lamb.

XVIII

Non ebur neque aureum
  mea renidet in domo lacunar,
non trabes Hymettiae
  premunt columnas ultima recisas

Africa, neque Attali
  ignotus heres regiam occupavi,
nec Laconicas mihi
  trahunt honestae purpuras clientae.

at fides et ingeni
  benigna vena est, pauperemque dives   10
me petit : nihil supra
  deos lacesso nec potentem amicum

largiora flagito,
  satis beatus unicis Sabinis.
truditur dies die,
  novaeque pergunt interire lunae.

tu secanda marmora
  locas sub ipsum funus et sepulcri
immemor struis domos,
  marisque Bais obstrepentis urges   20

ODE XVIII

The Vanity of Riches

NOT ivory or gilded panel gleams in my home, nor do beams of Hymettian marble rest on pillars quarried in farthest Africa, nor have I, as heir of Attalus,[1] become unwittingly the owner of a palace, nor for me do high-born dames trail robes of Laconian purple. But I have loyalty and a kindly vein of genius, and me, though poor, the rich man courts. I importune the gods for nothing more, and of my friend in power I crave no larger boon, happy enough in my cherished Sabine farm. Day treads upon the heel of day, and new moons haste to wane; yet thou on the grave's verge dost contract for the cutting of marble slabs, and, forgetful of the tomb, dost rear a palace, eager to build out the coast of the sea that thunders by Baiae,

[1] In 133 B.C. Attalus III., King of Pergamus, had made the Roman people his heir.

summovere litora,
   parum locuples continente ripa.
quid quod usque proximos
   revellis agri terminos et ultra

limites clientium
   salis avarus? pellitur paternos
in sinu ferens deos
   et uxor et vir sordidosque natos.

nulla certior tamen
   rapacis Orci fine destinata   30
aula divitem manet
   erum. quid ultra tendis? aequa tellus

pauperi recluditur
   regumque pueris, nec satelles Orci
callidum Promethea
   revexit auro captus. hic superbum

Tantalum atque Tantali
   genus coercet, hic levare functum
pauperem laboribus
   vocatus atque non vocatus audit.   40

not rich enough in the mainland shore. What, that thou tearest down each neighbouring post that marks thy farm, and in thy greed dost overleap the boundaries of thy tenants! Man and wife are driven forth bearing in their arms their household gods and ragged children. And yet no hall more certainly awaits the wealthy lord than greedy Orcus' destined bourne. Why strive for more and more? For all alike doth Earth unlock her bosom—for the poor man and for princes' sons. Nor could Orcus' minion be bribed by gold to ferry back Prometheus, the crafty. Proud Tantalus and the son of Tantalus he holdeth fast, and, summoned or unsummoned, lends an ear to free the poor man when his toils are o'er.

XIX

BACCHVM in remotis carmina rupibus
vidi docentem—credite posteri—
    Nymphasque discentes et auris
        capripedum Satyrorum acutas.

euhoe, recenti mens trepidat metu,
plenoque Bacchi pectore turbidum
    laetatur.   euhoe, parce, Liber,
        parce, gravi metuende thyrso.

fas pervicaces est mihi Thyiadas
vinique fontem lactis et uberes   10
    cantare rivos atque truncis
        lapsa cavis iterare mella;

fas et beatae coniugis additum
stellis honorem tectaque Penthei
    disiecta non leni ruina
        Thracis et exitium Lycurgi.

tu flectis amnes, tu mare barbarum,
tu separatis uvidus in iugis
    nodo coerces viperino
        Bistonidum sine fraude crines.   20

ODE XIX

Bacchus, Thine's the Power!

BACCHUS I saw on distant crags—believe me, ye of
after time—teaching hymns, and I beheld the nymphs
his pupils, and the goat-footed satyrs with their
pointed ears. Evoe! My heart thrills with fear
still fresh, and tumultuously rejoices, since my breast
is full of the god. Evoe! Liber! Spare me, oh,
spare me, thou god to be dreaded for thy mighty
thyrsus! 'Tis meet for me to sing of the tireless
Bacchanals, to tell of the fountains of wine, the rich
streams of milk, and the honey distilling from
hollow tree-trunks. Meet, too, it is to sing of the
crown of thy consort deified, set now among the stars,
and Pentheus' palace overthrown in dire destruction,
and the fatal end of Thracian Lycurgus. Thou bendest
to thy sway the streams and the savage sea. On
distant peaks, flushed with wine, thou bindest the
hair of the Bistonian women with harmless knot of

tu, cum parentis regna per arduum
cohors Gigantum scanderet impia,
    Rhoetum retorsisti leonis
        unguibus horribilique mala;

quamquam choreis aptior et iocis
ludoque dictus non sat idoneus
    pugnae ferebaris; sed idem
        pacis eras mediusque belli.

te vidit insons Cerberus aureo
cornu decorum, leniter atterens   30
    caudam, et recedentis trilingui
        ore pedes tetigitque crura.

serpents. Thou, too, when the impious crew of giants through the steep sky strove to mount to the realms of Jove, didst hurl back Rhoetus with the dread lion's claw and tooth. Though called fitter for dance and mirth and game, and said to be ill-suited for the fight, yet thou didst share in war as well as peace. Thee, too, glorious with thy horn of gold, Cerberus looked upon and harmed thee not, brushing thee fondly with his tail, and at thy going touched thy legs and feet with his triple tongue.

XX

Non usitata nec tenui ferar
pinna biformis per liquidum aethera
   vates, neque in terris morabor
    longius invidiaque maior

urbes relinquam. non ego, pauperum
sanguis parentum, non ego, quem vocas,
   dilecte Maecenas, obibo
    nec Stygia cohibebor unda.

iam iam residunt cruribus asperae
pelles, et album mutor in alitem   10
   superne, nascunturque leves
    per digitos umerosque plumae.

iam Daedaleo notior[1] Icaro
visam gementis litora Bosphori
   Syrtesque Gaetulas canorus
    ales Hyperboreosque campos.

me Colchus et, qui dissimulat metum
Marsae cohortis, Dacus et ultimi
   noscent Geloni, me peritus
    discet Hiber Rhodanique potor.   20

absint inani funere neniae
luctusque turpes et querimoniae;
   compesce clamorem ac sepulcri
    mitte supervacuos honores.

[1] *inferior MSS.* ocior: tutior *Bentley.*

ODE XX

The Poet prophesies his own Immortality

On no common or feeble pinion shall I soar in double form through the liquid air, a poet still, nor linger more on earth, but victorious over envy I shall quit the towns of men. Not I, the son of parents poor, not I, who hear your voice, beloved Maecenas, shall perish, or be confined by waters of the Styx. Even now the wrinkled skin is gathering on my ankles, and I am changing to a snowy swan above, and o'er my arms and shoulders is spreading a plumage soft. Soon, a tuneful bird, I shall visit the shores of the moaning Bosphorus, more renowned than Icarus, born of Daedalus; I shall visit the Gaetulian Syrtes and the plains of the Hyperboreans. Me the Colchian shall come to know, and the Dacian, who feigns to feel no dread of our Marsian cohorts, and the far Geloni; by the study of my writings the Spaniard shall become learned and they who drink the waters of the Rhone.

Let dirges be absent from what you falsely deem my death, and unseemly show of grief and lamentation! Restrain all clamour and forgo the idle tribute of a tomb!

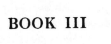

BOOK III

LIBER III

I

ODI profanum vulgus et arceo;
favete linguis.   carmina non prius
   audita Musarum sacerdos
    virginibus puerisque canto.

regum timendorum in proprios greges,
reges in ipsos imperium est Iovis,
   clari Giganteo triumpho,
    cuncta supercilio moventis.

est ut viro vir latius ordinet
arbusta sulcis, hic generosior   10
   descendat in Campum petitor,
    moribus hic meliorque fama

contendat, illi turba clientium
sit maior; aequa lege Necessitas
   sortitur insignes et imos:
    omne capax movet urna nomen.

BOOK III

ODE I

Simplicity

I HATE the uninitiate crowd and keep them far away.
Observe a reverent silence! I, the Muses' priest,
sing for maids and boys songs not heard before.

The rule of dreaded kings is over their own
peoples; but over the kings themselves is the rule
of Jove, glorious for his victory o'er the Giants, and
controlling all things with the nod of his brow.

'Tis true that one man plants his vineyards over
wider acres than his fellow; that one candidate for
office who comes down to the Campus is of nobler
birth, another of greater worth and fame, while still
another has a larger band of followers; yet with
impartial justice Necessity allots the fates of high
and low alike. The ample urn keeps tossing every
name.

destrictus ensis cui super impia
cervice pendet, non Siculae dapes
    dulcem elaborabunt saporem,
        non avium citharaeque cantus   20

somnum reducent.   somnus agrestium
lenis virorum non humiles domos
    fastidit umbrosamque ripam,
        non zephyris agitata Tempe.

desiderantem quod satis est neque
tumultuosum sollicitat mare
    nec saevus Arcturi cadentis
        impetus aut orientis Haedi,

non verberatae grandine vineae
fundusque mendax, arbore nunc aquas   30
    culpante, nunc torrentia agros
        sidera, nunc hiemes iniquas.

contracta pisces aequora sentiunt
iactis in altum molibus : huc frequens
    caementa demittit redemptor
        cum famulis dominusque terrae

fastidiosus.   sed Timor et Minae
scandunt eodem quo dominus, neque
    decedit aerata triremi et
        post equitem sedet atra Cura.   40

Over whose impious head [1] the drawn sword hangs,
for him Sicilian feasts will produce no savour sweet,
nor will music of birds or lutes bring back sleep to his
couch.   Soft slumber scorns not the humble cottage of
the peasant, nor the shady bank, nor the valley by
the zephyrs fanned.   He who longs for only what he
needs is troubled not by stormy seas, not by the fierce
onslaught of setting Arcturus or rising Haedus—not
by the lashing of his vineyards with the hail, nor by
the treachery of his farm, the trees complaining now
of too much rain, now of the dog-star parching the
fields, now of the cruel winters.

The fishes note the narrowing of the waters by
piers of rock laid in their depths.   Here the builder
with his throng of slaves, and the master who disdains
the land, let down the rubble.   But Fear and Threats
climb to the selfsame spot the owner does ; nor does
black Care quit the brass-bound galley and even takes
her seat behind the horseman.

1 An allusion to "the sword of Damocles." When Damocles
extolled the great felicity of the tyrant Dionysius, the latter
placed him at a sumptuous banquet where Damocles saw a
sword suspended over his head by a single hair.

quodsi dolentem nec Phrygius lapis
nec purpurarum sidere clarior
   delenit usus nec Falerna
      vitis Achaemeniumque costum,

cur invidendis postibus et novo
sublime ritu moliar atrium?
   cur valle permutem Sabina
      divitias operosiores?

But if neither Phrygian marble nor purple brighter than the stars nor Falernian wine nor Persian nard can soothe one in distress, why should I rear aloft in modern style a hall with columns to stir envy? Why should I change my Sabine dale for the greater burden of wealth?

II

ANGVSTAM amice pauperiem pati
robustus acri militia puer
   condiscat et Parthos feroces
     vexet eques metuendus hasta,

vitamque sub divo et trepidis agat
in rebus. illum ex moenibus hosticis
   matrona bellantis tyranni
     prospiciens et adulta virgo

suspiret: " eheu, ne rudis agminum
sponsus lacessat regius asperum   10
   tactu leonem, quem cruenta
     per medias rapit ira caedes."

dulce et decorum est pro patria mori.
mors et fugacem persequitur virum,
   nec parcit imbellis iuventae
     poplitibus timidove tergo.

Virtus, repulsae nescia sordidae,
intaminatis fulget honoribus,
   nec sumit aut ponit secures
     arbitrio popularis aurae.   20

ODE II

Endurance, and Fidelity to One's Trust

LET the youth, hardened by active service, learn to bear with patience trying hardships! Let him, a horseman dreaded for his lance, harass the warlike Parthians and pass his life beneath the open sky amid stirring deeds! At sight of him from foeman's battlements may the consort of the warring tyrant and the ripe maiden sigh: " Ah, let not our royal lover, unpractised in the fray, rouse the lion fierce to touch, whom rage for blood hurries through the midst of carnage !"

'Tis sweet and glorious to die for fatherland. Yet Death o'ertakes not less the runaway, nor spares the limbs and coward backs of faint-hearted youths.

True worth, that never knows ignoble defeat, shines with undimmed glory, nor takes up nor lays aside the axes at the fickle mob's behest. True worth,

Virtus, reeludens immeritis mori
caelum, negata temptat iter via,
   coetusque vulgares et udam
      spernit humum fugiente pinna.

est et fideli tuta silentio
merces: vetabo, qui Cereris sacrum
   volgarit arcanae, sub isdem
      sit trabibus fragilemque mecum

solvat phaselon; saepe Diespiter
neglectus incesto addidit integrum,   30
   raro antecedentem scelestum
      deseruit pede Poena claudo.

opening Heaven wide for those deserving not to die,
essays its course by a path denied to others, and
spurns the vulgar crowd and damp earth on fleeting
pinion.

There is a sure reward for trusty silence, too.   I
will forbid the man who has divulged the sacred rites
of mystic Ceres, to abide beneath the same roof or to
unmoor with me the fragile bark.   Often has outraged
Jupiter involved the innocent with the guilty ; but
rarely does Vengeance, albeit of halting gait, fail to
o'ertake the guilty, though he gain the start.

III

Ivstvm et tenacem propositi virum
non civium ardor prava iubentium,
   non vultus instantis tyranni
      mente quatit solida neque Auster,

dux inquieti turbidus Hadriae,
nec fulminantis magna manus Iovis ;
   si fractus inlabatur orbis,
      impavidum ferient ruinae.

hac arte Pollux et vagus Hercules
enisus arces attigit igneas,   10
   quos inter Augustus recumbens
      purpureo bibet[1] ore nectar.

hac te merentem, Bacche pater, tuae
vexere tigres, indocili iugum
   collo trahentes ; hac Quirinus
      Martis equis Acheronta fugit,

gratum elocuta consiliantibus
Iunone divis : "Ilion, Ilion
   fatalis incestusque iudex
      et mulier peregrina vertit   20

      [1] *Some MSS. read* bibit.

ODE III

Justice, and Steadfastness of Purpose

THE man tenacious of his purpose in a righteous cause is not shaken from his firm resolve by the frenzy of his fellow-citizens bidding what is wrong, not by the face of threatening tyrant, not by Auster, stormy master of the restless Adriatic, not by the mighty hand of thundering Jove. Were the vault of heaven to break and fall upon him, its ruins would smite him undismayed.

'Twas by such merits that Pollux and roving Hercules strove and reached the starry citadels, reclining among whom Augustus shall sip nectar with ruddy lips. 'Twas for such merits, Father Bacchus, that thy tigers drew thee in well-earned triumph, wearing the yoke on untrained neck. 'Twas for such merits that Quirinus escaped Acheron on the steeds of Mars, what time Juno, among the gods in council gathered, spake the welcome words: " Ilium, Ilium has been turned to dust by an umpire fateful

in pulverem, ex quo destituit deos
mercede pacta Laomedon, mihi
   castaeque damnatum Minervae
      cum populo et duce fraudulento.

iam nec Lacaenae splendet adulterae
famosus hospes nec Priami domus
   periura pugnaces Achivos
      Hectoreis opibus refringit,

nostrisque ductum seditionibus
bellum resedit.   protinus et graves   30
   iras et invisum nepotem,
      Troica quem peperit sacerdos,

Marti redonabo; illum ego lucidas
inire sedes, ducere [1] nectaris
   sucos et adscribi quietis
      ordinibus patiar deorum.

dum longus inter saeviat Ilion
Romamque pontus, qualibet exsules
   in parte regnanto beati;
      dum Priami Paridisque busto   40

insultet armentum et catulos ferae
celent inultae, stet Capitolium
   fulgens triumphatisque possit
      Roma ferox dare iura Medis.

[1] *Good MSS. also have* discere.

and impure, and by a foreign woman—Ilium given over to me and virgin Pallas, with its folk and treacherous king, ever since Laomedon cheated the gods of their covenanted pay. No longer does the infamous stranger dazzle the eyes of his Spartan paramour, nor does the perjured house of Priam with Hector's help longer baffle the contending Greeks; and the war our feuds had lengthened, now has ended. Henceforth I will abandon my fierce wrath and restore to Mars my hated grandson whom the Trojan priestess bore. Him will I suffer to enter the abodes of light, to quaff sweet nectar, and to be enrolled in the serene ranks of the gods.

Provided only a wide sea rage between Ilium and Rome, let the exiles reign happy in whatever place they choose; provided only the cattle trample over the tomb of Priam and of Paris, and the wild beasts hide their whelps there with impunity, let the Capitol stand gleaming, and let warlike Rome dictate terms to the conquered Medes! Held far and wide in awe,

horrenda late nomen in ultimas
extendat oras, qua medius liquor
   secernit Europen ab Afro,
     qua tumidus rigat arva Nilus,

aurum inrepertum et sic melius situm,
cum terra celat, spernere fortior   50
   quam cogere humanos in usus
     omne sacrum rapiente dextra.

quicumque mundo terminus obstitit,
hunc tangat armis, visere gestiens,
   qua parte debacchentur ignes,
     qua nebulae pluviique rores.

sed bellicosis fata Quiritibus
hac lege dico, ne nimium pii
   rebusque fidentes avitae
     tecta velint reparare Troiae.   60

Troiae renascens alite lugubri
fortuna tristi clade iterabitur
   ducente victrices catervas
     coniuge me Iovis et sorore.

ter si resurgat murus aëneus
auctore Phoebo, ter pereat meis
   excisus Argivis, ter uxor
     capta virum puerosque ploret."

let her spread her name to farthest coasts, where the Strait severs Europe from Africa, where the swollen Nile waters the corn-lands, stronger to spurn undiscovered gold (better so bestowed, while Earth yet hides it) than to gather it for human uses with a hand that plunders every sacred thing. Whatever limit bounds the world, this let her reach with her arms, eager to behold where tropic heats hold revel, where mists and dripping rains prevail.

But on this condition only do I foretell the fates to the martial Quirites : Let them not, too loyal and too trustful of their power, wish to renew the roofs of ancestral Troy ! If Troy's fortune revive again, it shall be under evil omen, and her doom shall be repeated with dire disaster, I, Jove's consort and sister, leading the conquering hosts. Should her walls thrice rise in bronze with Phoebus' help, thrice shall they perish, destroyed by my Argive warriors; thrice shall the captive wife mourn her husband and her children."

non hoc iocosae conveniet lyrae :

quo, Musa, tendis ?   desine pervicax   70

  referre sermones deorum et

    magna modis tenuare parvis.

But this will not befit the sportive lyre. On what, O Muse, art thou bent? Cease wantonly to report the councils of the gods and to belittle lofty themes with trivial measures!

IV

DESCENDE caelo et dic age tibia
regina longum Calliope melos,
    seu voce nunc mavis acuta
        seu fidibus citharaque Phoebi.

auditis, an me ludit amabilis
insania?   audire et videor pios
    errare per lucos, amoenae
        quos et aquae subeunt et aurae.

me fabulosae Volture in avio [1]
nutricis extra limen Apuliae [2]   10
    ludo fatigatumque somno
        fronde nova puerum palumbes

texere, mirum quod foret omnibus,
quicumque celsae nidum Acherontiae
    saltusque Bantinos et arvum
        pingue tenent humilis Forenti,

ut tuto ab atris corpore viperis
dormirem et ursis, ut premerer sacra
    lauroque conlataque myrto,
        non sine dis animosus infans.   20

    1 avio *Keller:* Apulo *MSS.*
    2 *Good MSS. also have* limina Pulliae.

ODE IV

Wisdom and Order

DESCEND from heaven, O Queen Calliope, and play upon the flute a long-continued melody, or sing with thy clear voice, dost thou prefer, or to the strings of Phoebus' lyre! Do ye hear, my mates? Or does some fond illusion mock me? Methinks I hear her and am straying through hallowed groves, where pleasant waters steal and breezes stir.

In childhood's days, on trackless Vultur, beyond the borders of old nurse Apulia, when I was tired with play and overcome with sleep, the doves of story covered me o'er with freshly fallen leaves, to be a marvel to all who dwell in lofty Acherontia's nest and Bantia's glades, and the rich fields of Forentum in the dale—how I slept safe from bears and black serpents, how I was overspread with sacred bay and gathered myrtle, with the gods' help a fearless child.

vester, Camenae, vester in arduos
tollor Sabinos, seu mihi frigidum
    Praeneste seu Tibur supinum
        seu liquidae placuere Baiae.

vestris amicum fontibus et choris
non me Philippis versa acies retro,
    devota non extinxit arbor,
        nec Sicula Palinurus unda.

utcumque mecum vos eritis, libens
insanientem navita Bosphorum   30
    temptabo et urentes harenas
        litoris Assyrii viator;

visam Britannos hospitibus feros
et laetum equino sanguine Concanum,
    visam pharetratos Gelonos
        et Scythicum inviolatus amnem.

vos Caesarem altum, militia simul
fessas cohortes addidit oppidis,
    finire quaerentem labores,
        Pierio recreatis antro.   40

vos lene consilium et datis et dato
gaudetis, almae.   scimus, ut impios
    Titanas immanemque turbam
        fulmine sustulerit caduco,

As yours, yes, yours, O Muses, do I climb to my lofty Sabine hills, or go to cool Praeneste, or sloping Tibur, or to cloudless Baiae, has it but caught my fancy. Friend of your springs and dancing choirs, not Philippi's rout destroyed me, nor that accursed tree, nor the Sicilian wave near Palinurus' headland. Whenever ye are with me, gladly will I as mariner essay the raging Bosphorus, or as wanderer the blazing sands of the Syrian shore. I'll visit all unscathed the Britons, no friends to strangers, the Concanian that delights in draughts of horses' blood, the Geloni that wear the quiver, and the Scythian stream.

'Tis ye who in Pierian grotto refresh our noble Caesar, when he seeks to soothe his cares, now that he has settled in the towns his cohorts wearied with campaigning. Ye give gentle counsel, and delight in giving it, ye goddesses benign. Full well we know how the impious Titans and their frightful horde were

qui terram inertem, qui mare temperat
ventosum et urbes regnaque tristia,
   divosque mortalesque turmas
     imperio regit unus aequo.

magnum illa terrorem intulerat Iovi
fidens iuventus horrida bracchiis   50
   fratresque tendentes opaco
     Pelion imposuisse Olympo.

sed quid Typhoeus et validus Mimas,
aut quid minaci Porphyrion statu,
   quid Rhoetus evulsisque truncis
     Enceladus iaculator audax

contra sonantem Palladis aegida
possent ruentes?   hinc avidus stetit
   Vulcanus, hinc matrona Iuno et
     numquam umeris positurus arcum,   60

qui rore puro Castaliae lavit
crines solutos, qui Lyciae tenet
   dumeta natalemque silvam,
     Delius et Patareus Apollo.

vis consili expers mole ruit sua:
vim temperatam di quoque provehunt
   in maius; idem odere vires
     omne nefas animo moventes.

struck down with the descending bolt by him who rules the lifeless earth, the wind-swept sea, cities, and the gloomy realms below, who alone with righteous sway governs the gods and throngs of men. Mighty terror had been brought on Jove by that insolent crew, bristling with hands, and by the brothers who strove to set Pelion on shadowy Olympus. But what could Typhoeus avail and mighty Mimas, what Porphyrion with his threatening mien, what Rhoetus and Enceladus, bold hurler of uprooted trees, in their rush against the ringing aegis of Minerva! On this side stood eager Vulcan, on that, matron Juno and he who from his shoulder shall never lay aside the bow, who laves his flowing locks in Castalia's pure dew, who haunts the Lycian thickets and the forests of his native isle, god of Delos and of Patara, Apollo's self.

Brute force bereft of wisdom falls to ruin by its own weight. Power with counsel tempered, even the gods make greater. But might that in its soul is bent

testis mearum centimanus Gyas [1]
sententiarum, notus et integrae   70
   temptator Orion Dianae,
     virginea domitus sagitta.

iniecta monstris Terra dolet suis
maeretque partus fulmine luridum
   missos ad Orcum; nec peredit
     impositam celer ignis Aetnen,

incontinentis nec Tityi iecur
reliquit ales, nequitiae additus
   custos; amatorem trecentae
     Pirithoum cohibent catenae.   80

[1] Gyas *Lambinus:* gigas *MSS.*

on all impiety, they hate.   Be hundred-handed Gyas the witness of my verdict, Orion too, well-known assailant of chaste Diana, subdued by the arrow of the maiden-goddess !   Earth, heaped upon her monstrous offspring, mourns and laments her progeny hurled down to murky Orcus by the thunderbolt.   Nor yet has the swift-darting flame eaten through Aetna's pile, nor does the vulture leave the breast of lawless Tityos, set as a watchman o'er his infamy.   And thrice a hundred chains hold fast the amorous Pirithous.

V

Caelo tonantem credidimus Iovem
regnare; praesens divus habebitur
    Augustus adiectis Britannis
        imperio gravibusque Persis.

milesne Crassi coniuge barbara
turpis maritus vixit et hostium
    (pro curia inversique mores!)
        consenuit socerorum in armis

sub rege Medo, Marsus et Apulus
anciliorum et nominis et togae   10
    oblitus aeternaeque Vestae,
        incolumi Iove et urbe Roma?

hoc caverat mens provida Reguli
dissentientis condicionibus
    foedis et exemplo trahentis[1]
        perniciem veniens in aevum,

si non periret immiserabilis
captiva pubes. "signa ego Punicis
    adfixa delubris et arma
        militibus sine caede" dixit   20

---

[1] trahentis *all MSS.:* trahenti *many editors.*

ODE V

Martial Courage

WE believe that Jove is king in heaven because we hear his thunders peal; Augustus shall be deemed a god on earth for adding to our empire the Britons and dread Parthians. Did Crassus' troops live in base wedlock with barbarian wives and (alas, our sunken Senate and our altered ways!) grow old in service of the foes whose daughters they had wedded —Marsian and Apulian submissive to a Parthian king, forgetful of the sacred shields, the Roman name, the toga, and eternal Vesta, while Jove's temples and the city Rome remained unharmed?

'Twas against this the far-seeing mind of Regulus had guarded when he revolted from the shameful terms and from such precedent foresaw ruin extending to the coming ages, should not the captive youth perish without pity. "With mine own eyes," he said, " have I seen our standards hung up in Punic shrines, and weapons

195

" derepta vidi, vidi ego civium
retorta tergo bracchia libero
   portasque non clausas et arva
     Marte coli populata nostro.

auro repensus scilicet acrior
miles redibit. flagitio additis
   damnum: neque amissos colores
     lana refert medicata fuco,

nec vera virtus, cum semel excidit,
curat reponi deterioribus.   30
   si pugnat extricata densis
     cerva plagis, erit ille fortis

qui perfidis se credidit hostibus,
et Marte Poenos proteret altero,
   qui lora restrictis lacertis
     sensit iners timuitque mortem.

hic, unde vitam sumeret inscius,
pacem duello miscuit. o pudor!
   o magna Carthago, probrosis
     altior Italiae ruinis!"   40

fertur pudicae coniugis osculum
parvosque natos ut capitis minor
   ab se removisse et virilem
     torvus humi posuisse voltum,

wrested from our soldiers without bloodshed; with mine own eyes have I seen the hands of freemen pinioned behind their backs, the gates (of Carthage) open wide, the fields once ravaged by our warfare tilled again. Redeemed by gold, forsooth, our soldiers will renew the strife with greater bravery! To shame ye are but adding loss; the wool with purple dyed never regains the hue it once has lost, nor does true manhood, when it once has vanished, care to be restored to degenerate breasts. If the doe gives fight when loosened from the close-meshed toils, then will *he* be brave who has trusted himself to perfidious foes, and *he* will crush the Carthaginians in a second war who has tamely felt the thongs upon his fettered arms and has stood in fear of death. Such a one, not knowing how to make his life secure, has confounded war with peace. Alas the shame! O mighty Carthage, raised higher on Italy's disgraceful ruins."

'Tis said he put away his chaste wife's kisses and his little children, as one bereft of civil rights, and sternly bent his manly gaze upon the ground, till he

donec labantis consilio patres
firmaret auctor numquam alias dato,
  interque maerentes amicos
    egregius properaret exsul.

atqui sciebat quae sibi barbarus
tortor pararet.   non aliter tamen
  dimovit obstantes propinquos
    et populum reditus morantem,

quam si clientum longa negotia
diiudicata lite relinqueret,
  tendens Venafranos in agros
    aut Lacedaemonium Tarentum.

50

should strengthen the Senate's wavering purpose by advice ne'er given before, and amid sorrowing friends should hurry forth a glorious exile.   Full well he knew what the barbarian torturer was making ready for him; and yet he pushed aside the kinsmen who blocked his path and the people who would stay his going, with no less unconcern than if some case in court had been decided, and he were leaving the tedious business of his clients, speeding to Venafran fields, or to Lacedaemonian Tarentum.

VI

Delicta maiorum immeritus lues,
Romane, donec templa refeceris
   aedesque labentes deorum et
     foeda nigro simulacra fumo.

dis te minorem quod geris, imperas:
hinc omne principium; huc refer exitum.
   di multa neglecti dederunt
     Hesperiae mala luctuosae.

iam bis Monaeses et Pacori manus
non auspicatos contudit impetus   10
   nostros et adiecisse praedam
     torquibus exiguis renidet.

paene occupatam seditionibus
delevit urbem Dacus et Aethiops,
   hic classe formidatus, ille
     missilibus melior sagittis.

fecunda culpae saecula nuptias
primum inquinavere et genus et domos:
   hoc fonte derivata clades
     in patriam populumque fluxit.   20

motus doceri gaudet Ionicos
matura virgo et fingitur artibus
   iam nunc et incestos amores
     de tenero meditatur ungui.

ODE VI

Religion and Purity

THY fathers' sins, O Roman, thou, though guiltless, shalt expiate, till thou dost restore the crumbling temples and shrines of the gods and their statues soiled with grimy smoke. 'Tis by holding thyself the servant of the gods that thou dost rule; with them all things begin; to them ascribe the outcome! Outraged, they have visited unnumbered woes on sorrowing Hesperia. Already twice Monaeses and the band of Pacorus have crushed our ill-starred onslaughts, and now beam with joy to have added spoil from us to their paltry necklaces. Beset with civil strife, the City has narrowly escaped destruction at the hands of Dacian and of Aethiop, the one sore dreaded for his fleet, the other better with the flying arrow. Teeming with sin, our times have sullied first the marriage-bed, our offspring, and our homes; sprung from this source, disaster's stream has overflowed the folk and fatherland. The maiden early takes delight in learning Grecian dances, and trains herself in coquetry e'en now, and plans unholy amours, with passion unrestrained.[1] Soon midst

---

[1] Literally : 'from her tender nail'; *i.e.* in every fibre of her being.

mox iuniores quaerit adulteros
inter mariti vina, neque eligit
   cui donet impermissa raptim
     gaudia luminibus remotis,

sed iussa coram non sine conscio
surgit marito, seu vocat institor   30
   seu navis Hispanae magister,
     dedecorum pretiosus emptor.

non his iuventus orta parentibus
infecit aequor sanguine Punico
   Pyrrhumque et ingentem cecidit
     Antiochum Hannibalemque dirum ;

sed rusticorum mascula militum
proles, Sabellis docta ligonibus
   versare glaebas et severae
     matris ad arbitrium recisos   40

portare fustes, Sol ubi montium
mutaret umbras et iuga demeret
   bobus fatigatis, amicum
     tempus agens abeunte curru.

damnosa quid non imminuit dies ?
aetas parentum, peior avis, tulit
   nos nequiores, mox daturos
     progeniem vitiosiorem.

her husband's revels she seeks younger paramours, nor stops to choose on whom she swiftly shall bestow illicit joys when lights are banished; but openly, when bidden, and not without her husband's knowledge, she rises, be it some peddler summons her, or the captain of some Spanish ship, lavish purchaser of shame.

Not such the sires of whom were sprung the youth that dyed the sea with Punic blood, and struck down Pyrrhus and great Antiochus and Hannibal, the dire; but a manly brood of peasant soldiers, taught to turn the clods with Sabine hoe, and at a strict mother's bidding to bring cut firewood, when the sun shifted the shadows of the mountain sides and lifted the yoke from weary steers, bringing the welcome time of rest with his departing car.

What do the ravages of time not injure! Our parents' age, worse than our grandsires', has brought forth us less worthy and destined soon to yield an offspring still more wicked.

VII

Qvid fles, Asterie, quem tibi candidi
primo restituent vere Favonii
    Thyna merce beatum,
      constantis iuvenem fide,

Gygen ?   ille Notis actus ad Oricum
post insana Caprae sidera frigidas
    noctes non sine multis
      insomnis lacrimis agit.

atqui sollicitae nuntius hospitae,
suspirare Chloen et miseram tuis   10
    dicens ignibus uri,
      temptat mille vafer modis.

ut Proetum mulier perfida credulum
falsis impulerit criminibus nimis
    casto Bellerophontae
      maturare necem refert ;

narrat paene datum Pelea Tartaro,
Magnessam Hippolyten dum fugit abstinens ;
    et peccare docentes
      fallax historias movet.[1]   20

---

[1] *Most MSS have* monet.

ODE VII

Constancy, Asterie !

WHY weepest thou, Asterie, for Gyges, whom at spring's first advent the cloudless zephyrs shall restore to thee, rich with Bithynian wares, thy constant lover ?   He, by east winds driven to Oricum, after the Goat's wild rising, passes the chill nights sleeplessly, not without many a tear.   And yet the messenger of his enamoured hostess, telling how wretched Chloë sighs and is consumed with affection for thy lover, craftily tempts him with a thousand arts. She tells how a perfidious woman by false charges drove credulous Proetus to bring swift death on over-chaste Bellerophon.   She tells of Peleus, all but doomed to Tartarus for righteous shunning of Magnessian Hippolyte ; and with subtle guile cites examples that encourage faithlessness.

frustra : nam scopulis surdior Icari
voces audit adhuc integer.   at tibi
  ne vicinus Enipeus
    plus iusto placeat cave ;

quamvis non alius flectere equum sciens
aeque conspicitur gramine Martio,
  nec quisquam citus aeque
    Tusco denatat alveo.

prima nocte domum claude neque in vias
sub cantu querulae despice tibiae,   30
  et te saepe vocanti
    duram difficilis mane.

Yet all in vain, for deafer than the cliffs of Icaros, he listens to her pleas, heart-whole as yet. But have *thou* a care lest to thee thy neighbour Enipeus prove more pleasing than he ought, though no one else is seen to be as skilful to guide his steed over the Campus' sward and no one swims so swiftly down the Tiber's channel. At nightfall close thy dwelling, nor bend thy gaze into the streets at the music of his plaintive flute, and though oft he call thee cruel, do thou remain unyielding.

VIII

MARTIIS caelebs quid agam Kalendis,
quid velint flores et acerra turis
plena miraris positusque carbo in
    caespite vivo,

docte sermones utriusque linguae.
voveram dulces epulas et album
Libero caprum prope funeratus
    arboris ictu.

hic dies anno redeunte festus
corticem adstrictum pice demovebit   10
amphorae fumum bibere institutae
    consule Tullo.

sume, Maecenas, cyathos amici
sospitis centum et vigiles lucernas
perfer in lucem : procul omnis esto
    clamor et ira.

mitte civiles super urbe curas :
occidit Daci Cotisonis agmen,
Medus infestus sibi luctuosis
    dissidet armis,   20

ODE VIII

A Glad Anniversary

WHAT I, a bachelor, am doing on the Martian Kalends, what mean the flowers, the casket full of incense, and the embers laid on fresh-cut turf—at this you marvel, you versed in the lore of either tongue! I had vowed to Liber a savoury feast and a pure-white goat, what time I narrowly escaped destruction by the falling tree. This festal day, each time the year revolves, shall draw a well-pitched cork forth from a jar set to drink the smoke [1] in Tullus' consulship. So drain, Maecenas, a hundred cyathi in celebration of your friend's escape, and keep the lamps alight till dawn! Banish far all angry brawls! Dismiss the cares of state! Crushed is the band of Dacian Cotiso; the hostile Parthians are fighting with each

[1] *I.e.* sealed.

209

servit Hispanae vetus hostis orae
Cantaber, sera domitus catena,
iam Scythae laxo meditantur arcu
   cedere campis.

neglegens, ne qua populus laboret,
parce privatus nimium cavere et
dona praesentis cape laetus horae ac
   linque severa.

other in disastrous strife; our old foe of the Spanish coast, the Cantabrian, at last in captive chains, is now our subject. Already the Scythians, with bows unstrung are planning to quit their plains. Be for the nonce a private citizen, care-free, and cease to be too much concerned lest in any way the people suffer! Gladly take the gifts of the present hour and abandon serious things!

IX

" Donec gratus eram tibi
  nec quisquam potior bracchia candidae
cervici iuvenis dabat,
  Persarum vigui rege beatior."

" donec non alia magis
  arsisti neque erat Lydia post Chloen,
multi Lydia nominis
  Romana vigui clarior Ilia."

" me nunc Thressa Chloe regit,
  dulces docta modos et citharae sciens,   10
pro qua non metuam mori,
  si parcent animae fata superstiti."

" me torret face mutua
  Thurini Calais filius Ornyti,
pro quo bis patiar mori,
  si parcent puero fata superstiti."

" quid si prisca redit Venus
  diductosque iugo cogit aëneo ?
si flava excutitur Chloe
  reiectaeque patet ianua Lydiae ? "   20

" quamquam sidere pulchrior
  ille est, tu levior cortice et improbo
iracundior Hadria,
  tecum vivere amem, tecum obeam libens ! "

ODES BOOK III

ODE IX

Reconciliation

" WHILE I was dear to thee and no more favoured youth flung his arms about thy dazzling neck, I lived in greater bliss than Persia's king."

" While thou wast enamoured of no other more than me, and Lydia ranked not after Chloë, in joy of my great fame I, Lydia, lived more glorious than Roman Ilia."

" Me Thracian Chloë now doth sway, skilled in sweet measures and mistress of the lyre ; for her I will not fear to die, if the Fates but spare my darling and suffer her to live."

" Me Calais, son of Thurian Ornytus, kindles with mutual flame ; for him right willingly I twice will die, if the Fates but spare the lad and suffer him to live."

" What if the old love come back again and join those now estranged beneath her compelling yoke ; if fair-haired Chloë be put aside and the door thrown open to rejected Lydia ? "

" Though he is fairer than the stars, and thou less stable than the tossing cork and stormier than the wanton Adriatic, with thee I fain would live, with thee I'd gladly die."

X

EXTREMVM Tanain si biberes, Lyce,
saevo nupta viro, me tamen asperas
porrectum ante fores obicere incolis
    plorares Aquilonibus.

audis, quo strepitu ianua, quo nemus
inter pulchra satum tecta remugiat
ventis, et positas ut glaciet nives
    puro numine Iuppiter?

ingratam Veneri pone superbiam,
ne currente retro funis eat rota: 10
non te Penelopen difficilem procis
    Tyrrhenus genuit parens.

o quamvis neque te munera nec preces
nec tinctus viola pallor amantium
nec vir Pieria paelice saucius
    curvat, supplicibus tuis

parcas, nec rigida mollior aesculo
nec Mauris animum mitior anguibus.
non hoc semper erit liminis aut aquae
    caelestis patiens latus.   20

ODE X

A Lover's Complaint

WERT thou wont to drink of Tanais' distant stream, O Lyce, wedded to some stern husband, yet wouldst thou be loth to expose me, stretched out before thy cruel portals, to the blasts of thy native North. Hearest thou how creaks the door, how the trees planted within thy fair abode are moaning in the gale; how in cloudless majesty Jupiter is glazing the fallen snow? Banish thy disdain, to Venus hateful, lest the rope run back as the wheel revolves![1] No Penelope art thou, unyielding to thy suitors, nor of Tuscan parents born. Though neither gifts nor prayers move thee, nor thy lovers' pallor tinged with saffron, nor thy husband's passion for a Thessalian mistress, yet spare thy suppliants, thou less pliant than the unbending oak, and in heart no gentler than Moorish serpents! Not for ever will my body endure thy threshold or the rain of heaven.

[1] A figure drawn from some mechanical appliance such as a windlass, of which control is lost.

XI

MERCVRI (nam te docilis magistro
movit Amphion lapides canendo),
tuque testudo resonare septem
    callida nervis,

nec loquax olim neque grata, nunc et
divitum mensis et amica templis,
dic modos, Lyde quibus obstinatas
    applicet aures,

quae velut latis equa trima campis
ludit exsultim metuitque tangi,   10
nuptiarum expers et adhuc protervo
    cruda marito.

tu potes tigres comitesque silvas
ducere et rivos celeres morari ;
cessit immanis tibi blandienti
    ianitor aulae,

Cerberus, quamvis furiale centum
muniant angues caput eius atque
spiritus taeter saniesque manet
    ore trilingui.   20

ODE XI

Take Warning, Lyde, from the Danaids!

O MERCURY (for taught by thee as master,
Amphion with his measures moved the rocks) and
thou, O shell, trained to respond with thy seven
strings, thou that once wast neither eloquent nor
lovely, but now art welcome at the tables of the
rich and in the temples of the gods, utter measures
to which Lyde may incline her reluctant ears, who
now, like a filly three years old, gambols o'er the
spreading plains, and shrinks from being touched, to
wedlock still a stranger, and not yet ripe for an eager
mate.

Thou hast power to draw tigers and the forests in
thy train, and canst stay the dashing streams. To
thy persuasive charms Cerberus, grim gateman of the
court of hell, surrendered, though a hundred snakes
guard his frightful head, and foul breath and gore

217

quin et Ixion Tityosque voltu
risit invito, stetit urna paulum
sicca, dum grato Danai puellas
    carmine mulces.

audiat Lyde scelus atque notas
virginum poenas et inane lymphae
dolium fundo pereuntis imo
    seraque fata,

quae manent culpas etiam sub Orco.
impiae (nam quid potuere maius ?)   30
impiae sponsos potuere duro
    perdere ferro.

una de multis face nuptiali
digna periurum fuit in parentem
splendide mendax et in omne virgo
    nobilis aevum,

" surge" quae dixit iuveni marito,
" surge, ne longus tibi somnus, unde
non times, detur ; socerum et scelestas
    falle sorores,   40

quae, velut nanctae vitulos leaenae,
singulos eheu lacerant : ego illis
mollior nec te feriam neque intra
    claustra tenebo.

flow from his three-tongued mouth. Nay, even Ixion
and Tityos smiled through their anguish, and for a
little while the jar stood dry, as with thy winning
notes thou Danaus' daughters didst beguile. Let
Lyde hear the tale of the maidens' sin and punishment
well-known, and their vessel ever empty of water
vanishing through the bottom, and the fate which,
though long deferred, awaits wrongdoing even in
Orcus' realms. Impious (for what greater crime could
they have compassed?), impious, they had the heart to
destroy their lovers with the cruel steel. One only of
the many was there, worthy of the marriage torch,
gloriously false to her perjured father, a maiden
noble for all time to come, who to her youthful
husband said : "Arise, arise ! lest unending slumber
visit thee from a source thou fearest not. Elude my
father and my wicked sisters, who like lionesses that
have seized young steers, alas ! are rending each her
own. I, softer of heart than they, will neither strike
thee nor hold thee under lock and bar. Me let my

me pater saevis oneret catenis,
quod viro clemens misero peperci;
me vel extremos Numidarum in agros
  classe releget.

i, pedes quo te rapiunt et aurae,
dum favet Nox et Venus; i secundo   50
omine, et nostri memorem sepulcro
  scalpe querellam."

father load with cruel chains, for that in mercy I did spare my hapless husband ! Let him with his ships send me in banishment to the farthest lands of the Numidians ! Go whither thy feet and the breezes hurry thee, while night and Venus are propitious ! God speed thee ! And carve upon my sepulchre an elegy in memory of me !"

XII

MISERARVM est neque amori dare ludum neque dulci
mala vino lavere aut exanimari metuentes
  patruae verbera linguae.

tibi qualum Cythereae puer ales, tibi telas
operosaeque Minervae studium aufert, Neobule,
  Liparaei nitor Hebri

simul unctos Tiberinis umeros lavit in undis,
eques ipso melior Bellerophonte, neque pugno
  neque segni pede victus,

catus idem per apertum fugientes agitato   10
grege cervos iaculari et celer arto latitantem
  fruticeto excipere aprum.

ODE XII

Neobule's Soliloquy

WRETCHED the maids who may not give play to love nor drown their cares in sweet wine, or who lose heart, fearing the lash of an uncle's tongue. From thee, O Neobule, Cytherea's winged child snatches away thy wool-basket, thy web, and thy devotion to busy Minerva, so soon as radiant Liparean Hebrus has bathed his well-anointed shoulders in Tiber's flood, a rider better even than Bellerophon, never defeated for fault of fist or foot, clever too to spear the stags flying in startled herd over the open plain, and quick to meet the wild boar lurking in the thick-set copse.

XIII

O fons Bandvsiae, splendidior vitro,
dulci digne mero non sine floribus,
    cras donaberis haedo,
        cui frons turgida cornibus

primis et venerem et proelia destinat.
frustra : nam gelidos inficiet tibi
    rubro sanguine rivos
        lascivi suboles gregis.

te flagrantis atrox hora Caniculae
nescit tangere, tu frigus amabile   10
    fessis vomere tauris
        praebes et pecori vago.

fies nobilium tu quoque fontium,
me dicente cavis impositam ilicem
    saxis, unde loquaces
        lymphae desiliunt tuae.

ODE XIII

To the Fountain Bandusia

O FOUNT BANDUSIA, brighter than crystal, worthy of sweet wine and flowers, to-morrow shalt thou be honoured with a firstling of the flock whose brow, with horns just budding, foretokens love and strife. Alas! in vain; for this offspring of the sportive flock shall dye thy cool waters with its own red blood. Thee the fierce season of the blazing dog-star cannot touch; to bullocks wearied of the ploughshare and to the roaming flock thou dost offer gracious coolness. Thou, too, shalt be numbered among the far-famed fountains, through the song I sing of the oak planted o'er the grotto whence thy babbling waters leap.

XIV

HERCVLIS ritu modo dictus, o plebs,
morte venalem petiisse laurum
Caesar Hispana repetit penates
    victor ab ora.

unico gaudens mulier marito
prodeat iustis operata divis
et soror clari ducis et decorae
    supplice vitta

virginum matres iuvenumque nuper
sospitum.   vos, o pueri et puellae   10
non virum expertae,[1] maleominatis [2]
    parcite verbis.

hic dies vere mihi festus atras
eximet curas; ego nec tumultum
nec mori per vim metuam tenente
    Caesare terras.

i, pete unguentum, puer, et coronas
et cadum Marsi memorem duelli,
Spartacum siqua potuit vagantem
    fallere testa.   20

[1] iam-expertae, *MSS.* non *Bentley ;* iam virum expertes,
Cuningham.
[2] male nominatis *most MSS.*

226

ODE XIV

The Return of Augustus

CAESAR, O citizens, who but now was said, like Hercules, to be in quest of the laurel purchased at the price of death, rejoins again his household gods, victoriously returning from the Spanish shore. Rejoicing in her peerless husband, let his consort, after offering sacrifice to the righteous gods, now advance, and the sister of our famous chief, and, with suppliant fillet decked, mothers of maids and sons just saved.

Do ye, O lads and maidens not yet wedded, refrain from ill-omened words! This day for me shall be truly festal and shall take away black cares. Neither civil strife nor death by violence will I fear, while Caesar holds the earth.

Go seek perfumes, lad, and garlands, and a jar that remembers the Marsian War, if a single one in any way hath been able to escape the roving Spartacus! Also

dic et argutae properet Neaerae
murreum nodo cohibere crinem ;
si per invisum mora ianitorem
    fiet, abito.

lenit albescens animos capillus
litium et rixae cupidos protervae ;
non ego hoc ferrem calidus iuventa
    consule Planco.

bid clear-voiced Neaera to make haste and fasten in a knot her chestnut locks!   If delay be caused by the hateful door-keeper, come away! My whitening hair softens a spirit prone to strife and wanton brawling; I had not brooked such insult when hot with youth in Plancus' consulship.

XV

Vxor pauperis Ibyci,
  tandem nequitiae fige modum tuae
famosisque laboribus;
  maturo propior desine funeri

inter ludere virgines
  et stellis nebulam spargere candidis.
non, si quid Pholoen, satis
  et te, Chlori, decet: filia rectius

expugnat iuvenum domos,
  pulso Thyias uti concita tympano.   10
illam cogit amor Nothi
  lascivae similem ludere capreae;

te lanae prope nobilem
  tonsae Luceriam, non citharae decent
nec flos purpureus rosae
  nec poti vetulam faece tenus cadi.

ODE XV

Old and Young

O WIFE of humble Ibycus, put an end at length to thy wantonness and thy disreputable arts! Since thou art nearing the fitting time for death, cease to sport among the maidens and to cast a cloud over the shining stars! What becomes Pholoë does not quite become thee also, Chloris. 'Tis fitter for thy daughter to storm the homes of gallants, like some Bacchanal roused by the beating drum. She, for love of Nothus, is forced to gambol like a sportive doe. The wool shorn near famed Luceria is meet for thee, not the lyre nor the dark red blossom of the rose, nor wine-jars drained to their dregs, old beldame that thou art!

XVI

Inclvsam Danaën turris aënea
robustaeque fores et vigilum canum
tristes excubiae munierant satis
    nocturnis ab adulteris,

si non Acrisium virginis abditae
custodem pavidum Iuppiter et Venus
risissent : fore enim tutum iter et patens
    converso in pretium deo.

aurum per medios ire satellites
et perrumpere amat saxa, potentius   10
ictu fulmineo : concidit auguris
    Argivi domus, ob lucrum

demersa exitio ; diffidit urbium
portas vir Macedo et subruit aemulos
reges muneribus ; munera navium
    saevos inlaqueant duces.

crescentem sequitur cura pecuniam
maiorumque fames.   iure perhorrui
late conspicuum tollere verticem,
    Maecenas, equitum decus.   20

ODES BOOK III

ODE XVI

Contentment

TOWER of bronze, doors of oak, and the strict guard of watch-dogs had quite protected imprisoned Danaë from nocturnal lovers, had not Jupiter and Venus laughed at Acrisius, anxious keeper of the hidden maiden. For they knew that the way would be safe and open, when the god had turned to gold. Gold loves to make its way through the midst of sentinels and to break through rocks, for 'tis mightier than the thunderbolt. 'Twas for the sake of gain that the house of the Argive prophet plunged to destruction and fell in ruins. 'Twas by gifts of gold that the Macedonian burst open gates of cities and overthrew rival kings; gifts ensnare bluff admirals, too. Yet as money grows, care and greed for greater riches follow after. With reason did I shrink from raising my head to be seen afar, Maecenas, thou glory of the equestrian

233

quanto quisque sibi plura negaverit,
ab dis plura feret : nil cupientium
nudus castra peto et transfuga divitum
    partes linquere gestio,

contemptae dominus splendidior rei,
quam si, quidquid arat impiger Apulus,
occultare meis dicerer horreis,
    magnas inter opes inops.

purae rivus aquae silvaque iugerum
paucorum et segetis certa fides meae   30
fulgentem imperio fertilis Africae
    fallit sorte beatior.

quamquam nec Calabrae mella ferunt apes,
nec Laestrygonia Bacchus in amphora
languescit mihi, nec pinguia Gallicis
    crescunt vellera pascuis :

importuna tamen pauperies abest,
nec si plura velim tu dare deneges.
contracto melius parva cupidine
    vectigalia porrigam,   40

quam si Mygdoniis regnum Alyattei
campis continuem.   multa petentibus
desunt multa ; bene est, cui deus obtulit
    parca quod satis est manu.

rank. The more a man denies himself, so much the more will he receive from the gods. Destitute myself, I seek the camp of those desiring naught, and, a renegade, am eager to leave the side of the rich, a more glorious master of the wealth I spurn than were I said to hide within my barns the produce of all the acres that the sturdy Apulian ploughs, a beggar in the midst of mighty wealth. My stream of pure water, my woodland of few acres, and sure trust in my crop of corn bring me more blessing than the lot of the dazzling lord of fertile Africa, though he know it not. Though neither Calabrian bees bring me honey, nor wine lies mellowing for me in Laestrygonian jar, nor thick fleeces are waxing for me in Gallic pastures, yet distressing poverty is absent; nor, did I wish more, wouldst thou refuse to grant it. By narrowing my desires I shall better enlarge my scanty revenues than were I to make the realm of Alyattes continuous with the Mygdonian plains. To those who seek for much, much is ever lacking; blest is he to whom the god with chary hand has given just enough.

XVII

Aeli vetusto nobilis ab Lamo,
quando et priores hinc Lamias ferunt
   denominatos et nepotum
     per memores genus omne fastos;

auctore ab illo ducis originem,
qui Formiarum moenia dicitur
   princeps et innantem Maricae
     litoribus tenuisse Lirim,

late tyrannus.   cras foliis nemus
multis et alga litus inutili   10
   demissa tempestas ab Euro
     sternet, aquae nisi fallit augur

annosa cornix.   dum potes, aridum
compone lignum; cras Genium mero
   curabis et porco bimenstri
     cum famulis operum solutis.

ODE XVII

Prepare for a Rainy Morrow!

O AELIUS, famed scion of ancient Lamus (since from him, they say, were named the Lamiae of old, and the whole line of their descendants through all recorded history), you draw your blood from him as founder who first is said to have held the walls of Formiae and the Liris where it floods Marica's shores, possessing lordship far and wide. To-morrow a tempest, from the East let loose, shall strew with many leaves the grove, and the shore with useless seaweed, unless the ancient raven, prophet of rain, this time prove false. Pile up dry fagots, while you may! To-morrow, attended by your household slaves from tasks released, cheer your soul with unmixed wine and a pig but two months old!

XVIII

Favne, Nympharum fugientum amator,
per meos fines et aprica rura
lenis incedas abeasque parvis
    aequus alumnis,

si tener pleno cadit haedus anno,
larga nec desunt Veneris sodali
vina craterae, vetus ara multo
    fumat odore.

ludit herboso pecus omne campo,
cum tibi nonae redeunt Decembres;   10
festus in pratis vacat otioso
    cum bove pagus;

inter audaces lupus errat agnos;
spargit agrestis tibi silva frondes;
gaudet invisam pepulisse fossor
    ter pede terram.

ODE XVIII

Thy Blessing, Faunus!

O Faunus, lover of the flying nymphs, with kindly
purpose mayst thou pass across my boundaries and
my sunny fields, and in thy going be propitious to the
young offspring of the flocks, if at the year's full tide
a tender kid falls sacrifice to thee and generous meed
of wine fails not the mixing bowl, comrade of Venus,
and the ancient altar smokes with store of incense.
All the flock gambols o'er the grassy field whene'er
December's Nones come round for thee; in festal
garb the country folk make holiday amid the meads,
along with resting steers; the wolf saunters among
lambs that know no fear; in thy honour the forest
sheds its woodland foliage; and the delver delights
in triple measure with his foot to beat the hated
ground.

XIX

QVANTVM distet ab Inacho
  Codrus pro patria non timidus mori
narras et genus Aeaci
  et pugnata sacro bella sub Ilio;

quo Chium pretio cadum
  mercemur, quis aquam temperet ignibus,
quo praebente domum et quota
  Paelignis caream frigoribus, taces.

da lunae propere novae,
  da noctis mediae, da, puer, auguris   10
Murenae: tribus aut novem
  miscentur cyathis pocula commodis.

qui Musas amat impares,
  ternos ter cyathos attonitus petet
vates; tres prohibet supra
  rixarum metuens tangere Gratia

nudis iuncta sororibus.
  insanire iuvat: cur Berecyntiae
cessant flamina tibiae?
  cur pendet tacita fistula cum lyra?   20

ODE XIX

Invitation to a Drinking-Bout

You tell how far removed in time from Inachus was Codrus, who feared not death for fatherland, and you detail the line of Aeacus and the wars waged beneath the walls of sacred Ilium; but you say not what price we shall pay for a jar of Chian wine, who with his fire shall heat the water, under whose roof and at what hour I am to escape the Paelignian cold.

A health without delay, my lad, to the new moon, to midnight, to Murena's augurship! With three cyathi, or with nine, as may be fitting, the draught is mixed! The rapt bard that loves the Muses of unequal number shall ask for cyathi three times three. The Grace hand in hand with her sisters nude, shrinking from brawls, forbids us to touch more than three. To revel madly is my delight. Why pause the measures of the Berecyntian flute? Why idly hangs the pipe beside the silent lyre?

parcentes ego dexteras
   odi : sparge rosas ; audiat invidus
dementem strepitum Lycus
   et vicina seni non habilis Lyco.

spissa te nitidum coma,
   puro te similem, Telephe, vespero
tempestiva petit Rhode ;
   me lentus Glycerae torret amor meae.

Hands that hold back, I hate. Fling round the roses! Let jealous Lycus hear our mad uproar, and the maid that dwells hard by, for aged Lycus not well-suited! Thee, glistening with thy clustering locks, O Telephus, like to the clear evening star, ripe Rhode seeks; myself a lingering love for my own Glycera burns.

XX

Non vides, quanto moveas periclo,
Pyrrhe, Gaetulae catulos leaenae?
dura post paulo fugies inaudax
   proelia raptor,

cum per obstantes iuvenum catervas
ibit insignem repetens Nearchum:
grande certamen, tibi praeda cedat,
   maior an illi.

interim, dum tu celeres sagittas
promis, haec dentes acuit timendos,   10
arbiter pugnae posuisse nudo
   sub pede palmam

fertur et leni recreare vento
sparsum odoratis umerum capillis,
qualis aut Nircus fuit aut aquosa
   raptus ab Ida.

ODES BOOK III

ODE XX

The Rivals

Seest thou not, Pyrrhus, at how great risk thou touchest the whelps of the Gaetulian lioness? Soon thou shalt shun fierce combats, a robber without spirit, when through the opposing crowd of youths she goes in quest of peerless Nearchus. Then great will be the struggle whether the prize is to fall to thee or rather to her. Meantime, as thou drawest thy swift arrows, and she is sharpening her dreadful teeth, the arbiter of the battle is said to have trampled the palm beneath his bare foot, and in the gentle breeze to be cooling his shoulders covered with perfumed locks, like unto Nireus or him that was carried off from many-fountained Ida.

XXI

O NATA mecum consule Manlio,
seu tu querellas sive geris iocos
 seu rixam et insanos amores
  seu facilem, pia testa, somnum,

quocumque lectum nomine Massicum
servas, moveri digna bono die,
 descende Corvino iubente
  promere languidiora vina.

non ille, quamquam Socraticis madet
sermonibus, te negleget horridus: 10
 narratur et prisci Catonis
  saepe mero caluisse virtus.

tu lene tormentum ingenio admoves
plerumque duro; tu sapientium
 curas et arcanum iocoso
  consilium retegis Lyaeo;

tu spem reducis mentibus anxiis
viresque et addis cornua pauperi,
 post te neque iratos trementi
  regum apices neque militum arma. 20

te Liber et si laeta aderit Venus
segnesque nodum solvere Gratiae
 vivaeque producent lucernae,
  dum rediens fugat astra Phoebus.

ODE XXI

In Praise of Wine

Thou faithful jar, born with me in Manlius' consulship, whether thou bringest lovers' plaints, or mirth,
or mad love and quarrels, or soft slumber—for whatever end was gathered the Massic that thou guardest,
fit to be brought out on some auspicious day—descend, since Corvinus gives the order to fetch forth a
mellower wine! Steeped though he be in Socratic
lore, he will not churlishly despise thee. Virtuous
old Cato, even, is said often to have warmed with
wine.

Pleasant compulsion dost thou apply to wits whose
wont is dullness; thou unlockest the thoughts of the
wise and their secret purpose by merry Bacchus'
spell; thou restorest hope to hearts distressed, and
addest power and courage to the poor man, who after
thee trembles not at the crowns of angry kings or
soldiers' weapons. Thee Liber and Venus, if she
lend her gracious presence, and the Graces, loth to
break their bond, and the burning lamps shall attend,
till returning Phoebus puts to flight the stars.

XXII

MONTIVM custos nemorumque, Virgo,
quae laborantes utero puellas
ter vocata audis adimisque leto,
    diva triformis,

imminens villae tua pinus esto,
quam per exactos ego laetus annos
verris obliquum meditantis ictum
    sanguine donem.

ODE XXII

Dedication of a Pine Tree to Diana

O MAIDEN goddess, guardian of hill and grove, thou that, thrice invoked, givest ear to young mothers when in travail and rescuest them from death, goddess of the triple form, thine be the pine that overhangs my dwelling, that gladly through the passing years I may offer to it the blood of a boar practising its first side-long thrusts!

XXIII

CAELO supinas si tuleris manus
nascente luna, rustica Phidyle,
   si ture placaris et horna
      fruge Lares avidaque porca:

nec pestilentem sentiet Africum
fecunda vitis nec sterilem seges
   robiginem aut dulces alumni
      pomifero grave tempus anno.

nam quae nivali pascitur Algido
devota quercus inter et ilices   10
   aut crescit Albanis in herbis
      victima, pontificum securis

cervice tinguet: te nihil attinet
temptare multa caede bidentium
   parvos coronantem marino
      rore deos fragilique myrto.

immunis aram si tetigit manus,
non sumptuosa blandior hostia,
   mollivit aversos Penates
      farre pio et saliente mica.   20

ODE XXIII

The Gods Love the Giver rather than the Gift

IF thou raise thy upturned palms to heaven each time the moon is born anew, O Phidyle, my country lass, if with incense, with grain of this year's harvest, and with a greedy swine thou appease the Lares, then thy teeming vine shall not feel the south wind's ravages, nor thy crop the barren blight, nor the young offspring of the flock the sickly season when autumn yields its fruits. For the destined victim that is grazing on snowy Algidus amid the oaks and ilexes, or is waxing fat on the Alban grass, shall dye the axes of the priests with its neck's blood. For thee there is no need to importune the gods with much sacrifice of sheep, if thou but crown their tiny images with rosemary and crisp myrtle. If pure hands have touched the altar, though commended by no costly victim, they appease estranged Penates even by sacred meal mingled with crackling salt.

CARMINVM LIBER III

XXIV

Intactis opulentior
  thesauris Arabum et divitis Indiae
caementis licet occupes
  terrenum[1] omne tuis et mare publicum;[2]

si figit adamantinos
  summis verticibus dira Necessitas
clavos, non animum metu,
  non mortis laqueis expedies caput.

campestres melius Scythae,
  quorum plaustra vagas rite trahunt domos, 10
vivunt et rigidi Getae,
  immetata quibus iugera liberas

fruges et Cererem ferunt,
  nec cultura placet longior annua,
defunctumque laboribus
  aequali recreat sorte vicarius.

illic matre carentibus
  privignis mulier temperat innocens,
nec dotata regit virum
  coniunx nec nitido fidit adultero.   20

[1] MSS. Tirrenum or Tyrrenum. *Lachmann reads* terrenum,
following Porphyrion's comment "non terram tantum . . .
occupantum."
[2] *So MSS.: less good ones* Ponticum *or* Apulicum:
the acceptance of Lachmann's conjecture involves reading
publicum.

252

ODE XXIV

The Curse of Mammon

THOUGH thou be richer than the unrifled treasuries of the Arabs or rich India, and with thy palaces encroach on all the land and the public sea, if dire Necessity plant her nails of adamant in thy topmost roof, thou shalt not free thy soul from fear nor thy head from the snare of Death. Far better live the Scythians of the steppes, whose wagons haul their homes from place to place, as is their wont; far better live the Getae stern, whose unallotted acres bring forth fruits and corn for all in common; nor with them is tillage binding longer than a year; another then on like conditions takes the place of him whose task is done.

There, matrons spare children of their mother reft, nor do them harm, nor does the dowered wife rule o'er her husband or put faith in dazzling paramour.

dos est magna parentium
  virtus et metuens alterius viri
certo foedere castitas,
  et peccare nefas aut pretium est mori.

o quisquis volet impias
  caedes et rabiem tollere civicam,
si quaeret " Pater urbium "
  subscribi statuis, indomitam audeat

refrenare licentiam,
  clarus postgenitis : quatenus, heu nefas,   30
virtutem incolumem odimus,
  sublatam ex oculis quaerimus, invidi.

quid tristes querimoniae,
  si non supplicio culpa reciditur ?
quid leges sine moribus
  vanae proficiunt ? si neque fervidis

pars inclusa caloribus
  mundi nec Boreae finitimum latus
durataeque solo nives
  mercatorem abigunt, horrida callidi   40

vincunt aequora navitae,
  magnum pauperies opprobrium iubet
quidvis et facere et pati,
  virtutisque viam deserit arduae.

Their noble dower is parents' worth and chastity
that shrinks in steadfast loyalty from the husband of
another. To sin is an abomination; or if they sin,
the penalty is death.

Whoe'er will banish impious slaughter and intes-
tine fury, whoe'er shall seek to have inscribed upon
his statues, "Father of Cities," let such have courage
to curb our lawless licence, and so win fame among
the men of after times; since we (alas, the shame!),
with envy filled, hate Virtue while it lives and
mourn it only when snatched from sight.

Of what avail are dismal lamentations, if wrong is
not repressed by penalties? Of what avail are empty
laws, if we lack principle; if neither the regions of
the world enclosed by burning heats nor the regions
near the North with snow hard-frozen on the ground
keep off the trader; if our skilful seamen outride
the stormy waves; and poverty, deemed a base re-
proach, bids us do all, suffer all, and quits the steep
path of Virtue?

vel nos in Capitolium,
  quo clamor vocat et turba faventium,
vel nos in mare proximum
  gemmas et lapides aurum et inutile,

summi materiem mali,
  mittamus, scelerum si bene paenitet.   50
eradenda cupidinis
  pravi sunt elementa et tenerae nimis

mentes asperioribus
  formandae studiis.   nescit equo rudis
haerere ingenuus puer
  venarique timet, ludere doctior,

seu Graeco iubeas trocho,
  seu malis vetita legibus alea,
cum periura patris fides
  consortem socium fallat et hospites   60

indignoque pecuniam
  heredi properet.   scilicet improbae
crescunt divitiae ; tamen
  curtae nescio quid semper abest rei.

To the Capitol, amid the plaudits of the noisy
crowd, or to the nearest sea let us send our gems
and jewels and our baneful gold, the cause of our
chiefest woe, if we repent us truly of our crimes.
Destroy the causes of our perverted greed, and let our
too feeble hearts be trained in sterner tasks! The
freeborn lad, unpractised, knows not how to ride his
steed; he fears to hunt, more skilled in games,
whether you bid him try with Grecian hoop or
rather with the dice the law forbids; while his perjured father defrauds his partner and his friends, and
hastens to lay up store of money for his unworthy
heir. His gains, ill-gotten, grow apace, 'tis true, yet
something is ever lacking to the fortune incomplete.

XXV

Qvo me, Bacche, rapis tui
  plenum? quae nemora aut quos agor in specus,
velox mente nova? quibus
  antris egregii Caesaris audiar

aeternum meditans decus
  stellis inserere et consilio Iovis?
dicam insigne, recens, adhuc
  indictum ore alio. non secus in iugis

exsomnis stupet Euhias,
  Hebrum prospiciens et nive candidam   10
Thracen ac pede barbaro
  lustratam Rhodopen, ut mihi devio

ripas et vacuum nemus
  mirari libet. o Naiadum potens
Baccharumque valentium
  proceras manibus vertere fraxinos,

nil parvum aut humili modo,
  nil mortale loquar. dulce periculum est,
o Lenaee, sequi deum
  cingentem viridi tempora pampino.   20

258

ODE XXV

A Dithyramb

WHITHER, O Bacchus, dost thou hurry me, o'erflowing with thy power? Into what groves or grottoes am I swiftly driven in fresh inspiration? In what caves shall I be heard planning to set amid the stars, and in Jove's council, peerless Caesar's immortal glory? I will sing of a noble exploit, recent, as yet untold by other lips. Just so upon the mountain-tops does the sleepless Bacchanal stand rapt, looking out o'er Hebrus and o'er Thrace glistening with snow, and Rhodope trodden by barbarian feet—even as I love to stray and to gaze with awe upon the unfrequented banks and groves.

O thou master of the Naiads and of the Bacchanals that have might to uproot lofty ash-trees with their hands, nothing trifling or of humble strain, nothing mortal will I utter. Sweet is the peril, O lord of the wine-press, to follow the god, crowning my temples with verdant vine-sprays.

XXVI

Vixi Puellis nuper idoneus
et militavi non sine gloria ;
    nunc arma defunctumque bello
      barbiton hic paries habebit,

laevum marinae qui Veneris latus
custodit. hic, hic ponite lucida
    funalia et vectes securesque [1]
      oppositis foribus minaces.

o quae beatam diva tenes Cyprum et
Memphin carentem Sithonia nive,   10
    regina, sublimi flagello
      tange Chloen semel arrogantem.

[1] securesque *Bentley :* et arcus *MSS.*

ODE XXVI

Love's Triumphs are Ended

TILL recently I lived fit for Love's battles and served not without renown. Now this wall that guards the left side of sea-born Venus shall have my weapons and the lyre that has done with wars. Here, O here, offer up the shining tapers and the levers and the axes that threaten opposing doors!

O goddess queen that holdest wealthy Cyprus and Memphis, free from Thracian snows, touch with thine uplifted lash, if only once, the haughty Chloë!

XXVII

Impios parrae recinentis omen
ducat et praegnas canis aut ab agro
rava decurrens lupa Lanuvino
    fetaque volpes;

rumpat et serpens iter institutum,
si per obliquum similis sagittae
terruit mannos: ego cui timebo,
    providus auspex,

antequam stantes repetat paludes
imbrium divina avis imminentum,   10
oscinem corvum prece suscitabo
    solis ab ortu.

sis licet felix, ubicumque mavis,
et memor nostri, Galatea, vivas;
teque nec laevus vetet ire picus
    nec vaga cornix.

sed vides, quanto trepidet tumultu
pronus Orion. ego quid sit ater
Hadriae novi sinus et quid albus
    peccet Iapyx.   20

ODE XXVII

Bon voyage!

MAY the wicked be guided by the omen of a scream-
ing lapwing and a pregnant dog or a red she-wolf
racing down from the Lanuvian fields, or a fox that
has just brought forth! May a serpent break
the journey they have begun, when, darting like
an arrow athwart the road, it has terrified the
ponies! But for whom I, as a prophetic augur,
cherish fear, for him will I rouse the singing raven
from the east with my entreaties, before the bird
that forebodes threatening showers re-seeks the
standing pools.

Mayst thou be happy, Galatea, wherever thou
preferrest to abide, and mayst thou live with
memories of me; nor may any woodpecker on the
left or any roving crow forbid thy going! But
thou seest with how great tumult sinking Orion
rages. Full well I know what Hadria's black gulf
can be and what the sins of clear Iapyx. May the

hostium uxores puerique caecos
sentiant motus orientis Austri et
aequoris nigri fremitum et trementes
    verbere ripas.

sic et Europe niveum doloso
credidit tauro latus et scatentem
beluis pontum mediasque fraudes
    palluit audax.

nuper in pratis studiosa florum et
debitae Nymphis opifex coronae   30
nocte sublustri nihil astra praeter
    vidit et undas.

quae simul centum tetigit potentem
oppidis Creten, "pater, o relictum
filiae nomen pietasque" dixit
    "victa furore.

unde quo veni? levis una mors est
virginum culpae. vigilansne ploro
turpe commissum an vitiis carentem
    ludit imago,   40

vana quae porta fugiens eburna
somnium ducit? meliusne fluctus
ire per longos fuit an recentes
    carpere flores?

wives and children of our foes be the ones to feel the blind onset of rising Auster and the roaring of the darkling sea, and the shores quivering with the shock!

So did Europa, too, entrust her snowy form to the treacherous bull and turn pale before the deep alive with monsters, and at the peril of mid-sea—she who before had been so bold. Erstwhile among the meadows, absorbed in flowers, and weaving a garland due the Nymphs, now she beheld naught in the glimmering night except the stars and waves. Soon as she touched Crete, mighty with its hundred cities, "O father," she exclaimed, "O name of daughter, that I forsook, and filial duty, by frenzy overmastered! Whence have I come and whither? A single death is too light for maidens' faults. Am I awake and do I lament a hideous deed, or am I free from sin and does some phantom mock me, that flying idly through the ivory gate, brings but a dream? Was it better to travel o'er the long waves, or to pluck fresh flowers? If anyone would now but

si quis infamem mihi nunc iuvencum
dedat iratae, lacerare ferro et
frangere enitar modo multum amati
    cornua monstri.

impudens liqui patrios Penates,
impudens Orcum moror.　o deorum   50
si quis haec audis, utinam inter errem
    nuda leones!

antequam turpis macies decentes
occupet malas teneraeque sucus
defluat praedae, speciosa quaero
    pascere tigris.

' vilis Europe,' pater urget absens:
' quid mori cessas?　potes hac ab orno
pendulum zona bene te secuta
    laedere collum.   60

sive te rupes et acuta leto
saxa delectant, age te procellae
crede veloci, nisi erile mavis
    carpere pensum

regius sanguis dominaeque tradi
barbarae paelex.' "　aderat querenti
perfidum ridens Venus et remisso
    filius arcu.

deliver the infamous bullock to my anger, I would strive to rend it with the steel and break the horns of the monstrous creature just now so fondly loved. Shameless, I left my household gods; shameless, I keep Orcus waiting. Oh, if any god hear these laments, let me wander naked among lions! Before hideous wasting seizes upon my comely cheeks and the fresh life-blood departs from the tender victim, while beauteous still, I seek to feed the tigers. 'Worthless Europa,' my father, though far distant, urges, 'why dost thou hesitate to die? On this ash thou canst hang thyself with the girdle that happily has followed thee. Or if the cliffs and rocks sharp for death allure thee, come! give thy body to the hurrying gale, if thou wilt not rather card a mistress' wool, thou of royal blood, and be given o'er, a concubine, to the mercies of some barbarian queen!'"

As she thus complained, Venus with treacherous laugh stood by, and her son with unstrung bow. Soon

mox ubi lusit satis, "abstineto"
dixit "irarum calidaeque rixae,   70
cum tibi invisus laceranda reddet
    cornua taurus.

uxor invicti Iovis esse nescis.
mitte singultus, bene ferre magnam
disce fortunam ; tua sectus orbis
    nomina ducet."

when the goddess had had sport enough, "Refrain from anger and hot passion," she exclaimed, "when the hated bull shall give thee his horns to be mangled! Thou knowest not that thou art the wife of Jove invincible. Cease thy sobs! Learn to bear becomingly thy great destiny! A region of the earth shall take thy name."

XXVIII

FESTO quid potius die
  Neptuni faciam ?   prome reconditum,
Lyde, strenua Caecubum
  munitaeque adhibe vim sapientiae.

inclinare meridiem
  sentis ac, veluti stet volucris dies,
parcis deripere horreo
  cessantem Bibuli consulis amphoram.

nos cantabimus invicem
  Neptunum et virides Nereidum comas ;   10
tu curva recines lyra
  Latonam et celeris spicula Cynthiae ;

summo carmine, quae Cnidon
  fulgentesque tenet Cycladas et Paphum
iunctis visit oloribus ;
  dicetur merita Nox quoque nenia.

ODE XXVIII

In Neptune's Honour

WHAT better could I do on Neptune's festal day? Nimbly bring forth, O Lyde, the Caecuban stored away, and make assault on wisdom's stronghold! Thou seest the day is waning, and yet, as though the fleeting hours were standing still, thou delayest to bring from out the store-room a waiting jar that dates from Bibulus' consulship.

In responsive song we will sing, I of Neptune and the Nereids' sea-green tresses. Thou, in answer, on thy curving lyre shalt hymn Latona and the shafts of swift-moving Cynthia; and in final song her who holds Cnidos and the shining Cyclades, and visits Paphos with her team of swans. Night also shall be celebrated with a fitting lay.

XXIX

Tyrrhena regum progenies, tibi
non ante verso lene merum cado
    cum flore, Maecenas, rosarum et
        pressa tuis balanus capillis

iam dudum apud me est : eripe te morae,
ne semper udum Tibur et Aefulae
    declive contempleris arvum et
        Telegoni iuga parricidae.

fastidiosam desere copiam et
molem propinquam nubibus arduis,   10
    omitte mirari beatae
        fumum et opes strepitumque Romae.

plerumque gratae divitibus vices
mundaeque parvo sub lare pauperum
    cenae sine aulacis et ostro
        sollicitam explicuere frontem.

iam clarus occultum Andromedae pater
ostendit ignem, iam Procyon furit
    et stella vesani Leonis
        sole dies referente siccos ;   20

ODES BOOK III

ODE XXIX

A Clear Conscience Makes Us Superior to Fortune

MAECENAS, scion of Tuscan kings, a jar of mellow wine as yet untouched has long been waiting for thee at my house, along with roses and balsam for thy locks expressed. Delay no more! Gaze not ever at well-watered Tibur and the sloping fields of Aefula and the heights of Telegonus, the parricide! Abandon cloying luxury and the pile that towers to the lofty clouds! Cease to wonder at the smoke, the riches, and the din of wealthy Rome! Often a change is pleasant to the rich, and a simple meal beneath the poor man's humble roof, without tapestries and purple, has smoothed the wrinkles on the care-worn brow.

Already Andromeda's shining father reveals his hidden fires; already Procyon rages and the star of furious Leo, as the sun brings back the days of drought. Now with his listless flock the weary

iam pastor umbras cum grege languido
rivumque fessus quaerit et horridi
    dumeta Silvani, caretque
        ripa vagis taciturna ventis.

tu civitatem quis deceat status
curas et urbi sollicitus times,
    quid Seres et regnata Cyro
        Bactra parent Tanaisque discors.

prudens futuri temporis exitum
caliginosa nocte premit deus,   30
    ridetque si mortalis ultra
        fas trepidat.   quod adest memento

componere aequus; cetera fluminis
ritu feruntur, nunc medio alveo
    cum pace delabentis Etruscum
        in mare, nunc lapides adesos

stirpesque raptas et pecus et domos
volventis una non sine montium
    clamore vicinaeque silvae,
        cum fera diluvies quietos   40

inritat amnes. ille potens sui
laetusque deget, cui licet in diem
    dixisse " vixi : cras vel atra
        nube polum pater occupato

shepherd seeks the shade and stream and shaggy
Silvanus' thickets, and the silent bank is forsaken by
the straying breeze.

Thy thoughts are set on what conditions fit the
State; anxious art thou for the City, fearing what
the Seres may be plotting, or Bactra once ruled by
Cyrus, and the discordant tribes on Tanais' banks.
With wise purpose does the god bury in the shades of
night the future's outcome, and laughs if mortals be
anxious beyond due limits. Remember to settle
with tranquil heart the problem of the hour! All
else is borne along like some river, now gliding
peacefully in mid-channel into the Tuscan Sea, now
rolling polished stones, uprooted trees, and flocks
and homes together, with echoing of the hills and
neighbouring woods, while the wild deluge stirs up
the peaceful streams.

Master of himself and joyful will that man live
who day by day can say: "I have lived to-day;
to-morrow let the Father fill the heaven with murky

vel sole puro ; non tamen irritum,
quodcumque retro est, efficiet, neque
   diffinget infectumque reddet,
     quod fugiens semel hora vexit.

Fortuna saevo laeta negotio et
ludum insolentem ludere pertinax   50
   transmutat incertos honores,
     nunc mihi, nunc alii benigna.

laudo manentem ; si celeres quatit
pinnas, resigno quae dedit et mea
   virtute me involvo probamque
     Pauperiem sine dote quaero.

non est meum, si mugiat Africis
malus procellis, ad miseras preces
   decurrere et votis pacisci,
     ne Cypriae Tyriaeque merces   60

addant avaro divitias mari :
tum me biremis praesidio scaphae
   tutum per Aegaeos tumultus
     aura feret geminusque Pollux."

clouds, or radiant sunshine ! Yet will he not render vain whatever now is past, nor will he alter and undo what once the fleeting hour has brought. Fortune, exulting in her cruel work, and stubborn to pursue her wanton sport, shifts her fickle favours, kind now to me, now to some other. I praise her while she stays ; but if she shake her wings for flight, I renounce her gifts, enwrap me in my virtue, and woo honest Poverty, undowered though she be. Not mine, when masts are groaning with the Afric gales, to have recourse to wretched prayers and with vows to strike a compact with the gods that my Cyprian and my Tyrian wares shall not add new riches to the devouring sea. Then the breezes and Pollux with his brother shall bear me through the tempests of the Aegean main, safely protected in my two-oared skiff."

XXX

Exegi monumentum aere perennius
regalique situ pyramidum altius,
quod non imber edax, non Aquilo impotens
possit diruere aut innumerabilis
annorum series et fuga temporum.
non omnis moriar multaque pars mei
vitabit Libitinam : usque ego postera
crescam laude recens.   dum Capitolium
scandet cum tacita virgine pontifex,
dicar, qua violens obstrepit Aufidus   10
et qua pauper aquae Daunus agrestium
regnavit populorum, ex humili potens
princeps Aeolium carmen ad Italos
deduxisse modos.   sume superbiam
quaesitam meritis et mihi Delphica
lauro cinge volens, Melpomene, comam.

ODE XXX

The Poet's Immortal Fame

I HAVE finished a monument more lasting than bronze and loftier than the Pyramids' royal pile, one that no wasting rain, no furious north wind can destroy, or the countless chain of years and the ages' flight. I shall not altogether die, but a mighty part of me shall escape the death-goddess. On and on shall I grow, ever fresh with the glory of after time. So long as the Pontiff climbs the Capitol with the silent Vestal, I, risen high from low estate, where wild Aufidus thunders and where Daunus in a parched land once ruled o'er a peasant folk, shall be famed for having been the first to adapt Aeolian song to Italian verse. Accept the proud honour won by thy merits, Melpomene, and graciously crown my locks with Delphic bays.

BOOK IV

LIBER IV

I

Intermissa, Venus, diu
    rursus bella moves.   parce, precor, precor.
non sum qualis eram bonae
    sub regno Cinarae.   desine, dulcium

mater saeva Cupidinum,
    circa lustra decem flectere mollibus
iam durum imperiis : abi,
    quo blandae iuvenum te revocant preces.

tempestivius in domum
    Pauli, purpureis ales oloribus,   10
comissabere Maximi,
    si torrere iecur quaeris idoneum.

namque et nobilis et decens
    et pro sollicitis non tacitus reis
et centum puer artium
    late signa feret militiae tuae;

BOOK IV

ODE I

Venus, Forbear!

THE contests long suspended thou, Venus, wouldst renew. Be merciful, I beg, I beg! I am not as I was under the sway of kindly Cinara. O cruel mother of sweet Cupids, strive no more to bend, when near fifty years are past, one now callous to thy soft commands! Hie thee rather to the place where the persuasive prayers of young men call. More suitably, borne by thy gleaming swans, shalt thou haste in joyous revelry to the house of Paulus Maximus, if thou dost seek to kindle a fitting heart. For noble is he and comely, an eloquent defender of anxious clients, a youth accomplished in a hundred arts; and he will bear the standard of thy service far and wide. And when prevailing

283

et quandoque potentior
  largi muneribus riserit aemuli,
Albanos prope te lacus
  ponet marmoream sub trabe citrea.   20

illic plurima naribus
  duces tura lyraeque et Berecyntiae
delectabere tibiae
  mixtis carminibus non sine fistula;

illic bis pueri die
  numen cum teneris virginibus tuum
laudantes pede candido
  in morem Salium ter quatient humum.

me nec femina nec puer
  iam nec spes animi credula mutui   30
nec certare iuvat mero
  nec vincire novis tempora floribus.

sed cur heu, Ligurine, cur
  manat rara meas lacrima per genas?
cur facunda parum decoro
  inter verba cadit lingua silentio?

nocturnis ego somniis
  iam captum teneo, iam volucrem sequor
te per gramina Martii
  Campi, te per aquas, dure, volubilis.   40

o'er the gifts of some lavish rival he shall laugh in triumph, beside the Alban lakes he'll set thy marble statue beneath a roof of citron wood.   Abounding incense shalt thou there inhale, and shalt take delight in the mingled strains of lyre and Berecyntian flute; nor shall the pipe be lacking. There twice each day shall boys, with maidens tender, hymning thy majesty, beat the ground with snowy feet, in triple time after the Salian fashion.

Me nor lad nor maid can more delight, nor trustful hope of love returned, nor drinking bouts nor temples bound with blossoms new.

But why, O Ligurinus, why steals now and then adown my cheek a tear? Why halts my tongue, once eloquent, with unbecoming silence midst my speech? In visions of the night, I now hold thee fast, now follow thee in flight o'er the Campus Martius' sward, now midst the whirling waves, O thou hard of heart!

II

PINDARVM quisquis studet aemulari,
Iule, ceratis ope Daedalea
nititur pinnis vitreo daturus
    nomina ponto.

monte decurrens velut amnis, imbres
quem super notas aluere ripas,
fervet immensusque ruit profundo
    Pindarus ore,

laurea donandus Apollinari,
seu per audaces nova dithyrambos   10
verba devolvit numerisque fertur
    lege solutis,

seu deos regesque canit, deorum
sanguinem, per quos cecidere iusta
morte Centauri, cecidit tremendae
    flamma Chimaerae,

sive quos Elea domum reducit
palma caelestes pugilemve equumve
dicit et centum potiore signis
    munere donat,   20

ODES BOOK IV

ODE II

Thou, Antonius, not I, shouldst Sing Great Caesar's Praise

WHOEVER strives, Iulus, to rival Pindar, relies on wings fastened with wax by Daedalean craft, and is doomed to give his name to some crystal sea.

Like a river from the mountain rushing down, which the rains have swollen above its wonted banks, so does Pindar seethe and, brooking no restraint, rush on with deep-toned voice, worthy to be honoured with Apollo's bays, whether he rolls new words through daring dithyrambs and is borne along in measures freed from rule, or sings of gods and kings, the progeny of gods, at whose hands the Centaurs fell in death deserved and by whom was quenched the fire of dread Chimaera; or when he sings of those whom the Elean palm leads home exalted to the skies, of boxer, or of steed, and endows them with a tribute more glorious than a hundred

flebili sponsae iuvenemve raptum
plorat et vires animumque moresque
aureos educit in astra nigroque
    invidet Orco.

multa Dircaeum levat aura cycnum,
tendit, Antoni, quotiens in altos
nubium tractus.   ego apis Matinae
    more modoque

grata carpentis thyma per laborem
plurimum circa nemus uvidique   30
Tiburis ripas operosa parvus
    carmina fingo.

concines maiore poeta plectro
Caesarem, quandoque trahet feroces
per sacrum clivum merita decorus
    fronde Sygambros ;

quo nihil maius meliusve terris
fata donavere bonique divi,
nec dabunt, quamvis redeant in aurum
    tempora priscum.   40

concines laetosque dies et urbis
publicum ludum super impetrato
fortis Augusti reditu forumque
    litibus orbum.

statues; or laments the young hero snatched from his tearful bride, and to the stars extols his prowess, his courage, and his golden virtue, begrudging them to gloomy Orcus.

A mighty breeze uplifts the Dircaean swan, Antonius, as oft as he essays a flight to the lofty regions of the clouds. I, after the way and manner of the Matinian bee, that gathers the pleasant thyme laboriously around full many a grove and the banks of well-watered Tibur, I, a humble bard, fashion my verses with incessant toil. Thou, a poet of loftier strain, shalt sing of Caesar, when, honoured with the well-earned garland, he shall lead in his train along the Sacred Slope the wild Sygambri; a sovereign than whom nothing greater, nothing better, have the Fates and gracious gods bestowed upon the world, nor shall bestow, even though the centuries roll backward to the ancient age of gold. Thou shalt sing of the festal days, of the city's public games to celebrate the return of brave Augustus in answer to our prayers, and of the Forum free from strife. Then,

tum meae, siquid loquar audiendum,
vocis accedet bona pars, et " O sol
pulcher, o laudande !" canam recepto
    Caesare felix.

tuque dum procedis,[1] io Triumphe !
non semel dicemus, " io Triumphe !"   50
civitas omnis dabimusque divis
    tura benignis.

te decem tauri totidemque vaccae,
me tener solvet vitulus, relicta
matre qui largis iuvenescit herbis
    in mea vota,

fronte curvatos imitatus ignis
tertium lunae referentis ortum,
qua notam duxit, niveus videri,
    cetera fulvus.   60

---

[1] teque dum procedis *all MSS. except B.C. (which give*
procedit): te *is then taken as referring to* Triumph : tuque
dum procedis *Peerlkamp, Keller.*

if I have aught deserving to be heard, the best powers of my voice shall swell the acclaim, and happy at Caesar's coming home, I'll sing: "O glorious day, with honour to be mentioned!" And as thou takest the lead along the ways, "Io triumphe!"[1] we will shout all of us together, and not only once: "Io triumphe!" and incense will we offer to the kindly gods.

Thy promises, ten bulls and as many kine shall satisfy; mine a tender calf, which, having left its dam, is growing on the generous pasturage to fulfil my vows, imitating with its brow the curving crescent of the moon at its third rising, snow-white where it bears a mark, but elsewhere tawny.

---

[1] *I.e.* " Hail! God of Triumph!"

III

Qvem tu, Melpomene, semel
  nascentem placido lumine videris,
illum non labor Isthmius
  clarabit pugilem, non equus impiger

curru ducet Achaico
  victorem, neque res bellica Deliis
ornatum foliis ducem,
  quod regum tumidas contuderit minas,

ostendet Capitolio ;
  sed quae Tibur aquae fertile praefluunt   10
et spissae nemorum comae
  fingent Aeolio carmine nobilem.

Romae principis urbium
  dignatur suboles inter amabiles
vatum ponere me choros,
  et iam dente minus mordeor invido.

o testudinis aureae
  dulcem quae strepitum, Pieri, temperas,
o mutis quoque piscibus
  donatura cycni, si libeat, sonum,   20

totum muneris hoc tui est,
  quod monstror digito praetereuntium
Romanae fidicen lyrae :
  quod spiro et placeo, si placeo, tuum est.

ODES BOOK IV

ODE III

My Glory is Thy Gift, O Muse

Whom thou, Melpomene, hast once beheld with favouring gaze at his natal hour, him no Isthmian toil shall make a famous boxer, no impetuous steed shall draw as victor in Achaean car, nor shall martial deeds show him to the Capitol, a captain decked with Delian bays, for having crushed the haughty threats of kings; but the waters that flow past fertile Tibur and the dense leafage of the groves shall make him famous for Aeolian song.

The children of Rome, queen of cities, deem it meet to rank me among the pleasant choirs of poets; and already am I less attacked by Envy's tooth. O thou Pierian maid that dost modulate the sweet tones of the golden shell, O thou that couldst lend the music of the swan even to dumb fishes, didst thou so desire, this is all thy gift, that I am pointed out by the finger of those passing by as the minstrel of the Roman lyre. That I am filled with the breath of song, and that I please, if please I do, is of thy bestowing.

IV

QVALEM ministrum fulminis alitem,
cui rex deorum regnum in aves vagas
   permisit expertus fidelem
     Iuppiter in Ganymede flavo,

olim iuventas et patrius vigor
nido laborum propulit inscium,
   vernique iam nimbis remotis
     insolitos docuere nisus

venti paventem, mox in ovilia
demisit hostem vividus impetus,   10
   nunc in reluctantes dracones
     egit amor dapis atque pugnae ;

qualemve laetis caprea pascuis
intenta fulvae matris ab ubere
   iam lacte depulsum leonem
     dente novo peritura vidit:

videre Raetis bella sub Alpibus
Drusum gerentem Vindelici ; (quibus
   mos unde deductus per omne
     tempus Amazonia securi   20

ODE IV

Drusus and the Claudian House

LIKE the winged bearer of the lightning, to whom
the king of gods gave dominion o'er the roving
birds, having found him faithful in the case of fair-
haired Ganymede—at first youth and native strength
drive him forth, ignorant of toils, from out his nest,
and the spring gales, now that storms are past, have
taught him unwonted efforts, despite his fears; next
with eager onset he swoops down as foe upon the
sheep-folds; then love of plunder and the fight drives
him against struggling snakes; or like some lion just
weaned from the rich milk of his tawny mother,
which a doe, intent on bounteous pasturage, has
espied, doomed to perish by its untried tooth: even
such was Drusus as the Vindelici beheld him waging
war beneath the Rhaetian Alps. Whence was de-
rived the custom that through all recorded time arms
their right hands with the Amazonian battle-axe, I

dextras obarmet, quaerere distuli,
nec scire fas est omnia) sed diu
    lateque victrices catervae
      consiliis iuvenis revictae

sensere quid mens, rite quid indoles
nutrita faustis sub penetralibus
    posset, quid Augusti paternus
      in pueros animus Nerones.

fortes creantur fortibus et bonis;
est in iuvencis, est in equis patrum   30
    virtus, neque imbellem feroces
      progenerant aquilae columbam.

doctrina sed vim promovet insitam,
rectique cultus pectora roborant;
    utcumque defecere mores.
      indecorant bene nata culpae.

quid debeas, o Roma, Neronibus,
testis Metaurum flumen et Hasdrubal
    devictus et pulcher fugatis
      ille dies Latio tenebris,   40

qui primus alma risit adorea,
dirus per urbes Afer ut Italas
    ceu flamma per taedas vel Eurus
      per Siculas equitavit undas.

have forborne to seek, nor is it vouchsafed to know all things; but the hordes long victorious on many a field were vanquished by the young hero's wisdom, and were made to feel the potency of head and heart fitly nurtured beneath an auspicious roof, and of Augustus' fatherly devotion to the youthful Neros.

'Tis only from the sturdy and the good that sturdy youths are born; in steers, in steeds, appear the merits of their sires; nor do fierce eagles beget timid doves. Yet training increases inborn worth, and righteous ways make strong the heart; whenever righteousness has failed, faults mar even what nature had made noble.

What, O Rome, thou owest to the Neros, the Metaurus River is a witness, and vanquished Hasdrubal, and that glorious day when the gloom from Latium was dispelled, the day that was the first to smile with blessed victory, since the dire Carthaginian dashed on his way through the Italian towns, like as the fire rages through the pines, or Eurus o'er the Sicilian waves. Thenceforth the Roman

297

post hoc secundis usque laboribus
Romana pubes crevit, et impio
    vastata Poenorum tumultu
        fana deos habuere rectos.

dixitque tandem perfidus Hannibal :
" cervi luporum praeda rapacium,   50
    sectamur ultro, quos opimus
        fallere et effugere est triumphus.

gens, quae cremato fortis ab Ilio
iactata Tuscis aequoribus sacra
    natosque maturosque patres
        pertulit Ausonias ad urbes,

duris ut ilex tonsa bipennibus
nigrae feraci frondis in Algido,
    per damna, per caedes ab ipso
        ducit opes animumque ferro.   60

non hydra secto corpore firmior
vinci dolentem crevit in Herculem,
    monstrumve submisere Colchi
        maius Echioniaeve Thebae.

merses profundo, pulchrior evenit ;
luctere, multa proruet integrum
    cum laude victorem geretque
        proelia coniugibus loquenda.

youth, through undertakings ever prosperous, waxed stronger, and the shrines laid waste by the impious havoc of the Carthaginians had their gods set up once more. And at last false Hannibal exclaimed: "Like deer, the prey of ravening wolves, we follow all in vain those whom it were a signal triumph to baffle and evade. The race which—sturdy still after Ilium's destruction—brought safe to the Ausonian towns, over tossing Tuscan seas, its sacred images, its children, and its aged sires, like some oak shorn of its leafy boughs by heavy axes on Mount Algidus rich in dark foliage, through loss, through slaughter, draws its strength and life from the very steel. Not the hydra, as its frame was hewn, grew mightier against Hercules, loth to yield; nor did the Colchians or Echionian Thebes rear a greater prodigy. Drown it in the depths! It comes forth fairer. Wrestle with it! It will throw with great renown a fresh opponent flushed with victory, and wage wars for wives to tell of. To

CARMINVM LIBER IV

Carthagini iam non ego nuntios
mittam superbos : occidit, occidit   70
   spes omnis et fortuna nostri
      nominis Hasdrubale interempto.

nil Claudiae non perficient manus,
quas et benigno numine Iuppiter
   defendit et curae sagaces
      expediunt per acuta belli. "

300

Carthage no more shall I send proud messengers; perished, perished is all hope and the fortune of our name since Hasdrubal's destruction.

Naught is there that the Claudian might shall not achieve, which Jupiter defends with power benign, and which wise counsels guide safely through war's perils.

V

Divis orte bonis, optime Romulae
custos gentis, abes iam nimium diu ;
maturum reditum pollicitus patrum
    sancto concilio redi.

lucem redde tuae, dux bone, patriae :
instar veris enim vultus ubi tuus
adfulsit populo, gratior it dies
    et soles melius nitent.

ut mater iuvenem, quem Notus invido
flatu Carpathii trans maris aequora   10
cunctantem spatio longius annuo
    dulci distinet a domo,

votis ominibusque et precibus vocat,
curvo nec faciem litore demovet :
sic desideriis icta fidelibus
    quaerit patria Caesarem.

tutus bos etenim rura perambulat,
nutrit rura Ceres almaque Faustitas,
pacatum volitant per mare navitae ;
    culpari metuit fides,   20

ODES BOOK IV

ODE V

The Blessings of Augustus' Sway

SPRUNG from the blessed gods, best guardian of the
race of Romulus, too long already art thou absent.
Come back, for thou didst pledge a swift return to
the sacred council of the Fathers. To thy country
give again, blest leader, the light of thy presence!
For when, like spring, thy face has beamed upon the
folk, more pleasant runs the day, and brighter shines
the sun. As with vows, with omens, and with prayers
a mother calls the son whom the South wind with his
envious gales keeps lingering far from his sweet home
across the stretch of the Carpathian Sea for longer
than a year, and from the curving shore turns not her
face; so, moved by loyal love, his country yearns for
Caesar. For when he is here, the ox in safety roams
the pastures; Ceres and benign Prosperity make rich
the crops; safe are the seas o'er which our sailors
course; Faith shrinks from blame; polluted by no

nullis polluitur casta domus stupris,
mos et lex maculosum edomuit nefas,
laudantur simili prole puerperae,
   culpam poena premit comes.

quis Parthum paveat, quis gelidum Scythen,
quis Germania quos horrida parturit
fetus, incolumi Caesare? quis ferae
   bellum curet Hiberiae?

condit quisque diem collibus in suis,
et vitem viduas ducit ad arbores;   30
hinc ad vina redit laetus et alteris
   te mensis adhibet deum;

te multa prece, te prosequitur mero
defuso pateris, et Laribus tuum
miscet numen, uti Graecia Castoris
   et magni memor Herculis.

"longas o utinam, dux bone, ferias
praestes Hesperiae!" dicimus integro
sicci mane die, dicimus uvidi,
   cum sol Oceano subest.   40

stain, the home is pure; custom and law have stamped out the taint of sin; mothers win praise because of children like unto their sires; while Vengeance follows close on guilt.

Who would fear the Parthian, who the icy Scythian, who the hordes rough Germany doth breed, while Caesar lives unharmed? Who would mind the war in wild Iberia? On his own hillside each man spends the day, and weds his vines to waiting trees; thence gladly repairs to the feast, and at the second course[1] invokes thee as a god. Thee with many a prayer, thee with pure wine poured from bowls, he worships; and mingles thy majesty with his household gods, like Greece mindful of Castor and great Hercules.

"Long holidays, blest leader, vouchsafe unto Hesperia!" So do we pray, dry-lipped, when day begins: so pray we, flushed with wine, when the sun sinks beneath the Ocean.

[1] When libations were poured to the deities before drinking began.

VI

Dive, quem proles Niobea magnae
vindicem linguae Tityosque raptor
sensit et Troiae prope victor altae
    Phthius Achilles,

ceteris maior, tibi miles impar,
filius quamvis Thetidis marinae
Dardanas turres quateret tremenda
    cuspide pugnax.

ille, mordaci velut icta ferro
pinus aut impulsa cupressus Euro,   10
procidit late posuitque collum in
    pulvere Teucro.

ille non inclusus equo Minervae
sacra mentito male feriatos
Troas et laetam Priami choreis
    falleret aulam;

sed palam captis gravis, heu nefas, heu,
nescios fari pueros Achivis
ureret flammis, etiam latentem
    matris in alvo,   20

ODES BOOK IV

ODE VI

Invocation to Apollo

O GOD, whom Niobe's offspring came to know as the punisher of boastful words, whom the robber Tityos felt and Phthian Achilles when well-nigh victorious over lofty Troy, mightier than others, yet no match for thee, though he was the son of sea-born Thetis and shook the Dardanian towers, fighting with his awful spear. He, like to some pine stricken with biting steel, or some cypress o'erturned by the Eastern wind, fell prostrate with his outstretched frame and bowed his neck in Trojan dust. He would not have hidden within the horse that feigned sacrifice to Minerva, nor striven to deceive the Trojans keeping ill-timed holiday, or Priam's court taking joy in dances; but with open cruelty to his captives (alas! alas! the horror) he would have burned with Grecian fires the speechless babes, yea, the very infant hidden in its mother's womb, had not the Father of the gods,

307

ni tuis victus Venerisque gratae
vocibus divom pater adnuisset
rebus Aeneae potiore ductos
    alite muros.

doctor argutae fidicen Thaliae,
Phoebe, qui Xantho lavis amne crinis,
Dauniae defende decus Camenae,
    levis Agyieu.

spiritum Phoebus mihi, Phoebus artem
carminis nomenque dedit poetae.   30
virginum primae puerique claris
    patribus orti,

Deliae tutela deae, fugacis
lyncas et cervos cohibentis arcu,
Lesbium servate pedem meique
    pollicis ictum,

rite Latonae puerum canentes,
rite crescentem face Noctilucam,
prosperam frugum celeremque pronos
    volvere menses.   40

nupta iam dices " ego dis amicum,
saeculo festas referente luces,
reddidi carmen docilis modorum
    vatis Horati."

won over by thy appeals and those of winsome Venus, promised to Aeneas' destiny walls built under better auspices.

O Phoebus, minstrel teacher of melodious Thalia, thou that lavest thy locks in Xanthus' stream, support the glory of the Daunian Muse, beardless Agyieus!

'Twas Phoebus lent me inspiration, Phoebus the art of song, and gave me the name of poet. O noblest of maids, and ye lads sprung from illustrious sires, wards of the Delian goddess, who with her bow stops the fleeing lynxes and the stags, observe the Lesbian measure and my finger's beat, as ye duly hymn Latona's son and the orb of night waxing with her torch, ripener of crops, and swift to speed the advancing months! Soon, when wedded, thou shalt boast, "I, trained in the measures of the bard Horatius, joined in rendering the hymn welcome to the gods, what time the cycle brought 'round again the festal days."

VII

Diffvgere nives, redeunt iam gramina campis
  arboribusque comae ;
mutat terra vices et decrescentia ripas
  flumina praetereunt ;

Gratia cum Nymphis geminisque sororibus audet
  ducere nuda choros.
immortalia ne speres, monet annus et almum
  quae rapit hora diem.

frigora mitescunt zephyris, ver proterit aestas
  interitura, simul   10
pomifer autumnus fruges effuderit, et mox
  bruma recurrit iners.

damna tamen celeres reparant caelestia lunae ;
  nos ubi decidimus,
quo pius Aeneas, quo Tullus dives et Ancus,
  pulvis et umbra sumus.

quis scit an adiciant hodiernae crastina summae
  tempora di superi ?
cuncta manus avidas fugient heredis, amico
  quae dederis animo.   20

310

ODE VII

Spring's Return

THE snow has fled; already the grass is returning to the fields and the foliage to the trees. Earth is going through her changes, and with lessening flood the rivers flow past their banks. The Grace, with the Nymphs and her twin sisters, ventures unrobed to lead her bands. The year and the hour that rob us of the gracious day warn thee not to hope for unending joys. The cold gives way before the zephyrs; spring is trampled underfoot by summer, destined likewise to pass away so soon as fruitful autumn has poured forth its harvest; and lifeless winter soon returns again.

Yet the swiftly changing moons repair their losses in the sky. We, when we have descended whither righteous Aeneas, whither rich Tullus and Ancus have gone, are but dust and shadow. Who knows whether the gods will add to-morrow's time to the sum of to-day? All things which thou grantest to thine own dear soul, shall escape the greedy clutches of thine heir.

311

cum semel occideris et de te splendida Minos
    fecerit arbitria,
non, Torquate, genus, non te facundia, non te
    restituet pietas;

infernis neque enim tenebris Diana pudicum
    liberat Hippolytum,
nec Lethaea valet Theseus abrumpere caro
    vincula Pirithoo.

When once thou hast perished and Minos has pronounced on thee his august judgment, not family, Torquatus, nor eloquence, nor righteousness shall restore thee again to life. For Diana releases not the chaste Hippolytus from the nether darkness, nor has Theseus power to break the Lethean chains of his dear Pirithous.

VIII

Donarem pateras grataque commodus,
Censorine, meis aera sodalibus,
donarem tripodas, praemia fortium
Graiorum, neque tu pessima munerum
ferres, divite me scilicet artium,
quas aut Parrhasius protulit aut Scopas,
hic saxo, liquidis ille coloribus
sollers nunc hominem ponere, nunc deum.
sed non haec mihi vis, non tibi talium
res est aut animus deliciarum egens.   10
gaudes carminibus : carmina possumus
donare et pretium dicere muneri.
non incisa notis marmora publicis,
per quae spiritus et vita redit bonis
post mortem ducibus, non celeres fugae
reiectaeque retrorsum Hannibalis minae,
non incendia Carthaginis impiae
eius, qui domita nomen ab Africa
lucratus rediit, clarius indicant
laudes quam Calabrae Pierides neque,   20
si chartae sileant quod bene feceris,
mercedem tuleris.   quid foret Iliae
Mavortisque puer, si taciturnitas

ODES BOOK IV

ODE VIII

In Praise of Poesy

GENEROUSLY would I give bowls and welcome bronzes
to my comrades, Censorinus, and tripods, prizes of the
manful Greeks, nor shouldst thou bear off the meanest
of my gifts, were I but rich, that is, in the treasures
which Parrhasius produced, or Scopas—skilful, the one
in marble, the other in liquid colours, to portray now
a hero, now a god. But I have no such store, nor
does thy condition or thy spirit crave such toys. In
songs is thy delight. Songs we can bestow, and can
name the worth of such a tribute.

Not marble graven with public records, whereby
breath and life return to goodly heroes after death,
nor the swift retreat of Hannibal and his threats re-
coiling on himself, nor the burning of wicked Carthage, declare more gloriously the fame of him
who came back home, having won his name from
Africa's subjection, than do the Muses of Calabria;
nor wouldst thou reap thy due reward, should the
parchment leave thy worthy deeds unheralded.
What to-day were the child of Ilia and Mars, had

obstaret meritis invida Romuli?
ereptum Stygiis fluctibus Aeacum
virtus et favor et lingua potentium
vatum divitibus consecrat insulis.
dignum laude virum Musa vetat mori.
caelo Musa beat. sic Iovis interest
optatis epulis impiger Hercules,   30
clarum Tyndaridae sidus ab infimis
quassas eripiunt aequoribus rates,
ornatus viridi tempora pampino
Liber vota bonos ducit ad exitus.

jealous silence blocked the path of Romulus' deserts?
The powers of gifted bards, their favour, and their
voice rescue Aeacus from the Stygian waves and win
for him a hallowed home in the Islands of the Blest.
'Tis the Muse forbids the hero worthy of renown to
perish. 'Tis the Muse bestows the boon of heaven.
'Tis thus that tireless Hercules shares Jove's hoped-
for table. 'Tis thus that Tyndareüs' sons, gleaming
fires, rescue storm-tossed ships from the sea's abyss,
and Liber, his temples decked with verdant vine-
sprays, brings vows to happy issue.

IX

Ne forte credas interitura quae
longe sonantem natus ad Aufidum
    non ante vulgatas per artes
        verba loquor socianda chordis:

non, si priores Maeonius tenet
sedes Homerus, Pindaricae latent
    Ceaeque et Alcaei minaces
        Stesichorique graves Camenae;

nec siquid olim lusit Anacreon
delevit aetas; spirat adhuc amor   10
    vivuntque commissi calores
        Aeoliae fidibus puellae.

non sola comptos arsit adulteri
crines et aurum vestibus illitum
    mirata regalesque cultus
        et comites Helene Lacaena,

primusve Teucer tela Cydonio
direxit arcu; non semel Ilios
    vexata; non pugnavit ingens
        Idomeneus Sthenelusve solus   20

ODE IX

In Praise of Lollius

THINK not the words will perish which I, born near far-sounding Aufidus, utter for linking with the lyre, by arts not hitherto revealed! E'en though Maeonian Homer holds the place of honour, yet Pindar's Muse is not unknown, or that of Ceos, of threatening Alcaeus, or of Stesichorus the stately. Nor has time destroyed whate'er Anacreon once sung in sport. Still breathes the love of the Aeolian maid, and lives her passion confided to the lyre.

Not Spartan Helen only became inflamed with love, marvelling at a paramour's trim locks, his gold-bespangled raiment, his princely pomp and followers; nor was Teucer first to speed the shaft from Cretan bow. Not once alone has an Ilium been beset; nor has great Idomeneus or Sthenelus alone fought

dicenda Musis proelia; non ferox
Hector vel acer Deiphobus graves
    excepit ictus pro pudicis
        coniugibus puerisque primus.

vixere fortes ante Agamemnona
multi; sed omnes inlacrimabiles
    urgentur ignotique longa
        nocte, carent quia vate sacro.

paulum sepultae distat inertiae
celata virtus.   non ego te meis   30
    chartis inornatum silebo,
        totve tuos patiar labores

impune, Lolli, carpere lividas
obliviones.   est animus tibi
    rerumque prudens et secundis
        temporibus dubiisque rectus,

vindex avarae fraudis et abstinens
ducentis ad se cuncta pecuniae,
    consulque non unius anni,
        sed quotiens bonus atque fidus   40

iudex honestum praetulit utili,
reiecit alto dona nocentium
    vultu, per obstantes catervas
        explicuit sua victor arma.

battles worthy to be sung by the Muses. Nor were doughty Hector and keen Deiphobus the first to encounter heavy blows for chaste wife and children. Many heroes lived before Agamemnon; but all are overwhelmed in unending night, unwept, unknown, because they lack a sacred bard. In the tomb, hidden worth differs little from cowardice. Not thee, O Lollius, will I leave unsung, unhonoured by my verse; nor will I suffer envious forgetfulness to prey undisturbed upon thy many exploits. A mind thou hast, experienced in affairs, well-poised in weal or woe, punishing greedy fraud, holding aloof from money that draws all things to itself, thou a consul not of a single year, but so oft as, a judge righteous and true, thou preferrest honour to expediency, rejectest with high disdain the bribes of guilty men, and bearest thine arms victorious through opposing hosts.

non possidentem multa vocaveris
recte beatum ; rectius occupat
   nomen beati, qui deorum
      muneribus sapienter uti

duramque callet pauperiem pati
peiusque leto flagitium timet,   50
   non ille pro caris amicis
      aut patria timidus perire

Not him who possesses much, would one rightly call the happy man; he more fitly gains that name who knows how to use with wisdom the blessings of the gods, to endure hard poverty, and who fears dishonour worse than death, not afraid to die for cherished friends or fatherland

X

O CRVDELIS adhuc et Veneris muneribus potens,
insperata tuae cum veniet pluma superbiae
et, quae nunc umeris involitant, deciderint comae,
nunc et qui color est puniceae flore prior rosae
mutatus, Ligurine, in faciem verterit hispidam :
dices "heu," quotiens te speculo videris alterum,
"quae mens est hodie, cur eadem non puero fuit,
vel cur his animis incolumes non redeunt genae ?"

ODE X

Beauty is Fleeting

O THOU, cruel still and dowered with Venus' gifts, when unexpected down shall come upon thy pride and the locks have fallen that now wave upon thy shoulders, and the bloom that now outvies the blossom of the crimson rose has faded, Ligurinus, and changed to a shaggy visage, then as often as thou gazest in the mirror on thy altered features, thou shalt say : " Alas ! why lacked I as a lad the purpose that I have to-day ? Or why to my present spirit do not my rosy cheeks return ? "

XI

Est mihi nonum superantis annum
plenus Albani cadus; est in horto,
Phylli, nectendis apium coronis;
    est hederae vis

multa, qua crines religata fulges;
ridet argento domus; ara castis
vincta verbenis avet immolato
    spargier agno;

cuncta festinat manus, huc et illuc
cursitant mixtae pueris puellae;   10
sordidum flammae trepidant rotantes
    vertice fumum.

ut tamen noris quibus advoceris
gaudiis, Idus tibi sunt agendae,
qui dies mensem Veneris marinae
    findit Aprilem,

iure sollemnis mihi sanctiorque
paene natali proprio, quod ex hac
luce Maecenas meus adfluentes
    ordinat annos.   20

ODE XI

A Joyous Birthday

I HAVE a jar full of Alban wine over nine years old; in my garden, Phyllis, is parsley for weaving garlands; there is goodly store of ivy, which, binding back thy hair, sets off thy beauty. The house gleams with silver vessels; the altar wreathed with sacred leafage yearns to be sprinkled with the blood of an offered lamb. The household all is hurrying; hither and thither rushes the mingled throng of lads and maids; the flames are dancing as they roll the sooty smoke aloft in wreaths. Yet that thou mayst know to what joys thou art invited, 'tis to celebrate the Ides that cleave in twain April, the month of sea-born Venus; with reason a festal day to me, and honoured almost more than my own natal day, because from this dawn my Maecenas reckons his on-gliding years.

Telephum, quem tu petis, occupavit
non tuae sortis iuvenem puella
dives et lasciva tenetque grata
   compede vinctum.

terret ambustus Phaëthon avaras
spes, et exemplum grave praebet ales
Pegasus terrenum equitem gravatus
   Bellerophontem,

semper ut te digna sequare et ultra
quam licet sperare nefas putando   30
disparem vites.   age iam, meorum
   finis amorum,

(non enim posthac alia calebo
femina) condisce modos, amanda
voce quos reddas : minuentur atrae
   carmine curae.

Telephus, whom thou seekest, a lad above thy station, a maiden rich and wanton has secured and holds him bound with pleasing chain. Scorched Phaëthon serves as a warning to ambitious hopes; and wingèd Pegasus, who brooked not Bellerophon, his earth-born rider, affords a weighty lesson, to follow ever what befits thee, and to shun an ill-assorted mate, deeming it wrong to hope for more than is permitted.

Come, now, ot all my loves the last (for hereafter I shall glow with passion for no other woman), learn verses to render with thy lovely voice! Black care shall be made to wane by the help of song.

XII

Iam veris comites, quae mare temperant,
impellunt animae lintea Thraciae;
iam nec prata rigent nec fluvii strepunt
   hiberna nive turgidi.

nidum ponit, Ityn flebiliter gemens,
infelix avis et Cecropiae domus
aeternum opprobrium, quod male barbaras
   regum est ulta libidines.

dicunt in tenero gramine pinguium
custodes ovium carmina fistula   10
delectantque deum, cui pecus et nigri
   colles Arcadiae placent.

adduxere sitim tempora, Vergili;
sed pressum Calibus ducere Liberum
si gestis, iuvenum nobilium cliens,
   nardo vina merebere.

nardi parvus onyx eliciet cadum,
qui nunc Sulpiciis adcubat horreis,
spes donare novas largus amaraque
   curarum eluere efficax.   20

ODE XII

The Delights of Spring

ALREADY the Thracian breezes, Spring's attendants, that calm the sea, are swelling the sails of ships; no longer are the meadows frozen, nor do the rivers roar, swollen with winter's snow. Making tearful moan for Itys, the ill-fated swallow builds her nest, everlasting disgrace of the Cecropian house, for that she avenged too cruelly the barbarous lust of kings.

On the soft grass the keepers of the fat sheep play songs upon the pipe, and delight the god to whom are dear Arcadia's flocks and sombre hills.

The season has brought thirst, O Virgil; but if thou, a follower of noble patrons, art eager to quaff a wine pressed at Cales, thou must earn the cup by bringing spikenard. A tiny shell of spikenard shall lure forth a jar that now reposes in Sulpicius' storehouse, rich in promise to bestow fresh hopes, and powerful to wash away the bitterness of care.

ad quae si properas gaudia, cum tua
velox merce veni : non ego te meis
immunem meditor tingere poculis,
     plena dives ut in domo.

verum pone moras et studium lucri
nigrorumque memor, dum licet, ignium
misce stultitiam consiliis brevem ;
     dulce est desipere in loco.

If thou art eager for such joys, come quickly with thy wares! If thou comest without thy portion, I purpose not, like some rich lord in well-stocked house, to steep thee in my cups. But put aside delay and thirst for gain, and, mindful of Death's dark fires, mingle, while thou mayst, brief folly with thy wisdom! 'Tis sweet at the fitting time to cast serious thoughts aside.

XIII

AVDIVERE, Lyce, di mea vota, di
audivere, Lyce : fis anus et tamen
   vis formosa videri
     ludisque et bibis impudens

et cantu tremulo pota Cupidinem
lentum sollicitas.   ille virentis et
   doctae psallere Chiae
     pulchris excubat in genis.

importunus enim transvolat aridas
quercus, et refugit te, quia luridi   10
   dentes te, quia rugae
     turpant et capitis nives.

nec Coae referunt iam tibi purpurae
nec cari lapides tempora, quae semel
   notis condita fastis
     inclusit volucris dies.

quo fugit Venus, heu, quove color? decens
quo motus?   quid habes illius, illius,
   quae spirabat amores,
     quae me surpuerat mihi,   20

ODE XIII

Retribution

THE gods have heard my prayer, O Lyce, aye, the gods have heard it. Thou art becoming old, and yet desirest to seem beauteous and joinest in the merriment and drinkest hard and, already maudlin, seekest with quavering song to rouse unwilling Cupid. He keeps his watch on the fair cheeks of blooming Chia, skilled in playing on the harp. For disdainfully he flies past withered oaks, and shrinks from thee, because yellow teeth and wrinkles and snowy locks disfigure thee.

No more do robes of Coan purple or costly jewels bring back to thee the days that time in its flight has once laid away and locked up in the archives known to all.

Whither has fled thy grace, alas! or thy bloom whither? Whither thy comely carriage? What dost thou retain of her, of her, I ask, who once breathed love, who stole me from myself, thou happy

felix post Cinaram notaque et artium
gratarum facies ?   sed Cinarae breves
   annos Fata dederunt,
     servatura diu parem

cornicis vetulae temporibus Lycen,
possent ut iuvenes visere fervidi
   multo non sine risu
     dilapsam in cineres facem.

after Cinara was gone, once famous for thy beauty and thy winning ways ? Brief years the Fates to Cinara granted, resolved on keeping Lyce long, to match the age of the ancient crow, so that hot youths with many a laugh might come to see the torch to ashes fallen.

XIV

QVAE cura patrum quaeve Quiritium
plenis honorum muneribus tuas,
    Auguste, virtutes in aevum
      per titulos memoresque fastus

aeternet, o, qua sol habitabiles
inlustrat oras, maxime principum,
    quem legis expertes Latinae
      Vindelici didicere nuper,

quid Marte posses.   milite nam tuo
Drusus Genaunos, implacidum genus,   10
    Breunosque [1] veloces et arces
      Alpibus impositas tremendis

deiecit acer plus vice simplici;
maior Neronum mox grave proelium
    commisit immanesque Raetos
      auspiciis pepulit secundis,

spectandus in certamine Martio
devota morti pectora liberae
    quantis fatigaret ruinis,
      indomitas prope qualis undas   20

[1] Breunos: *some inferior MSS. have* Brennos.

ODES BOOK IV

ODE XIV

Drusus and Tiberius

WHAT care of Fathers and Quirites, O Augustus, shall
with full meed of honours immortalise thy prowess
by inscriptions and commemorative records, thou
mightiest of princes where'er the sun shines on
habitable coasts, thou whose power in war the Vindelici, free till now from Latin rule, have learned
of late to know. For thine were the troops where-
with keen Drusus, with more than like requital, hurled
the Genauni down, a clan implacable, the swift
Breuni, and their strongholds set upon the awful
Alps. Soon too the elder Nero joined deadly battle
and overcame the savage Rhaetians under happy
auspices, a wonder to behold in martial combat for
the havoc with which he crushed hearts dedicated to
the death of freemen; almost as the south wind when
he frets the unconquerable waves, when the band of

exercet Auster Pleiadum choro
scindente nubes, impiger hostium
    vexare turmas et frementem
        mittere equum medios per ignes.

sic tauriformis volvitur Aufidus,
qui regna Dauni praefluit Apuli,
    cum saevit horrendamque cultis
        diluviem minitatur agris,

ut barbarorum Claudius agmina
ferrata vasto diruit impetu   30
    primosque et extremos metendo
        stravit humum sine clade victor,

te copias, te consilium et tuos
praebente divos.   nam tibi quo die
    portus Alexandrea supplex
        et vacuam patefecit aulam,

Fortuna lustro prospera tertio
belli secundos reddidit exitus,
    laudemque et optatum peractis
        imperiis decus adrogavit.   40

te Cantaber non ante domabilis
Medusque et Indus, te profugus Scythes
    miratur, o tutela praesens
        Italiae dominaeque Romae.

Pleiads cleaves the clouds; eager to harry the hosts of the foe and to drive his snorting charger through the midst of fiery tumult. So does bull-formed Aufidus roll on, flowing past the realms of Apulian Daunus, when he rages and threatens awful deluge to the well-tilled fields, even as Claudius o'erwhelmed with destructive onslaught the mail-clad hosts of savages, and strewed the ground, mowing down van and rear, victorious without loss,—the troops, the plan, the favouring gods provided all by thee. For on the selfsame day that suppliant Alexandria opened her harbours and her empty palace to thee, propitious Fortune, three lustrums later, brought a happy issue to the war and bestowed fame and hoped-for glory upon the deeds wrought in fulfilment of thy commands.

At thee marvels the Cantabrian never before subdued, at thee the Mede and Indian, at thee the roving Scythian, thou mighty guardian of Italy and

te, fontium qui celat origines,
Nilusque et Hister, te rapidus Tigris,
   te beluosus qui remotis
      obstrepit Oceanus Britannis,

te non paventis funera Galliae
duraeque tellus audit Hiberiae   50
   te caede gaudentes Sygambri
      compositis venerantur armis.

imperial Rome. To thee the Nile gives ear, the Nile that hides the sources of its springs; to thee the Danube, the swirling Tigris, the Ocean teeming with monsters, that roars around the distant Britons; to thee the land of Gaul that recks not death, and stubborn Iberia. Before thee stand in awe the slaughter-loving Sygambri, with weapons laid to rest.

XV

Phoebvs volentem proelia me loqui
victas et urbes increpuit lyra,
   ne parva Tyrrhenum per aequor
      vela darem.   tua, Caesar, aetas

fruges et agris rettulit uberes
et signa nostro restituit Iovi
   derepta Parthorum superbis
      postibus et vacuum duellis

Ianum Quirini clausit et ordinem
rectum evaganti frena licentiae   10
   iniecit emovitque culpas
      et veteres revocavit artes,

per quas Latinum nomen et Italae
crevere vires famaque et imperi
   porrecta maiestas ad ortus
      solis ab Hesperio cubili.

custode rerum Caesare non furor
civilis aut vis exiget otium,
   non ira, quae procudit enses
      et miseras inimicat urbes.   20

ODES BOOK IV

ODE XV

Augustus

WHEN I wished to sing of fights and cities won, Apollo
checked me, striking loud his lyre, and forbade my
spreading tiny sails upon the Tuscan Sea. Thy age,
O Caesar, has restored to farms their plenteous crops
and to our Jove the standards stript from the proud
columns of the Parthians ; has closed Quirinus' fane
empty of war ; has put a check on licence, passing
righteous bounds ; has banished crime and called
back home the ancient ways whereby the Latin
name and might of Italy waxed great, and the fame
and majesty of our dominion were spread from the
sun's western bed to his arising.

While Caesar guards the state, not civil rage, nor
violence, nor wrath that forges swords, embroiling
hapless towns, shall banish peace. Not they that

non qui profundum Danuvium bibunt
edicta rumpent Iulia, non Getae,
   non Seres infidive Persae,
      non Tanain prope flumen orti.

nosque et profestis lucibus et sacris
inter iocosi munera Liberi
   cum prole matronisque nostris,
      rite deos prius adprecati,

virtute functos more patrum duces
Lydis remixto carmine tibiis   30
   Troiamque et Anchisen et almae
      progeniem Veneris canemus.

drink the Danube deep shall break the Julian laws, nor Getae, Seres, faithless Parthians, nor they by Tanais born. On common and on sacred days, amid the gifts of merry Bacchus, with wife and child we first will duly pray the gods; then after our fathers' wont, in measures joined to strains of Lydian flutes, we will hymn the glories of the heroic dead, Troy and Anchises and benign Venus' offspring.

CARMEN SAECULARE

CARMEN SAECVLARE

Phoebe silvarumque potens Diana,
lucidum caeli decus, o colendi
semper et culti, date quae precamur
    tempore sacro,

quo Sibyllini monuere versus
virgines lectas puerosque castos
dis quibus septem placuere colles
    dicere carmen.

alme Sol, curru nitido diem qui
promis et celas aliusque et idem   10
nasceris, possis nihil urbe Roma
    visere maius !

rite maturos aperire partus
lenis, Ilithyia, tuere matres,
sive tu Lucina probas vocari
    seu Genitalis.

diva, producas subolem patrumque
prosperes decreta super iugandis
feminis prolisque novae feraci
    lege marita,   20

CARMEN SAECULARE

O Phoebus, and Diana, queen of forests, radiant glory of the heavens, O ye ever cherished and ever to be cherished, grant the blessings that we pray for at the holy season when the verses of the Sibyl have commanded chosen maidens and spotless youths to sing the hymn in honour of the gods who love the Seven Hills.

O quickening Sun, that in thy shining car usherest in the day and hidest it, and art reborn another and yet the same, ne'er mayst thou be able to view aught greater than the city of Rome!

O Ilithyia, that, according to thy office, art gracious to bring issue in due season, protect our matrons, whether thou preferrest to be invoked as " Lucina " or as " Genitalis."   Rear up our youth, O goddess, and bless the Fathers' edicts concerning wedlock and the marriage-law, destined, we pray, to be prolific in new offspring, that the sure cycle of ten times eleven

CARMEN SAECVLARE

certus undenos deciens per annos
orbis ut cantus referatque ludos
ter die claro totiensque grata
    nocte frequentes.

vosque veraces cecinisse, Parcae,
quod semel dictum stabilisque rerum
terminus servet,[1] bona iam peractis
    iungite fata.

fertilis frugum pecorisque tellus
spicea donet Cererem corona;   30
nutriant fetus et aquae salubres
    et Iovis aurae.

condito mitis placidusque telo
supplices audi pueros, Apollo;
siderum regina bicornis, audi,
    Luna, puellas.

Roma si vestrum est opus Iliaeque
litus Etruscum tenuere turmae,
iussa pars mutare Lares et urbem
    sospite cursu,   40

cui per ardentem sine fraude Troiam
castus Aeneas patriae superstes
liberum munivit iter, daturus
    plura relictis:

[1] servat: *Orelli.*

years may bring round again music and games thronged thrice by bright daylight and as often by gladsome night!

And ye, O Fates, truthful in your oracles, as has once been ordained, and may the unyielding order of events confirm it, link happy destinies to those already past.

Bountiful in crops and cattle, may Mother Earth deck Ceres with a crown of corn; and may Jove's wholesome rains and breezes give increase to the harvest!

Do thou, Apollo, gracious and benign, put aside thy weapon and give ear to thy suppliant sons! And do thou, O Luna, the constellations' crescent queen to the maidens lend thine ear!

If Rome be your handiwork, and if from Ilium hailed the bands that gained the Tuscan shore (the remnant bidden to change their homes and city in auspicious course), they for whom righteous Aeneas, survivor of his country, unscathed 'mid blazing Troy, prepared a way to liberty, destined to bestow more

353

di, probos mores docili iuventae,
di, senectuti placidae quietem,
Romulae genti date remque prolemque
    et decus omne.

quaeque vos bobus veneratur albis
clarus Anchisae Venerisque sanguis,   50
impetret, bellante prior, iacentem
    lenis in hostem.

iam mari terraque manus potentes
Medus Albanasque timet secures,
iam Scythae responsa petunt superbi
    nuper et Indi.

iam Fides et Pax et Honor Pudorque
priscus et neglecta redire Virtus
audet, apparetque beata pleno
    copia cornu.   60

augur et fulgente decorus arcu
Phoebus acceptusque novem Camenis,
qui salutari levat arte fessos
    corporis artus,

si Palatinas videt aequus aras,
remque Romanam Latiumque felix
alterum in lustrum meliusque semper
    proroget [1] aevum,

---

[1] proroget : *excellent MSS. also have* prorogat.

than had been left behind,—then do ye, O gods, make teachable our youth and grant them virtuous ways; to the aged give tranquil peace; and to the race of Romulus, riches and offspring and every glory!

And what the glorious scion of Anchises and of Venus, with sacrifice of milk-white steers, entreats of you, that may he obtain, triumphant o'er the warring foe, but generous to the fallen! Now the Parthian fears the hosts mighty on land and sea, and fears the Alban axes. Now the Indians and Scythians, but recently disdainful, are asking for our answer. Now Faith and Peace and Honour and old-time Modesty and neglected Virtue have courage to come back, and blessèd Plenty with her full horn is seen.

May Phoebus, the prophet, who goes adorned with the shining bow, who is dear to the Muses nine, and with his healing art relieves the body's weary frame —may he, if he looks with favour on the altars of the Palatine, prolong the Roman power and Latium's prosperity to cycles ever new and ages ever better!

quaeque Aventinum tenet Algidumque,
quindecim Diana preces virorum   70
curet et votis puerorum amicas
    applicet aures.

haec Iovem sentire deosque cunctos
spem bonam certamque domum reporto
doctus et Phoebi chorus et Dianae
    dicere laudes.

CARMEN SAECULARE

And may Diana, who holds Aventine and Algidus, heed the entreaty of the Fifteen Men and incline gracious ears to the children's prayers! That such is the purpose of Jove and all the gods, we bear home the good and steadfast hope, we the chorus trained to hymn the praises of Phoebus and Diana.

THE EPODES

EPODON

1

Ibis Liburnis inter alta navium,
    amice, propugnacula,
paratus omne Caesaris periculum
    subire, Maecenas, tuo.
quid nos, quibus te vita si superstite
    iucunda, si contra, gravis?
utrumne iussi persequemur otium
    non dulce ni tecum simul,
an hunc laborem mente laturi, decet
    qua ferre non molles viros?   10
feremus, et te vel per Alpium iuga
    inhospitalem et Caucasum
vel Occidentis usque ad ultimum sinum
    forti sequemur pectore.
roges, tuum labore [1] quid iuvem meo,
    imbellis ac firmus parum?
comes minore sum futurus in metu,
    qui maior absentes habet:

---

[1] labore *Glareanus*: laborem *MSS.*

360

THE EPODES

EPODE I

Friendship's Tribute

On Liburnian galleys shalt thou go, my friend
Maecenas, amid vessels with towering bulwarks,
ready to encounter at thine own risk every peril that
threatens Caesar. But what of us, to whom, with thee
surviving, life is a delight, but else is full of heaviness?
Shall we, as bidden, devote ourselves to ease, that is
not sweet except with thee? Or shall we bear these
hardships with such resolve as befitteth stalwart men?
Bear them we will, and whether o'er the ridges of
the Alps and savage Caucasus, or to the very farthest
corners of the West, thee will we follow with stout
heart. Thou askest how by my hardships I am to
lighten thine—I for war unfit and in strength not
rugged? I shall have less fear, attending thee, for
fear lays hold with greater power on those away,—

ut adsidens implumibus pullis avis
    serpentium adlapsus timet   20
magis relictis, non ut adsit auxili
    latura plus praesentibus.
libenter hoc et omne militabitur
    bellum in tuae spem gratiae,
non ut iuvencis inligata pluribus
    aratra nitantur mea,
pecusve Calabris ante sidus fervidum
    Lucana mutet pascuis,
neque ut superni villa candens Tusculi
    Circaea tangat moenia.   30
satis superque me benignitas tua
    ditavit : haud paravero,
quod aut avarus ut Chremes terra premam,
    discinctus aut perdam nepos.

just as a brooding mother-bird more keenly dreads attacks of gliding serpents on her unfledged nestlings when she has left them, though she could lend them no more aid were she at hand.

This war and every war shall be gladly undertaken in hope to win thy favour—not that more straining bullocks may be mine, yoked to the plough, nor that my flocks may change Calabrian for Lucanian pastures before the blazing dog-star's season, nor that I may have a gleaming villa close to the Circean walls of lofty Tusculum. Enough has thy bounty enriched me and more; I will not lay up treasure, either to bury in the ground, like miser Chremes, or to squander like some reckless spendthrift.

II

" Beatvs ille qui procul negotiis,
    ut prisca gens mortalium,
paterna rura bobus exercet suis
    solutus omni faenore,
neque excitatur classico miles truci,
    neque horret iratum mare,
Forumque vitat et superba civium
    potentiorum limina.
ergo aut adulta vitium propagine
    altas maritat populos,   10
aut in reducta valle mugientium
    prospectat errantes greges,
inutilesque falce ramos amputans
    feliciores inserit,
aut pressa puris mella condit amphoris,
    aut tondet infirmas oves ;
vel cum decorum mitibus pomis caput
    Autumnus agris extulit,
ut gaudet insitiva decerpens pira
    certantem et uvam purpurae,   20
qua muneretur te, Priape, et te, pater
    Silvane, tutor finium.

THE EPODES

EPODE II

Country Joys

" Happy the man who, far away from business cares,
like the pristine race of mortals, works his ancestral
acres with his steers, from all money-lending free ;
who is not, as a soldier, roused by the wild clarion,
nor dreads the angry sea; he avoids the Forum and
proud thresholds of more powerful citizens; and so
he either weds his lofty poplar-trees to well-grown
vines, or in secluded dale looks out upon the rang-
ing herds of lowing cattle, and, cutting off useless
branches with the pruning-knife, engrafts more
fruitful ones, or stores away pressed honey in clean
jars, or shears the helpless sheep. Or when Autumn
in the fields has reared his head crowned with
ripened fruits, how he delights to pluck the grafted
pears, and grapes that with the purple vie, with
which to honour thee, Priapus, and thee, Father
Silvanus, guardian of boundaries.

libet iacere modo sub antiqua ilice,
    modo in tenaci gramine.
labuntur altis interim ripis [1] aquae,
    queruntur in silvis aves,
fontesque [2] lymphis obstrepunt manantibus,
    somnos quod invitet leves.
at cum tonantis annus hibernus Iovis
    imbres nivesque comparat,   30
aut trudit acris hinc et hinc multa cane
    apros in obstantes plagas,
aut amite levi rara tendit retia,
    turdis edacibus dolos,
pavidumque leporem et advenam laqueo gruem
    iucunda captat praemia.
quis non malarum, quas amor curas habet,
    haec inter obliviscitur?
quod si pudica mulier in partem iuvet
    domum atque dulces liberos,   40
Sabina qualis aut perusta solibus
    pernicis uxor Apuli,
sacrum vetustis extruat lignis focum
    lassi sub adventum viri,
claudensque textis cratibus laetum pecus
    distenta siccet ubera,
et horna dulci vina promens dolio
    dapes inemptas adparet:

---

[1] *Good MSS. also have* rivis.
[2] fontes *MSS. :* frondes (Markland's conj.) *many edd.*

THE EPODES, ii

'Tis pleasant, now to lie beneath some ancient
ilex-tree, now on the matted turf. Meanwhile the
rills glide between their high banks; birds warble
in the woods; the fountains plash with their flowing
waters, a sound to invite soft slumbers. But when
the wintry season of thundering Jove brings rains
and snow, with his pack of hounds one either drives
fierce boars from here and there into the waiting
toils, or on polished pole stretches wide-meshed nets,
a snare for greedy thrushes, and catches with the
noose the timid hare and the crane that comes from
far—sweet prizes! Amid such joys, who does not
forget the wretched cares that passion brings?

But if a modest wife shall do her part in tending
home and children dear, like to some Sabine woman
or the well-tanned mate of sturdy Apulian, piling
high the sacred hearth with seasoned firewood
against the coming of her weary husband, penning
the frisking flock in wattled fold, draining their
swelling udders, and, drawing forth this year's sweet
vintage from the jar, prepare an unbought meal,—then

non me Lucrina iuverint conchylia
    magisve rhombus aut scari,   50
si quos Eois intonata fluctibus
    hiems ad hoc vertat mare ;
non Afra avis descendat in ventrem meum,
    non attagen Ionicus
iucundior quam lecta de pinguissimis
    oliva ramis arborum
aut herba lapathi prata amantis et gravi
    malvae salubres corpori
vel agna festis caesa Terminalibus
    vel haedus ereptus lupo.   60
has inter epulas ut iuvat pastas oves
    videre properantes domum,
videre fessos vomerem inversum boves
    collo trahentes languido
postosque vernas, ditis examen domus,
    circum renidentes Lares."
haec ubi locutus faenerator Alfius,
    iam iam futurus rusticus,
omnem redegit Idibus pecuniam,
    quaerit Kalendis ponere.   70

not Lucrine oysters would please me more, nor scar, nor turbot, should winter, thundering on the eastern waves, turn them to our coasts; not Afric fowl nor Ionian pheasant would make for me a repast more savoury than olives gathered from the richest branches of the trees, or the plant of the meadow-loving sorrel, and mallows wholesome to the ailing body, or than a lamb slain at the feast of Terminus, or a kid rescued from the wolf. Amid such feasts, what joy to see the sheep hurrying homeward from pasture, to see the wearied oxen dragging along the upturned ploughshare on their listless necks, and the home-bred slaves, troop of a wealthy house, ranged around the gleaming Lares! "

When the usurer Alfius had uttered this, on the very point of beginning the farmer's life, he called in all his funds upon the Ides—and on the Kalends seeks to put them out again !

EPODON LIBER

III

Parentis olim si quis impia manu
 senile guttur fregerit,
edit cicutis allium nocentius,
 o dura messorum ilia!
quid hoc veneni saevit in praecordiis?
 num viperinus his cruor
incoctus herbis me fefellit? an malas
 Canidia tractavit dapes?
ut Argonautas praeter omnes candidum
 Medea mirata est ducem,
ignota tauris inligaturum iuga
 perunxit hoc Iasonem;
hoc delibutis ulta donis paelicem
 serpente fugit alite.
nec tantus umquam siderum insedit vapor
 siticulosae Apuliae,
nec munus umeris efficacis Herculis
 inarsit aestuosius.
at si quid umquam tale concupiveris,
 iocose Maecenas, precor,
manum puella savio opponat tuo,
 extrema et in sponda cubet.

THE EPODES

EPODE III

That Wicked Garlic!

IF ever any man with impious hand strangle an aged parent, may he eat of garlic, deadlier than the hemlock! Ah! what tough vitals reapers have! What venom this that rages in my frame? Has vipers' blood without my knowledge been brewed into these herbs? Or has Canidia tampered with the poisonous dish? When Medea was enraptured with the hero Jason, fair beyond all the Argonauts, 'twas with this she anointed him, as he essayed to fasten upon the steers the unfamiliar yoke; 'twas with presents steeped in this, that she took vengeance on her rival ere she fled on her winged dragon. Never o'er parched Apulia did such heat of dog-star brood, nor did Nessus' gift burn with fiercer flame into the shoulders of Hercules, that wrought mighty deeds. But if ever, my merry Maecenas, you wish to repeat the jest, I pray your sweetheart may put her hands before your kisses, and lie on the farthest edge of the couch.

EPODON LIBER

IV

Lvpis et agnis quanta sortito obtigit,
    tecum mihi discordia est,
Hibericis peruste funibus latus
    et crura dura compede.
licet superbus ambules pecunia,
    Fortuna non mutat genus.
videsne, Sacram metiente te Viam
    cum bis trium ulnarum toga,
ut ora vertat huc et huc euntium
    liberrima indignatio ?   10
" sectus flagellis hic triumviralibus
    praeconis ad fastidium
arat Falerni mille fundi iugera
    et Appiam mannis terit
sedilibusque magnus in primis eques
    Othone contempto sedet.
quid attinet tot ora navium gravi
    rostrata duci pondere
contra latrones atque servilem manum,
    hoc, hoc tribuno militum ? "   20

THE EPODES

EPODE IV

The Upstart

As great as is the enmity between lambs and wolves,
by Nature's laws decreed, so great is that 'twixt me
and you—you whose flanks are scarred by the Spanish
rope, and whose legs are callous with hard shackles.
Though you strut about in pride of wealth, yet
Fortune does not change your breed. See you not,
as with toga three yards wide you parade from end
to end the Sacred Way, how indignation unrestrained
spreads over the faces of the passers-by? "This
fellow, scourged with the triumvir's lashes till the
tired beadle wearied of the task, now ploughs a
thousand acres of Falernian ground, and with his
ponies travels the Appian Way. Braving Otho's law,
he takes his place with the importance of a knight
in the foremost rows of seats! What boots it for so
many well-beaked ships of massive burden to be led
against the pirates and hordes of slaves, when a fellow
such as this is tribune of the soldiers!"

V

" At o deorum quicquid in caelo regit
    terras et humanum genus,
quid iste fert tumultus et quid omnium
    vultus in unum me truces?
per liberos te, si vocata partubus
    Lucina veris adfuit,
per hoc inane purpurae decus precor,
    per improbaturum haec Iovem,
quid ut noverca me intueris aut uti
    petita ferro belua?"   10
ut haec trementi questus ore constitit
    insignibus raptis puer,
impube corpus, quale posset impia
    mollire Thracum pectora:
Canidia, brevibus implicata viperis
    crines et incomptum caput,
iubet sepulcris caprificos erutas,
    iubet cupressus funebres
et uncta turpis ova ranae sanguine
    plumamque nocturnae strigis   20
herbasque quas Iolcos atque Hiberia
    mittit venenorum ferax,
et ossa ab ore rapta ieiunae canis
    flammis aduri Colchicis.

THE EPODES

EPODE V

Canidia's Incantation

" But in the name of all the gods in heaven that rule
the world and race of men, what means this tumult,
and what the savage looks of all of you bent on me
alone? By thy children, I implore thee, if Lucina,
when invoked, came to help an honest birth, by this
bauble of my purple dress, by Jupiter, sure to dis-
approve these acts, why like a stepmother dost thou
gaze at me, or like a wild beast brought to bay with
hunting-spear?"

When, after making these complaints with quivering lip, the lad stood still, stripped of boyhood's emblems, a youthful form, such as might soften the impious breasts of Thracians, Canidia, her locks and
dishevelled head entwined with short vipers, orders
wild fig-trees uprooted from the tombs, funereal
cypresses, eggs and feathers of a night-roving screech-
owl smeared with the blood of a hideous toad, herbs
that Iolcos and Iberia, fertile in poisons, send, and
bones snatched from the jaws of a starving bitch—all
these to be burned in the magic flames. But high-girt

at expedita Sagana, per totam domum
  spargens Avernales aquas,
horret capillis ut marinus asperis
  echinus aut currens aper.
abacta nulla Veia conscientia
  ligonibus duris humum   30
exhauriebat, ingemens laboribus,
  quo posset infossus puer
longo die bis terque mutatae dapis
  inemori spectaculo,
cum promineret ore, quantum exstant aqua
  suspensa mento corpora :
exsecta uti medulla et aridum iecur
  amoris esset poculum,
interminato cum semel fixae cibo
  intabuissent pupulae.   40
non defuisse masculae libidinis
  Ariminensem Foliam
et otiosa credidit Neapolis
  et omne vicinum oppidum,
quae sidera excantata voce Thessala
  lunamque caelo deripit.
hic inresectum saeva dente livido
  Canidia rodens pollicem
quid dixit aut quid tacuit ? " o rebus meis
  non infideles arbitrae,   50
Nox et Diana, quae silentium regis,
  arcana cum fiunt sacra,

Sagana, sprinkling through all the house water from Lake Avernus, bristles with streaming hair, like some sea-urchin or a racing boar; and Veia, by no sense of guilt restrained, groaning o'er her labours, with stout mattock was digging up the ground, that, buried there, the lad might perish gazing at food changed twice and thrice during the tedious day, his face protruding only so much as swimmers, when hanging in the water by the chin—and all for this, that his marrow and his liver, cut out and dried, might form a love-charm, when once his eye-balls, fixed on the forbidden food, had wasted all away. Gossiping Naples and every neighbouring town believed that Folia of Ariminum, the wanton hag, was also there—Folia, who with Thessalian incantation bewitches stars and moon and plucks them down from heaven. Then fierce Canidia, gnawing her uncut nail with malignant tooth—what did she say, or rather what did she leave unsaid!

"O faithful witnesses of my deeds, Night and Diana, thou that art mistress of the silent hour when mystic

nunc, nunc adeste, nunc in hostiles domos
    iram atque numen vertite.
formidulosis cum latent silvis ferae
    dulci sopore languidae,
senem, quod omnes rideant, adulterum
    latrent Suburanae canes,
nardo perunctum, quale non perfectius
    meae laborarint manus.   60
quid accidit?   cur dira barbarae minus
    venena Medeae valent,
quibus superbam fugit ulta paelicem,
    magni Creontis filiam,
cum palla, tabo munus imbutum, novam
    incendio nuptam abstulit?
atqui nec herba nec latens in asperis
    radix fefellit me locis.
indormit unctis omnium cubilibus
    oblivione paelicum.   70
a! a! solutus ambulat veneficae
    scientioris carmine!
non usitatis, Vare, potionibus,
    o multa fleturum caput,
ad me recurres, nec vocata mens tua
    Marsis redibit vocibus.
maius parabo, maius infundam tibi
    fastidienti poculum,
priusque caelum sidet inferius mari
    tellure porrecta super,   80

rites are wrought, now, even now, lend me your
help! Now against hostile homes turn your wrath
and power! While in the awesome woods the wild
beasts lie in hiding, wrapped in soft slumber, may
Subura's dogs bark at the old rake,—a sight for all
to laugh at—anointed with an essence such as my
hands ne'er made more perfect! What has befallen?
Why fail to work the dire philtres of the barbarian
Medea, with which before her flight she took vengeance on the haughty paramour, mighty Creon's
daughter, what time the robe, a gift steeped in
poisoned gore, snatched away in fire the new-made
bride? And yet no herb nor root, lurking in rough
places, escaped me. He lies asleep on perfumed
couch, forgetful of all mistresses. Aha! He walks at
will, freed by the charm of some cleverer enchantress.
By no wonted potions, Varus, thou creature doomed
bitterly to weep, shalt thou return to me; and, summoned by no Marsian spells, shall thy devotion be
revived. A stronger draught I will prepare, a
stronger draught pour out, to meet thy scorn; and
sooner shall the heaven sink below the sea, with
earth spread out above, than thou shouldst fail to

quam non amore sic meo flagres uti
    bitumen atris ignibus."
sub haec puer iam non, ut ante, mollibus
    lenire verbis impias,
sed dubius unde rumperet silentium,
    misit Thyesteas preces:
" venena maga non fas nefasque, non valent [1]
    convertere humanam vicem.
diris agam vos; dira detestatio
    nulla expiatur victima.   90
quin, ubi perire iussus exspiravero,
    nocturnus occurram Furor,
petamque vultus umbra curvis unguibus,
    quae vis deorum est Manium,
et inquietis adsidens praecordiis
    pavore somnos auferam.
vos turba vicatim hinc et hinc saxis petens
    contundet obscenas anus;
post insepulta membra different lupi
    et Esquilinae alites,   100
neque hoc parentes, heu mihi superstites,
    effugerit spectaculum."

[1] venena maga non *Haupt*: venena magnum *MSS*.

burn with love for me, even as burns the pitch in the smoky flame."

At this the lad no longer, as before, essayed to soothe the impious creatures with gentle speech, but, doubtful with what words to break the silence, hurled forth Thyestean curses: " Your magic spells have not the power to alter right and wrong, nor to avert human retribution. With curses I will hound you; by no sacrifice shall my awful execration be warded off. Nay, even when, doomed to die, I have breathed my last, at night I will meet you as a fury; and as a ghost I will tear your faces with crooked claws, as is the Manes' power; and seated on your restless bosoms, I will banish sleep with terror. The rabble, pelting you with stones on every side along the streets, shall crush you, filthy hags. Then by and by the wolves and birds that haunt the Esquiline shall scatter far and wide your unburied limbs, nor shall this sight escape my parents,— surviving me, alas!"

VI

Qvid immerentes hospites vexas, canis
    ignavus adversum lupos?
quin huc inanes, si potes, vertis minas,
    et me remorsurum petis?
nam qualis aut Molossus aut fulvus Lacon,
    amica vis pastoribus,
agam per altas aure sublata nives,
    quaecumque praecedet fera;
tu, cum timenda voce complesti nemus,
    proiectum odoraris cibum.   10
cave, cave: namque in malos asperrimus
    parata tollo cornua,
qualis Lycambae spretus infido gener
    aut acer hostis Bupalo.
an, si quis atro dente me petiverit,
    inultus ut flebo puer?

THE EPODES

EPODE VI

The Blackmailer

WHY dost thou worry unoffending strangers, thou cur
when facing wolves ? Why not hither, if thou darest,
turn thy idle threats and make assault on me, who
will bite thee in return ? For, like Molossian hound
or tawny Laconian, the shepherd's sturdy friends, with
ear upraised I'll follow amid deep snow whatever
beast of prey goes before. Thou, when thou hast
filled the woods with thy fearful yelps, sniffest
around at the food that has been flung thee. Beware,
beware ! For full fiercely do I lift my ready horns
against evil-doers, even as the slighted son in-law
of perfidious Lycambes, or as Bupalus' keen foe.
Or if any one with venomous tooth assail me, shall
I forgo revenge and whimper like a child ?

VII

Qvo, quo scelesti ruitis? aut cur dexteris
    aptantur enses conditi?
parumne campis atque Neptuno super
    fusum est Latini sanguinis?
non ut superbas invidae Carthaginis
    Romanus arces ureret,
intactus aut Britannus ut descenderet
    Sacra catenatus Via,
sed ut secundum vota Parthorum sua
    urbs haec periret dextera.   10
neque hic lupis mos nec fuit leonibus,
    numquam [1] nisi in dispar feris.
furorne caecus an rapit vis acrior
    an culpa? responsum date!
tacent, et ora pallor albus inficit,
    mentesque perculsae stupent.
sic est: acerba fata Romanos agunt
    scelusque fraternae necis,
ut immerentis fluxit in terram Remi
    sacer nepotibus cruor.   20

[1] numquam *Bentley:* unquam *MSS.*

THE EPODES

EPODE VII

A Threatened Renewal of Civil Strife

WHITHER, whither are ye rushing to ruin in your wicked frenzy? Or why are your hands grasping the swords that have once been sheathed? Has too little Roman blood been shed on field and flood—not that the Roman might burn the proud towers of jealous Carthage, or that the Briton, as yet unscathed, might descend the Sacred Way in fetters, but that, in fulfilment of the Parthians' prayers, this city might perish by its own right hand? Such habit ne'er belonged to wolves or lions, whose fierceness is turned only against beasts of other kinds. Does some blind frenzy drive us on, or some stronger power, or guilt? Give answer!—They speak not; a ghastly pallor o'erspreads their faces; and dazed are their shattered senses. 'Tis so: a bitter fate pursues the Romans, and the crime of a brother's murder, ever since blameless Remus' blood was spilt upon the ground, to be a curse upon posterity.

VIII

Rogare longo putidam te saeculo,
  vires quid enervet meas,
cum sit tibi dens ater et rugis vetus
  frontem senectus exaret,
hietque turpis inter aridas natis
  podex velut crudae bovis!
sed incitat me pectus et mammae putres,
  equina quales ubera,
venterque mollis et femur tumentibus
  exile suris additum.   10
esto beata, funus atque imagines
  ducant triumphales tuum.
nec sit marita, quae rotundioribus
  onusta bacis ambulet.
quid quod libelli Stoici inter Sericos
  iacere pulvillos amant?
inlitterati num minus nervi rigent,
  minusve languet fascinum?
quod ut superbo provoces ab inguine
  ore adlaborandum est tibi.   20

THE EPODES

EPODE VIII

THE idea that you should ask all this long time what it is that unnerves my strength—you stinking hag! —when you've got one black tooth, when old age furrows your forehead with wrinkles, when a shameful hole like a cow's with diarrhoea gapes between ugly buttocks. But what stirs me up is that flabby chest, those flabby breasts, like a mare's teats, and that spongy belly and skinny thigh perched on top of swollen legs. Bless you then, and I hope likenesses of triumphant men-folk will lead your funeral. May there be no wife who may walk along laden with rounder blobs of pearls than yours. There are Stoic treatises which tend to lie among neat little pillows of silk. What of it? Surely those unlearned sinews stiffen no less? That poker doesn't droop any less, does it? However, to stir that up from a proud groin one's got to work hard with one's mouth.

IX

Qvando repostum Caecubum ad festas dapes
    victore laetus Caesare
tecum sub alta—sic Iovi gratum—domo,
    beate Maecenas, bibam
sonante mixtum tibiis carmen lyra,
    hac Dorium, illis barbarum ?
ut nuper, actus cum freto Neptunius
    dux fugit ustis navibus,
minatus urbi vincla, quae detraxerat
    servis amicus perfidis.   10
Romanus eheu—posteri negabitis—
    emancipatus feminae
fert vallum et arma, miles et spadonibus
    servire rugosis potest,
interque signa turpe militaria
    sol adspicit conopium.
ad hoc [1] frementes verterunt bis mille equos
    Galli, canentes Caesarem,
hostiliumque navium portu latent
    puppes sinistrorsum citae.   20
io triumphe, tu moraris aureos
    currus et intactas boves ?

[1] ad hoc *Bentley* : ad hunc *MSS.*

THE EPODES

EPODE IX

After Actium

When, happy Maecenas, within thy lofty palace,—
such is Jove's pleasure,—shall I with thee, in joy at
Caesar's triumph, drink the Caecuban stored away
for festal banquets, while flute and lyre make music
with their mingled melody of Phrygian and Dorian
strains? Just as lately, when the Neptunian leader,[1]
his ships consumed, was driven from the sea in
flight, though he had threatened the City with the
shackles he had taken from faithless slaves, his
friends! The Roman, alas! (ye, O men of after
times, will deny the charge)—the Roman bears stakes
and weapons at a woman's behest, and, a soldier,
can bring himself to become the minion of withered
eunuchs, while amid the soldiers' standards the
sun shines on the shameful Egyptian pavilion. At
sight of this, twice a thousand Gauls, chanting the
name of Caesar, turned away their snorting steeds;
and the ships of the foe, when summoned to the
left, lay hidden in the harbour! Io, Triumphe![2]
Dost thou keep back the golden cars and the unsullied

[1] Sextus Pompeius.
[2] *I.e.* "Hail! O God of Triumph."

389

ıo triumphe, nec Iugurthino parem
    bello reportasti ducem
neque Africanum, cui super Carthaginem
    virtus sepulcrum condidit.
terra marique victus hostis punico
    lugubre mutavit sagum.
aut ille centum nobilem Cretam urbibus,
    ventis iturus non suis,   30
exercitatas aut petit Syrtes Noto,
    aut fertur incerto mari.
capaciores adfer huc, puer, scyphos
    et Chia vina aut Lesbia,
vel quod fluentem nauseam coerceat
    metire nobis Caecubum.
curam metumque Caesaris rerum iuvat
    dulci Lyaeo solvere.

kine? Io, Triumphe! Neither in Jugurtha's war didst thou bring back so glorious a captain; nor was Africanus such,—he whose valour reared for him a shrine o'er Carthage. Vanquished on sea and land, the foe has changed the scarlet cape for sable, and against baffling winds is either making for Crete famed for her hundred cities, or is seeking the Syrtes by Notus tossed, or is borne upon uncertain seas. Bring hither, lad, more generous bowls, and Chian wine or Lesbian, or pour out for us Caecuban, to check our rising qualms. 'Tis sweet to banish anxious fear for Caesar's fortunes with Bacchus' mellow gift.

EPODON LIBER

X

MALA soluta navis exit alite,
   ferens olentem Mevium.
ut horridis utrumque verberes latus,
   Auster, memento, fluctibus.
niger rudentes Eurus inverso mari
   fractosque remos differat;
insurgat Aquilo, quantus altis montibus
   frangit trementes ilices.
nec sidus atra nocte amicum appareat,
   qua tristis Orion cadit;   10
quietiore nec feratur aequore
   quam Graia victorum manus,
cum Pallas usto vertit iram ab Ilio
   in impiam Aiacis ratem.
o quantus instat navitis sudor tuis
   tibique pallor luteus
et illa non virilis heiulatio
   preces et aversum ad Iovem,
Ionius udo cum remugiens sinus
   Noto carinam ruperit.   20
opima quod si praeda curvo litore
   porrecta mergos iuveris,
libidinosus immolabitur caper
   et agna Tempestatibus.

THE EPODES

EPODE X

Bad Luck to Mevius

UNDER evil omen the ship sets sail, bearing unsavoury Mevius. With fearful waves, O Auster, remember to lash both her sides! Let lowering Eurus scatter sheet and broken oars on upturned sea! Let Aquilo arise in all the fury with which he rends the quivering oaks on lofty mountain-tops! And may no friendly star appear on the murky night when grim Orion sets! And on no gentler sea may he be borne than was the host of the victorious Greeks, when Pallas turned her wrath from Ilium's ashes against Ajax' impious bark! Oh! What toil awaits thy sailors! And thyself, what ghastly pallor, and what unmanly wailing, and prayers to Jove estranged, when the Ionian Sea whistling with rainy Notus, shall wreck thy vessel! But if, stretched out as fat carrion on the curving shore, thou give pleasure to the gulls, then a sportive goat and a lamb shall be offered to the gods of storms.

XI

Petti, nihil me sicut antea iuvat
    scribere versiculos amore percussum gravi,
amore, qui me praeter omnes expetit
    mollibus in pueris aut in puellis urere.
hic tertius December, ex quo destiti
    Inachia furere, silvis honorem decutit.
heu me, per urbem, nam pudet tanti mali,
    fabula quanta fui! conviviorum et paenitet,
in quis amantem languor et silentium
    arguit et latere petitus imo spiritus.   10
" contrane lucrum nil valere candidum
    pauperis ingenium!" querebar adplorans tibi,
simul calentis inverecundus deus
    fervidiore mero arcana promorat loco.
" quod si meis inaestuet praecordiis
    libera bilis, ut haec ingrata ventis dividat
fomenta, vulnus nil malum levantia,
    desinet imparibus certare summotus pudor."
ubi haec severus te palam laudaveram,
    iussus abire domum ferebar incerto pede   20
ad non amicos heu mihi postis et heu
    limina dura, quibus lumbos et infregi latus.

394

THE EPODES

EPODE XI
Cupid's Power

O Pettius, no more do I delight as formerly to write
my verses, for I am stricken with the heavy dart of
Love, yea of Love who seeks to kindle me beyond all
others with passion for tender boys and maids. The
third December is now shaking the glory from the
woods since I lost my infatuation for Inachia. Ah
me! (for I'm ashamed of such a sore affliction), how
people talked of me throughout the town! I hate
to recall the feasts at which my listlessness and silence
and the sighs drawn from my bosom's depths proved
my love-lorn state. "To think that a poor man's
guileless heart can naught avail against the power
of gold," did I oft complain, unburdening my grief
to thee, so soon as the god that banishes reserve had
warmed me with the quickening wine and brought my
secrets from their hiding-place. "But if a righteous
indignation should boil up within my heart, so as to
scatter to the winds these thankless consolations
that nowise ease my grievous suffering, I'll banish
modesty and cease to vie with rivals not my peers."
When with stern resolve I had praised this course
before thee, bidden go home, I went my way with
step irresolute towards door-posts to me, alas! un-
friendly, and to thresholds hard, on which I racked

nunc gloriantis quamlibet mulierculam
  vincere mollitia amor Lycisci me tenet ;
unde expedire non amicorum queant
  libera consilia nec contumeliae graves,
sed alius ardor aut puellae candidae
  aut teretis pueri, longam renodantis comam.

my loins and side. Affection for Lyciscus now en-
thrals me, for Lyciscus, who claims in tenderness to
outdo any woman, and from whom no friends' frank
counsels or stern reproaches have power to set me
free, but only another flame, either for some fair
maid or slender youth, with long hair gathered in a
knot.

XII

Qvid tibi vis, mulier nigris dignissima barris ?
  munera cur mihi quidve tabellas
mittis, nec firmo iuveni neque naris obesae ?
  namque sagacius unus odoror,
polypus an gravis hirsutis cubet hircus in alis,
  quam canis acer, ubi lateat sus.
qui sudor vietis et quam malus undique membris
  crescit odor, cum pene soluto
indomitam properat rabiem sedare, neque illi
  iam manet umida creta colorque   10
stercore fucatus crocodili, iamque subando
  tenta cubilia tectaque rumpit.
vel mea cum saevis agitat fastidia verbis :
  " Inachia langues minus ac me ;
Inachiam ter nocte potes, mihi semper ad unum
  mollis opus.   pereat male, quae te
Lesbia quaerenti taurum monstravit inertem,

THE EPODES

EPODE XII

" WHAT possesses you, woman, highly worthy of any
big black jumbo? Why send me presents and
letters? I'm not yet a thorough youth and have no
nasty fat nose yet. You see I smell out shrewdly
whether a polyp or a goaty stench is bedded in the
armpits, and do it better than a hound with its
keen scent finds where the boar-sow lies hidden."
Oh! what a sweat, what a bad smell spreads all over
her shrivelled limbs when, the poker lying all slack,
she tries in a hurry to calm down that indomitable
madness; the damp cosmetic chalk and her tinted
make-up dyed with a crocodile's dung no longer
stay on her; by now too she makes the hard-strained
mattress and canopy of the bed burst in her heat.
Or again, when she attacks my distaste with savage
jibes, she says: " You get tired with that girl
Inachia less than with me. You can do her three
times a night; for me you are pliant for the works
just once. To hell with that Lesbia who showed

cum mihi Cous adesset Amyntas,
cuius in indomito constantior inguine nervos,
    quam nova collibus arbor inhaeret.   20
muricibus Tyriis iteratae vellera lanae
    cui properabantur ?   tibi nempe,
ne foret aequales inter conviva, magis quem
    diligeret mulier sua quam te.
o ego non felix, quam tu fugis, ut pavet acres
    agna lupos capreaeque leones !"

you to be impotent when I looked for a bull, when I had Amyntos of Cos handy, in whose unconquerable groin sticks tight a sinew more firmly than a young tree on the hills. Those fleeces of wool dyed again and again in purples of Tyre—for whom were they hurriedly prepared? For you to be sure, lest there should be found among your agemates a fellow-guest whose woman loved him more than she loved you. Oh dear, I'm not happy—you run away from me just as a lamb is frightened by fierce wolves and roe-deer by lions!"

XIII

HORRIDA tempestas caelum contraxit, et imbres
    nivesque deducunt Iovem; nunc mare, nunc siluae
Threicio Aquilone sonant.   rapiamus, amici,
    occasionem de die, dumque virent genua
et decet, obducta solvatur fronte senectus.
    tu vina Torquato move consule pressa meo.
cetera mitte loqui : deus haec fortasse benigna
    reducet in sedem vice.   nunc et Achaemenio
perfundi nardo iuvat et fide Cyllenea
    levare diris pectora sollicitudinibus,   10
nobilis ut grandi cecinit Centaurus alumno :
    "invicte, mortalis dea nate puer Thetide,
te manet Assaraci tellus, quam frigida parvi
    findunt Scamandri flumina lubricus et Simois,
unde tibi reditum certo subtemine Parcae
    rupere, nec mater domum caerula te revehet.
illic omne malum vino cantuque levato,
    deformis aegrimoniae dulcibus alloquiis."

THE EPODES

EPODE XIII

Defiance to the Storm : Make Merry !

A DREADFUL storm has narrowed heaven's expanse, and
rain and snow are bringing Jove to earth. The sea,
the woods, now roar with the Thracian north wind.
Let us snatch our opportunity from the day, my
friends, and while our limbs are strong and the time
is fitting, let seriousness be banished from the clouded
brow ! Bring thou forth a vintage trodden in my
Torquatus' year. Cease of aught else to speak ! The
god perchance with kindly change will mend our
present ills. Now is the pleasing time to anoint the
head with Persian nard, and with Cyllenian lyre to
relieve our hearts of dread anxieties, even as the far-
famed Centaur once sang to his stalwart foster-child :
" O thou invincible, thou mortal child of goddess
Thetis, thee the land of Assaracus awaits, through
which the tiny Scamander's cooling waters flow and
gliding Simois, whence the Fates by fixed decree
have cut off thy return ; nor shall thy sea-blue
mother bear thee home again. When there, lighten
every ill with wine and song, sweet consolations for
unlovely sorrow ! "

XIV

Mollis inertia cur tantam diffuderit imis
    oblivionem sensibus,
pocula Lethaeos ut si ducentia somnos
    arente fauce traxerim,
candide Maecenas, occidis saepe rogando :
    deus, deus nam me vetat
inceptos, olim promissum carmen, iambos
    ad umbilicum adducere.
non aliter Samio dicunt arsisse Bathyllo
    Anacreonta Teium,   10
qui persaepe cava testudine flevit amorem
    non elaboratum ad pedem.
ureris ipse miser : quod si non pulchrior ignis
    accendit obsessam Ilion,
gaude sorte tua ; me libertina, nec uno
    contenta, Phryne macerat.

THE EPODES

EPODE XIV

Promises Unfulfilled

You distress me, honest Maecenas, by asking oft, why soft indolence has diffused as great forgetfulness over my inmost senses as if with parchèd throat I had drained the bowl that brings Lethean sleep; for 'tis the god, yea 'tis the god, that forbids me to bring to an end the iambics already begun, the song long promised. Not otherwise enamoured of Samian Bathyllus, do they say, was Teian Anacreon, who on his hollow shell sang full oft his plaintive strains of love in simple measure. You yourself are the victim of Love's fires; but if no fairer flame kindled beleaguered Ilium, then be happy in your lot! *I* am consumed with love for Phryne, a freedwoman, with a single lover not content.

EPODON LIBER

XV

Nox erat et caelo fulgebat Luna sereno
    inter minora sidera,
cum tu, magnorum numen laesura deorum,
    in verba iurabas mea,
artius atque hedera procera adstringitur ilex
    lentis adhaerens bracchiis,
dum pecori lupus et nautis infestus Orion
    turbaret hibernum mare,
intonsosque agitaret Apollinis aura capillos,
    fore hunc amorem mutuum.   10
o dolitura mea multum virtute Neaera!
    nam si quid in Flacco viri est,
non feret adsiduas potiori te dare noctes,
    et quaeret iratus parem;
nec semel offensae[1] cedet constantia formae,
    si certus intrarit dolor.
et tu, quicumque es felicior atque meo nunc
    superbus incedis malo,
sis pecore et multa dives tellure licebit
    tibique Pactolus fluat,   20
nec te Pythagorae fallant arcana renati,
    formaque vincas Nirea,
eheu, translatos alio maerebis amores.
    ast ego vicissim risero.

---

[1] offensi : *Bentley.*

THE EPODES

EPODE XV
Faithless!

Twas night, and in a cloudless sky the moon was
shining amid the lesser lights, when thou, soon to
outrage the majesty of the mighty gods, didst pledge
thy loyalty, clinging to me more closely with thy
twining arms than the lofty ilex is girt by the ivy, and
didst swear that as long as the wolf should be hostile
to the flock, as long as Orion, the sailors' foe, should
toss the wintry sea, as long as the breeze should wave
Apollo's unshorn locks, so long should last our love for
one another.   O Neaera, doomed bitterly to rue my
manhood!   For if there is a spark of the man in
Flaccus, he'll not allow thee to give night after night
to a more favoured rival, but in his anger he will
seek a fitting mate; nor will his stern resolve yield
to thy beauty's charms, now become hateful to him
once fixed resentment has entered his soul.   And
thou, whoe'er thou art, that now paradest happier
than I and proud o'er my distress, though thou be
rich in flocks and acres broad, though for thee
Pactolus flow, and the secrets of Pythagoras rein-
carnate elude thee not, though in beauty thou
shouldst surpass even Nireus, alas! thou art doomed
to mourn her love flown to another.   But I in turn
shall laugh.

XVI

ALTERA iam teritur bellis civilibus aetas,
  suis et ipsa Roma viribus ruit.
quam neque finitimi valuerunt perdere Marsi
  minacis aut Etrusca Porsenae manus,
aemula nec virtus Capuae nec Spartacus acer
  novisque rebus infidelis Allobrox
nec fera caerulea domuit Germania pube
  parentibusque abominatus Hannibal:
impia perdemus devoti sanguinis aetas,
  ferisque rursus occupabitur solum.   10
barbarus heu cineres insistet victor et urbem
  eques sonante verberabit ungula,
quaeque carent ventis et solibus ossa Quirini,
  nefas videre!   dissipabit insolens.
forte, quod ¹ expediat, communiter aut melior pars
  malis carere quaeritis laboribus?
nulla sit hac potior sententia, Phocaeorum
  velut profugit exsecrata civitas
agros atque lares patrios, habitandaque fana
  apris reliquit et rapacibus lupis,   20
ire, pedes quocumque ferent, quocumque per undas
  Notus vocabit aut protervus Africus.

¹ quod *inferior MSS :* quid *best MSS*

THE EPODES

EPODE XVI
The Woes of Civil Strife.   A Remedy

ALREADY a second generation is being ground to pieces by civil war, and Rome through her own strength is tottering. The city that neither the neighbouring Marsians had the power to ruin, nor the Etruscan host of threatening Porsena, nor Capua's rival might, nor fierce Spartacus, nor the Gaul, disloyal in time of tumult, nor wild Germany, with its blue-eyed youth, nor Hannibal by parents hated,—this selfsame city we ourselves shall ruin, we, an impious generation, of stock accurst; and the ground shall again be held by beasts of prey. The savage conqueror shall stand, alas! upon the ashes of our city, and the horseman shall trample it with clattering hoof, and (impious to behold!) shall scatter wantonly Quirinus' bones, that now are sheltered from the wind and sun.

Perchance all ye (and this were the wiser course), or at least the better part, seek to escape this dire distress? As once the Phocean folk, having cursed their fields and ancestral gods, went into exile and left their shrines to be the dwelling-place of boars and ravening wolves, so with us let no other plan be preferred to this: To go wheresoever our feet shall bear us, wheresoever o'er the waves Notus or

409

sic placet? an melius quis habet suadere?
   secunda
  ratem occupare quid moramur alite?
sed iuremus in haec: simul imis saxa renarint
  vadis levata, ne redire sit nefas;
neu conversa domum pigeat dare lintea, quando
  Padus Matina laverit cacumina,
in mare seu celsus procurrerit Appenninus,
  novaque monstra iunxerit libidine   30
mirus amor, iuvet ut tigres subsidere cervis,
  adulteretur et columba miluö,
credula nec ravos timeant armenta leones,
  ametque salsa levis hircus aequora.
haec et quae poterunt reditus abscindere dulces
  eamus omnis exsecrata civitas,
aut pars indocili melior grege; mollis et exspes
  inominata perprimat cubilia!
vos, quibus est virtus, muliebrem tollite luctum,
  Etrusca praeter et volate litora.   40
nos manet Oceanus circumvagus; arva, beata
  petamus arva divites et insulas,
reddit ubi Cererem tellus inarata quotannis
  et imputata floret usque vinea,
germinat et numquam fallentis termes olivae,
  suamque pulla ficus ornat arborem,
mella cava manant ex ilice, montibus altis
  levis crepante lympha desilit pede.
illic iniussae veniunt ad mulctra capellae,
  refertque tenta grex amicus ubera,   50

boisterous Africus shall call. Is such your pleasure?
Or has some one better counsel? Why, with omens
fair, do we delay to board the ship? But let us swear
to this: So soon as rocks shall rise from Ocean's depths
and float again, then let it be no sin to return! Nor
let us be loth to shift our canvas and trim it for the
voyage home, when the Po shall wash the Matinian
heights, when the lofty Apennines shall jut out into
the sea, when strange affection shall join monsters in
unnatural desire, so that tigers shall love to mate with
deer, and the dove shall pair with the kite, the trustful
herd fear not the tawny lion, and the goat, grown
smooth with scales, shall love the briny waters of the
sea. Having vowed these solemn pledges and whatever can prevent our sweet return, let us go forth, the
State entire, or the portion better than the ignorant
herd! Let the weak and hopeless remnant rest on
their ill-fated couches!

Ye who have manhood, away with womanish laments,
and speed past the Etruscan coasts! Us the encom-
passing Ocean awaits. Let us seek the Fields, the
Happy Fields, and the Islands of the Blest, where
every year the land, unploughed, yields corn, and
ever blooms the vine unpruned, and buds the shoot of
the never-failing olive ; the dark fig graces its native
tree ; honey flows from the hollow oak ; from the
lofty hill, with plashing foot, lightly leaps the fountain.
There the goats come unbidden to the milking-pail,
and the willing flock brings swelling udders home ;

nec vespertinus circumgemit ursus ovile,
   neque intumescit alta viperis humus ;
pluraque felices mirabimur, ut neque largis
   aquosus Eurus arva radat imbribus,
pinguia nec siccis urantur semina glaebis,
   utrumque rege temperante caelitum.[1]
non huc Argoo contendit remige pinus,
   neque impudica Colchis intulit pedem ;
non huc Sidonii torserunt cornua nautae,
   laboriosa nec cohors Ulixei.   60
nulla nocent pecori contagia, nullius astri
   gregem aestuosa torret impotentia.
Iuppiter illa piae secrevit litora genti,
   ut inquinavit aere tempus aureum ;
aere, dehinc ferro duravit saecula, quorum
   piis secunda vate me datur fuga.

   [1] *The arrangement of the lines from 56 on varies with different
editors.*

THE EPODES, xvi

nor does the bear at eventide growl 'round the sheep-
fold, nor the ground swell high with vipers. And at yet
more marvels shall we wonder in our good fortune,—
how rainy Eurus does not deluge the cornland with
his showers; and how the fertile seeds are not burnt
up in the hard-baked clods, since the king of the gods
tempers both heat and cold. Hither came no ship of
pine with straining Argo's oarsmen, nor here did any
shameless Colchian queen set foot; no Sidonian
mariners hither turned their spars, nor Ulysses' toiling
crew. No murrain blights the flock; no planet's
blazing fury scorches the herd. Jupiter set apart
these shores for a righteous folk, ever since with
bronze he dimmed the lustre of the Golden Age.
With bronze and then with iron did he harden the
ages, from which a happy escape is offered to the
righteous, if my prophecy be heeded.

XVII

" Iam iam efficaci do manus scientiae,
supplex et oro regna per Proserpinae,
per et Dianae non movenda numina,
per atque libros carminum valentium
refixa caelo devocare sidera,
Canidia, parce vocibus tandem sacris
citumque retro solve, solve turbinem!
movit nepotem Telephus Nereium,
in quem superbus ordinarat agmina
Mysorum et in quem tela acuta torserat.   10
unxere [1] matres Iliae addictum feris
alitibus atque canibus homicidam Hectorem,
postquam relictis moenibus rex procidit,
heu! pervicacis ad pedes Achillei.
saetosa duris exuere pellibus
laboriosi remiges Ulixei
volente Circa membra, tunc mens et sonus
relapsus atque notus in vultus honor.
dedi satis superque poenarum tibi,
amata nautis multum et institoribus.   20
fugit iuventas et verecundus color
reliquit; ossa pelle amicta lurida,

---

[1] unxere: *good MSS. also have* luxere.

THE EPODES

EPODE XVII

A Palinode

"At length I yield to thy potent skill, and on
bended knee I beg—by the realms of Proserpine,
by Diana's inviolable majesty, and by the books of
incantations that have power to unfix the stars and
call them down from heaven—Canidia, cease at
length thy magic spells, and let the whirling wheel
go back, go back! Telephus moved to pity Nereus'
grandson, against whom in defiance he had marshalled
the hosts of the Mysians and had hurled his pointed
darts. Man-slaying Hector, though given o'er to
birds of prey and dogs, the Ilian dames were suffered to anoint for funeral rites, after the king,
leaving the city walls, fell, ah! piteous sight, at the
feet of Achilles hard of heart! By Circe's will
the oarsmen of toil-worn Ulysses put off the limbs
bristling with tough hides; then returned wit and
speech, and to their features the wonted grace.
Enough of penalty and more have I paid to thee,
thou much beloved of sailors and of peddlers!
My youth has sped; departed is my rosy bloom; my

tuis capillus albus est odoribus,
nullum ab labore me reclinat otium ;
urget diem nox et dies noctem, neque est
levare tenta spiritu praecordia.
ergo negatum vincor ut credam miser,
Sabella pectus increpare carmina
caputque Marsa dissilire nenia.
quid amplius vis ? o mare et terra, ardeo,   30
quantum neque atro delibutus Hercules
Nessi cruore, nec Sicana fervida
virens in Aetna flamma ; tu, donec cinis
iniuriosis aridus ventis ferar,
cales venenis officina Colchicis.
quae finis aut quod me manet stipendium ?
effare ; iussas cum fide poenas luam,
paratus expiare, seu poposceris
centum iuvencos, sive mendaci lyra
voles sonari : tu pudica, tu proba   40
perambulabis astra sidus aureum.
infamis Helenae Castor offensus vicem
fraterque magni Castoris, victi prece,
adempta vati reddidere lumina :
et tu—potes nam—solve me dementia,
o nec paternis obsoleta sordibus
nec in sepulcris pauperum prudens anus
novendiales dissipare pulveres.
tibi hospitale pectus et purae manus

bones are covered with a yellow skin; with thy
essences my hair is white; no respite relieves me
from torment; night follows close on day, and day on
night; nor is it possible to ease my straining breast
by taking breath. And so, ill-fated, I am driven to
believe what I once denied: that Sabellian incantations can confuse the heart, and that by Marsian
spells the head is rent asunder. What more dost thou
desire? O sea and earth! I burn as neither Hercules,
steeped in the black blood of Nessus, nor the live
Sicilian flame in blazing Aetna. But thou art a
glowing shop of magic drugs, to the end that I may
become dry ashes and be carried off by the wanton
winds. What end or penalty awaits me? Speak
out! The punishments commanded, I faithfully will
pay, ready to make expiation, whether thou de-
mandest a hundred bullocks, or wouldst have thy
praises sounded on mendacious lute. Chaste and
righteous, thou shalt be made to walk amid the
stars, a golden constellation. Castor and mighty
Castor's brother, incensed at the affront to Helen,
were yet won o'er by prayers, and to the bard restored the sight they had taken away; do thou—
for thou art powerful—relieve me of my madness,
O thou sullied by no ancestral taint, thou no hag
deft in scattering funeral ashes amid the graves of
the poor! Kindly is thy heart and pure thy hands;

417

tuosque venter Pactumeius, et tuo 50
cruore rubros obstetrix pannos lavit,
utcumque fortis exsilis puerpera."
" quid obseratis auribus fundis preces?
non saxa nudis surdiora navitis
Neptunus alto tundit hibernus salo.
inultus ut tu riseris Cotytia
volgata, sacrum liberi Cupidinis,
et Esquilini pontifex venefici
impune ut urbem nomine impleris meo?
quid proderit ditasse Paelignas anus 60
velociusve miscuisse toxicum?
sed tardiora fata te votis manent;
ingrata misero vita ducenda est in hoc,
novis ut usque suppetas laboribus.
optat quietem Pelopis infidi pater,
egens benignae Tantalus semper dapis,
optat Prometheus obligatus aliti,
optat supremo collocare Sisyphus
in monte saxum; sed vetant leges Iovis.
voles modo altis desilire turribus, 70
modo ense pectus Norico recludere,
frustraque vincla gutturi nectes tuo,
fastidiosa tristis aegrimonia.
vectabor umeris tunc ego inimicis eques,

Pactumeius is thy offspring, and thine the blood that
stained the cloths the midwife washed, however
sturdily thou trippest forth after thy travail."

"Why dost thou pour forth prayers to ears whose
gates are barred? Not deafer to shipwrecked sailors
are the cliffs that wintry Neptune beats with swelling
surge! Thou to laugh with impunity at divulging the
Cotytian rites and the orgies of Cupid unrestrained!
Thou, the minister of Esquiline incantation, to fill
the town with talk of me and reap no punishment!
What use to have enriched Paelignian dames, or to
have learned to mix a swifter poison! But a fate
awaits thee more lingering than thy prayers implore.
Wretch! Thou must drag out a weary life for this:
to be ever present for fresh sufferings. For rest,
longs Tantalus, the sire of faithless Pelops, yearning
ever for the bounteous feast; for rest, Prometheus
too, chained to the bird of prey. Sisyphus longs to
set the rock upon the mountain's crest, but the laws
of Jove forbid. Thy wish shall be, now to plunge
down from lofty towers, now to pierce thy bosom
with the Noric blade; and in vain shalt thou reeve
the noose about thy throat, sick at heart with weary
loathing. Then as a horseman I'll ride upon thy
hated shoulders, and the earth shall give way before

meaeque terra cedet insolentiae.
an quae movere cereas imagines,
ut ipse nosti curiosus, et polo
deripere lunam vocibus possim meis,
possim crematos excitare mortuos
desiderique temperare pocula,   80
plorem artis in te nil agentis exitum ? "

my unexampled might. Shall I, who can make waxen
images to feel (as thou, prying creature, thyself dost
know), I who by incantations can snatch down the
moon from heaven, can raise the ashes of the dead,
and mix the potion that creates desire,—shall I
lament the issue of my craft, futile against thee
alone ! "

INDEX OF PROPER NAMES

References preceded by " C.S." are to the " Carmen Saecu-
lare"; those preceded by " Epod." are to the Epodes ;
others are to the Odes.

422

INDEX OF PROPER NAMES

423

INDEX OF PROPER NAMES

INDEX OF PROPER NAMES

INDEX OF PROPER NAMES

426

INDEX OF PROPER NAMES

427

INDEX OF PROPER NAMES

INDEX OF PROPER NAMES

INDEX OF PROPER NAMES

430

INDEX OF PROPER NAMES

INDEX OF PROPER NAMES

432

INDEX OF PROPER NAMES

INDEX OF PROPER NAMES

INDEX OF FIRST LINES

435

INDEX OF FIRST LINES

INDEX OF FIRST LINES

INDEX OF FIRST LINES